THE
ATONEMENT:

IN ITS RELATIONS TO

THE COVENANT, THE PRIESTHOOD, THE INTERCESSION OF OUR LORD.

BY

HUGH MARTIN, D.D.,

AUTHOR OF 'CHRIST'S PRESENCE IN GOSPEL HISTORY,' 'THE SHADOW OF CALVARY,'
'THE PROPHET JONAH,' ETC. ETC.

'Lo, I come; in the volume of the book it is written of me,
I delight to do Thy will, O my God.'—Ps. xl. 7, 8; Heb. x. 7.

EDINBURGH:
JAMES GEMMELL GEORGE IV. BRIDGE.
1882.

CONTENTS.

CHAP.		PAGE
I.	ATONEMENT AND THE COVENANT OF GRACE,	9
II.	ATONEMENT AND THE FEDERAL THEOLOGY,	25
III.	ATONEMENT AND CHRIST'S PRIESTLY OFFICE,	49
IV.	CHRIST'S PRIESTLY ACTION IN HIS DEATH,	76
V.	ATONEMENT AND INTERCESSION:—I. THE DIRECT ARGUMENT,	104
VI.	ATONEMENT AND INTERCESSION:—II. THE INVERSE ARGUMENT,	128
VII.	ATONEMENT AND REMISSION,	169
VIII.	THE COUNTER-IMPUTATIONS OF SIN AND RIGHTEOUSNESS,	198
IX.	ROBERTSON OF BRIGHTON'S VIEWS OF VICARIOUS SACRIFICE,	232
X.	ATONEMENT, AND THE DISTINCTIVE PECULIARITY OF MORAL LAW,	255
	APPENDIX:—A DISCOURSE ON GOD'S BLESSEDNESS AND HIS STATUTES,	291

Windham Press is committed to bringing the lost cultural heritage of ages past into the 21st century through high-quality reproductions of original, classic printed works at affordable prices.

This book has been carefully crafted to utilize the original images of antique books rather than error-prone OCR text. This also preserves the work of the original typesetters of these classics, unknown craftsmen who laid out the text, often by hand, of each and every page you will read. Their subtle art involving judgment and interaction with the text is in many ways superior and more human than the mechanical methods utilized today, and gave each book a unique, hand-crafted feel in its text that connected the reader organically to the art of bindery and book-making.

We think these benefits are worth the occasional imperfection resulting from the age of these books at the time of scanning, and their vintage feel provides a connection to the past that goes beyond the mere words of the text.

As bibliophiles, we are always seeking perfection in our work, and so please notify us of any errors in this book by emailing us at corrections@windhampress.com. Our team is motivated to correct errors quickly so future customers are better served. Our mission is to raise the bar of quality for reprinted works by a focus on detail and quality over mass production.

To peruse our catalog of carefully curated classic works, please visit our online store at www.windhampress.com.

PREFACE.

THIS volume, it will be obvious, does not profess to be a systematic treatise on the great Doctrine of the Atonement. For that reason, I would have been glad to give it the unpretending title, "*Papers on the Atonement;*" and I was anxious to have done so. But it was represented to me, by a friend in whose judgment I have confidence, that such a designation would convey the impression that the following discussions are miscellaneous and fragmentary,—which a glance at the Table of Contents will show is far from being the case. Hence I have qualified the general title, "THE ATONEMENT, by the supplementary clause, "*In its relations to the Covenant, the Priesthood, the Intercession of our Lord.*" And this indicates pretty exactly the real scope of the volume.

In a word, my object is to indicate certain *conditions* under which the Doctrine of the Atonement ought to be discussed; and that with a twofold view. *First*, in order to clear away at the outset all temptation to à *priori* speculation, seeing that it is not an abstract and philosophical *theory* of Atonement we have to deal with, but the revealed reality of the actual sacrifice of the Son of God on Calvary. And, *secondly*, because—as I think the intelligent reader of these pages, after perusing them, will be prepared to admit—the discussion, when conducted under the conditions indicated, can be pointed with the very greatest ease, and with extreme brevity of treatment, to the overthrow of all those current speculations of the day which have in view to set aside the Catholic Doctrine of the Cross. Their refutation comes out in the shape of corollaries, that are all but intuitively obvious, and, as I believe, utterly indisputable.

It is only in the view of such occasionally occurring corollaries, or inferences, in refutation of error, that this book can in any sense be called controversial. Properly speaking, a controversial volume it is not. And there is not a tinge of *party* in it. Such portions of it as have appeared already in another form have met with remarkably kind acceptance from all parties. For I have attempted to set aloft, in the intelligent and adoring admiration of Christian men, the thorough efficaciousness and boundless glory of the propitiatory sacrifice of Calvary; and to do so, if possible, in such fashion that the numerous perversions of the doctrine of the Cross may give intelligent Christian men little or no trouble.

The writing of these pages has been very pleasant work,—an opportunity for usefulness for which I am truly grateful. If it please God, I may resume my pen in further prosecution of the same exhaustless theme. Again and again I have abstained, with a sort of fond regret, from following out a tempting line of thought as I could have wished. And the investigation of the relations between Atonement and Conscience would alone afford materials for a volume as large as this. Meantime, however, I lay down my pen now, just as the great doctrine of the Atonement seems about to be discussed afresh, on the issue, Calvinism *versus* Amyraldism. May the Eternal Spirit, through whom Christ offered Himself without spot to God, direct that discussion to the triumphant vindication of the efficaciousness of the Atonement.

H. M.

CHAPTER I.

ATONEMENT AND THE COVENANT OF GRACE.

IF we would investigate the very doctrine of Atonement which God's Word sets forth,—avoiding arbitrary and capricious speculations, and illegitimate and useless trains of thought,—it must be laid down at the outset, as a proposition of transcendent importance,—

That the Doctrine of the Atonement ought to be discussed and defended as inside the Doctrine of the Covenant of Grace.

I. It will not be denied nor doubted that the doctrine of the Covenant of Grace is a larger category than the doctrine of the Atonement. It is wider; comprehending the Atonement within its provisions; affording to it also both explanation and support.

Now it surely is extremely injudicious and impolitic for defenders of the faith to discuss any scriptural doctrine, and particularly to profess to do so fully and exhaustively, outside of any greater category to which the doctrine properly and natively belongs. For by doing so they place it in a position of unnecessary danger, and assign to themselves a greater difficulty in defending it than Scripture assigns to them. They rob it of the illustration, and they rob it of the protection, which the higher category affords. They deprive it of the benefit of scriptural considerations in the light of which their defence might be comparatively easy, and would be found, indeed, presented to their hand; and, by the isolated position to which they have consigned it, they give advantages to the enemy which the abler and more acute of their number are not slow to seize. For instance: The plausible objection against a truly expiatory sacrifice, to the effect that it is unjust that the innocent should suffer that the guilty may escape, is seen to be a mere misrepresentation when the doctrine of the Covenant has been put forward as explaining and conditioning the Atonement; the objection losing all its plausibility in the light of Christ's covenant-headship and responsibility, and of the covenant oneness with Him of those whose sins He expiates by dying in their stead and room. Moreover, by this impolitic and unscientific procedure, theologians place themselves under the necessity—or at least subject themselves to the strong temptation—of betaking themselves to general and abstract reasoning to an extent that is extremely riskful, and for which not the doctrine but themselves are responsible. We have no desire to exclude all abstract reasoning from the discussion of those great scriptural themes which must ever exercise all earnest minds and are found to fascinate so many.

Abstract reasoning is in many cases eminently serviceable in showing the thorough consistency of theological truth with philosophy and science truly so called. And the wise defenders of the faith will be forward to show that there is no incongruity, and indeed no want of mutual support, between theology, the Queen of Sciences, and her many handmaids in every department of solid thought and legitimate investigation. And when a great ultimate scriptural truth is set forth in its own magnificent proportions, and on its own appropriate evidence, it is one of the worthiest exercises of the human intellect to show that it conflicts with nothing that the intellect of man has discovered or trustworthily accepted. This is to assign to theology its own proper sphere, and to leave theology in its own unaided majesty.

But it is a totally different thing when a scriptural doctrine, isolated from the place which it holds in the great scheme of revelation, has been inadequately discussed—as in such a case inadequately discussed and still more inadequately defended it must inevitably be—it is a totally different thing in such a case to introduce abstract and philosophical discussion in order to supplement a deficiency which theology herself, when rightly questioned, is found to have abundant materials at hand to supply. This is not to illustrate the harmony of philosophy and theology, thereby providing some confirmation of theological truth from philosophical considerations. It is, in so far, *to turn theology into a philosophy*—a very different matter indeed, and a course of procedure against which theologians would always do well to be upon their guard. The science of theology is perfectly competent within her own sphere for discharging all the duty which lies to her hand. She is under no necessity to confess inadequacy of materials in her own proper department for her own proper work: and when she is tempted to feel under any such necessity, it must be either because she has carried her investigations and efforts outside her own proper sphere, or has not exhausted the materials within it.

II. Remarkable instances of the truth and value of these considerations are to be met with in Dr CUNNINGHAM'S magnificent work on Historical Theology. Two in particular occur to us.

The first is his sagacious declinature to receive help in establishing the fundamental truths of Calvinism from the doctrine of what is called philosophical necessity. He wisely declines binding up the validity of a purely theological demonstration with the fate or the foundations of a philosophical theory. But the second instance is more directly in point to our present purpose, because in it we have this great theologian discarding a philosophical or metaphysical defence of divine truth, and falling back for the only real and satisfying defence of it upon the doctrine of federality. It occurs in his chapter on the Bondage of the Will. He has been considering the objection—so ready to be raised against the doctrine of man's total inability to will any spiritual good accompanying salvation—to the effect, namely, that such inability would be incompatible with responsibility. And he has subjected to a very searching and very beautifully acute investigation the distinction that has so often been relied upon in answering this objection —the distinction between natural and moral inability. Admitting this distinction as a *real* distinction, and in its own place important, he expresses himself as dissatisfied with it, as not affording any real answer to the objection, or solution of the difficulty. He says:—" I am not persuaded that any solution meets the difficulty of asserting that man is responsible for his sins and shortcomings *notwithstanding* his inability to will and to do what is good, except by showing that he is responsible *for* his inability." And to provide *this* answer —which his subtlety and sagacity and ingenuousness all combined to lead him to see and acknowledge to be fairly desiderated—he falls back on the covenant oneness of the race in Adam. " We are satisfied," he says, " that the principle which contributes more fully than any other to furnish an answer to the objection—an explanation of the difficulty—is just the scriptural doctrine which leads us to regard man in his whole history, fallen and unfallen, or the whole human race collectively in their relation to God, *as virtually one and indivisible*, so far as regards their legal standing and responsibilities, —to contemplate the whole history of the human race as virtually the history of one and the same man, or, what is substantially and practically the same thing, to regard the inability of will to anything spiritually good —which can be proved to attach to man *de facto*—as a penal infliction, a punishment justly imposed upon account of previous guilt—the guilt, of course, of Adam's first sin imputed to his posterity." "And with respect to the difficulty about responsibility, the substance of our position in answer to the objection is just this: That man is responsible for not willing and doing good, *notwithstanding* his inability to will and to do good, *because* he is answerable *for* that inability itself, having, as legally answerable for Adam's sin, inherited the inability, as part of the forfeiture penally due for that first transgression."

It is in this manner that divine truths are most convincingly established and successfully defended,—when placed, that is, in their due order and in their right relations of subordination to each other: and an illustrious instance of this, such as that which we have now given, ought not to be without its due weight with us. For instance: Let the objection to the Atonement about punishing the innocent and allowing the transgressors to escape, be referred back upon the Covenant of Grace, precisely as Dr CUNNINGHAM refers back upon the covenant of works the asserted incompatibility between inability and responsibility; and how easily is it rebutted. Bring in, that is to say, the scriptural doctrine which teaches us to regard Christ and the Church collectively in their relation to God, *as virtually one and indivisible*, so far as regards their legal standing and responsibilities; and the objection is not merely seen at once to be false, but to be irrelevant and inept. It requires no answer, in the light of the covenant oneness of Christ and His members: it simply disappears. We have before us "virtually the history of one and the same man,"—the Second Man, the last Adam. The death of Christ is then seen to be the real infliction of the originally threatened curse. No one considered as innocent suffers, and no one continuing guilty escapes. Righteousness and Peace are seen to kiss each other, and Justice goes before Him to set us in the way of His steps.

The objection, in this light, we have said, disappears. And that is true. But it reappears as an utterly unanswerable objection to the scheme of those who deny the doctrine of satisfaction for sin, and yet acknowledge the historical facts of Christ's sinlessness and His death on Calvary. For unless these facts are denied, or are accounted for as the theology of the Covenant of Grace accounts for them, then Christ did die precisely under the character of one in every sense and in every light innocent; and if His death was thus beneficial to sinners without being vicarious—if it issues in their good without having been suffered in their stead—then sinners, still considered as guilty, do escape by means of it. That the innocent suffer and the guilty escape thereby, is an assertion not merely without ground, but without meaning, when made against a vicarious sacrifice such as that which is explained and safe-guarded by the Covenant of Grace. But it carries in it all its plain meaning, and rests on unanswerable grounds, when affirmed against any theory that admits that Christ was a truly righteous man, that He truly died, and by dying did not effectually expiate sin, but merely give a display of God's character, or bring into play some influence to act beneficially on the destinies and character of men. The doctrine of the Covenant, and of the covenant oneness of Christ and His people, enables us not merely to rebut but to retort the objection; and the unity of plan or principle on which the scriptural doctrine is thus both established, on the one hand, and defended, on the other, is at once very glorifying to the truth of God, and most satisfactory to the intellect of man.

III. A correct and comprehensive scheme of federal theology, in fact, commends itself very powerfully to every logical mind by the readiness with which it may be brought to bear on the exposure of the various aberrations that have manifested themselves on the doctrine of the Atonement. Take, for instance, Dr WARDLAW'S erroneous views, and place them in the light of the federal theology: they are immediately robbed of all their plausibility.

Dr WARDLAW[*] held the notion of a universal, unlimited, or indefinite atonement, undertaken literally

---

[*] Discourses on the Nature and Extent of the Atonement. By Ralph Wardlaw, D.D. Glasgow, 1844.

for all men, and accomplishing as much for every human being as for any. And being a believer in the doctrines of election and of the necessity of the Spirit's regenerating grace, he held that the sovereign purpose of God comes in afterwards, in the order of nature, to determine to whom the Atonement shall be rendered actually fruitful of saving results. This, of course, is to acknowledge, in some sense, intentionally at least, a covenant of grace. But it is a covenant conditioning not Christ's work, but merely the Spirit's. Of such a covenant, however, the Scriptures contain not a single trace. The covenant which we deduce, by a large and satisfactory induction of particulars from Holy Scripture, is a covenant with Christ, concerning Christ's own work,—its nature, its objects, its beneficiaries, its rewards. And it is a covenant with the Spirit, only because it is a covenant with the CHRIST—the immeasurably Anointed One of God, anointed of the Holy Ghost, and endued with power to give the Spirit to as many as the Father hath given Him. To dislocate here, is to derange everything. To place Christ and His work outside this covenant, in order to give His redemption the aspect of larger graciousness and indefinite relations to all men universally, is to pervert the entire doctrine of the Covenant,—to turn aside, at its very fountain-head, that river the streams whereof make glad the city of God.

Moreover, under pretence of enlarging the aspects of Grace, it achieves most effectually a precisely opposite result. For, to bring in a covenant of grace in order to *limit* the application and circumscribe the effectual results of an atonement in its own nature and accomplished merit unlimited, is surely one of the most perverted and perverting schemes that could be adopted. To introduce a covenant of any kind as an instrument of limitation of a mercy, and of the actual blessings of a mercy, already in the field without limit, is surely too offensive to expect acceptance with thoughtful and generous minds—unless indeed very overwhelming evidence can be presented of its being verily the Divine method, clearly and unmistakably revealed to us. But to introduce a covenant of *grace*, as an instrument for the *limitation* of grace, is at once an insult to the human understanding and a travesty of the Divine wisdom. In any such view of its action and intent, it must assuredly cease to be called a covenant of grace. The grace is all in the prior arrangement or achievement, which it has been agreed on this scheme to call the Atonement; and the covenant is a covenant circumscribing the grace into limits narrower than its own. It is, therefore, a covenant, not of grace, but of alarming judgment.

Nay, more: it is a covenant of reasonless, arbitrary and capricious judgment. For it is utterly vain to call in, in arrest of this condemnatory criticism, any reference to the sovereignty of God. The Divine sovereignty is legitimately referred to at the *earlier* stage, as arranging a real Covenant of Grace—grace true and pure and simple—taking action from the first to provide and accept and apply a definite and complete atonement for the full and free and sure salvation of the lost and guilty. Sovereignty is in its true place there and then: and its action there and then may be defended against all cavils whatsoever by the answers which the Spirit of God has provided against them: "May I not do what I will with my own?" "Who art thou, O man, that repliest against God?" For, from that point of view, and at that stage in the order of nature, sinners are contemplated *as sinners simply*,—in the eye of Divine justice guilty and righteously exposed to the wrath of God, helpless to relieve themselves from it, and with nothing as yet achieved by Heaven for their relief. And the question, Why is not atonement provided for all? is answered by the question, Why is atonement provided for any? To fall back on the Divine sovereignty here is perfectly legitimate, and indeed inevitable. But to fall back on the Divine sovereignty at a *later* stage, as Dr WARDLAW'S capricious scheme of doctrine does, is utterly useless and unwarrantable. For if the sovereignty of God is called in at the later stage, at which a universal and unlimited atonement is seen, so to speak, to have already taken the field, then sinners must be viewed, not as simply sinners now, but *as sinners whose sin has been atoned for* —whatever, on this scheme, that may mean. And a covenant coming into play at such a stage, to exclude, in point of fact, vast multitudes from all beneficial effects of an atonement, which, in its own nature, had as beneficial bearings on them as on any and all of those who are ultimately to be saved,—a covenant such as this, it is utter folly to call a covenant of grace. It is not a covenant of grace in any sense, but a covenant of judgment; and not a covenant of sovereignty, but of arbitrary and reasonless and terrific judgment. The objection, therefore, in deference to which a definite, effectual, and sure atonement is disparaged and set aside in favour of one that is indefinite and unlimited,—and from all the benefits of which, whatever these may be, an imaginary covenant interposes to exclude vast numbers of its beneficiaries,—reappears against the erroneous doctrine itself in a form the most aggravated and offensive, with relevancy which it is impossible to deny, and with a force which it is impossible to rebut.

IV. A correct application of the doctrine of the Covenant is, in like manner, eminently serviceable in refuting the argument for an indefinite atonement based on the alleged necessity of providing a foundation for a universal gospel call. For—not to speak of the very obvious consideration that the command of God is sufficient warrant to "go into all the world and preach the gospel to every creature"—any intellectual difficulty that reverential minds may feel on this point should be allayed, if not indeed removed, by observing the relation in which the Gospel Call stands to the Covenant of Grace.

That relation is very intimate. The gospel call comes

forth from the covenant, and summons sinners into it. It is a voice from within the covenant, addressed to those that are without, with the view of bringing them within. Its administration is itself one of the stipulations of the covenant: "Behold, thou shalt call a nation that thou knewest not" (Isa. lv. 5). And its success is equally guaranteed by the covenant: "And nations that knew not thee shall run unto thee, because of the Lord thy God, and for the Holy One of Israel; for he hath glorified thee" (*idem*). Such is the covenant intercommunion of the Father and the Son concerning the gospel call, stipulating that it shall be given, and that when given it shall not be without success. And it is, as it were, fresh from rehearsing and recording what he hath been a witness to between the Father and the Son concerning the gospel call, that the Spirit turns to us and ministers it to us, shining fresh in the light of covenant Divine counsels concerning it:—"Seek ye the Lord while he may be found; call ye upon him while he is near" (see vers. 6–13). It is therefore a sure source of inevitable error to overlook the relations between the call and the covenant; and, more particularly, it must most manifestly derange all scriptural and correct views, to seek for the call a basis broader than the covenant supplies. The call is a voice from within the covenant, summoning sinners to come within its gracious bonds. Of course, therefore, it is a universal call. The one thing which it takes for granted is that sinners are out side the covenant. This is all that is requisite to render them fit subjects for its gracious proposal and authoritative requirement. It is, of course, therefore, a universal call, because it is a call addressed to those that are without. Is there any inconsistency between this and the fact that it calls them to come within the covenant, itself therefore coming from within, and resting on grounds not wider than those on which the covenant rests? Could it call sinners into the covenant if itself rested on grounds outside the covenant? Whatever is without the covenant, outside its limits — as an indefinite, unlimited atonement is—has nothing to do with the gospel call; can impart to it no validity, no strength, no enlargement; can constitute for it no real basis or foundation. An indefinite atonement, therefore, as pleaded for by some in the interests of the freeness of the gospel call, is one of the most self-contradictory and self-negativing devices that can be imagined.

Besides, it ought to be ever borne in mind that in the giving of the gospel call the preachers of the gospel are ambassadors, and ambassadors merely. We are ministers. We give the call ministerially. He who really calls is Christ. And when Christ, by His ambassadors, and in His instituted ordinances, gives forth the gospel call, it is a glorious exercise of His kingly office. But Christ executes His kingly office by covenant. The exercise of His kingly office cannot possibly be placed on any wider, broader, more gracious foundation than the Covenant of Grace. Not any more, therefore, can the gospel call. For, as we have said, the solitary thing which it takes for granted is that sinners are not inside—not yet interested in—this blessed covenant or constitution; that they are aliens from the blessed kingdom of which it is the charter. It is, therefore, in its essential nature obviously a universal call. It is so because it is a call *to* the covenant. What possible contradiction or want of harmony can there be between this and the fact that the call comes from *within* the covenant,—resting, therefore, on foundations as broad, neither more nor less, as those on which the covenant itself rests? For my part, I do not see what it is that is supposed to require, or even permit of reconciliation. On the contrary, to make the Call proceed upon grounds broader than the Covenant, and on considerations not contained within it, is, in my opinion, to create a necessity for reconciling and harmonising to an extent and of a kind which it will be found in strict reason utterly impossible to meet. The Call itself is destroyed in all the intrinsic worth and in all the professed design of it, as a call *to* the Covenant, and to all its free grace and sure and saving blessings, if it be a call coming from any quarter but the Covenant itself—be it even from Christ, if it be not from Christ as the covenant-head. It is in fact simply impossible to regard it as resting on any grounds, or as based on any considerations, save those which the Covenant embraces.

These considerations have been somewhat abstract as well as miscellaneous. But we propose to resume the subject in the following chapter, treating it in a somewhat more directly scriptural manner. For we should like to commend the federal theology to the younger preachers and students of our Churches. It seems to us to have fallen too much out of view; for what reason it is not easy to see. It is a noble category of revealed truth. It is a thoroughly scientific generalisation, commending itself by the ease with which it ranges, in their right positions and relations to each other, the great leading truths of the Word of God as these bear on the redemption that is in Christ: and it is unrivalled as an instrument of defence against the various attacks that are at present being made on the doctrine of Christ's sacrifice as a true expiation of the sins of His people. We can compare it, in a strategic point of view, to nothing more aptly than to the lines of Torres Vedras in the old Peninsular campaign, —affording both a base of operation for forward movement, and an impregnable protection against hostile assault. Nor is it only or chiefly in a controversial point of view that we value the federal theology. The exposition of it adapts with the greatest ease, and with uniform acceptability, to the instruction of those who have believed the Gospel. It is always welcome to the children of God. And we should not like to see the day in Scotland when the least acceptable of candidates for the office of the ministry should be he who expounds most explicitly and richly the doctrine of the Covenant of Grace.

CHAPTER II.

ATONEMENT AND THE FEDERAL THEOLOGY.

IT is scarcely possible to exaggerate the advantages of grounding the exposition and defence of the Scriptural theory of the Atonement on a sound and comprehensive doctrine of the Covenant of Grace.

This is a doctrine—the doctrine of the Covenant—which even the best and safest of our German theologians entirely overlook. It is, of course, unnecessary to say that it is a doctrine wholly unknown to British writers of the type of Maurice and Jowett. And what between the attempt to answer the latter class of writers on their own ground, and the study of the German authors—on the part even of such as peruse them for the sake of what is valuable in their learned and laborious productions—it has come to pass, we fear, that the federal theology is at present suffering a measure of neglect which does not bode well for the immediate future of the Church amongst us. It is with the view, if we may, of counteracting this present tendency, that we would respectfully submit some considerations fitted to commend the study of the federal theology to our younger preachers, as well as to the members of the Church generally.

It is quite possible that, in attempting this, we may be met by the objection that the doctrine of the Covenant of Grace is *old-fashioned.*

Well; it can hardly be very old-fashioned yet. There are not many congregations of the Church that, if questioned on the subject, would as yet feel themselves driven to give an answer analogous to what Paul once got from "certain disciples" at Ephesus: "We have not so much as heard whether there be any" Covenant of Grace! On the contrary, the pious eldership, and the patriarchal piety of the Church generally, are familiar with the doctrine of the covenants, and are not insensible of the great extent to which their own vitality and vigour are bound up with the intelligent appreciation of it. We venture to say that, in very many districts of the Church, our probationers and younger ministers could not take a course more fitted to commend them to the love, esteem, and gratitude of our pious people, than just to expound to them,—to use a well-remembered phrase of Dr CUNNINGHAM'S—"the provisions and arrangements of the Covenant of Grace." If there is a feeling abroad, to the effect that the standard of the preaching of the Disruption ministry is not being maintained by the race that is succeeding them, it might be well to inquire whether the explanation of this be not found in the direction we have indicated. The preaching of the Disruption ministers was largely leavened, or rather was pervadingly characterised, by the large place assigned in it to the covenants —those great schemes of the Divine dispensation with mankind. And the consequence was, that the intelligent hearers acquired large views of Divine truth; could perceive the relations subsisting between different departments thereof; could refer a topic to its proper place in the system; and could accordingly realise themselves to be conscious of growing in knowledge—of acquiring real power to make attainments and advancement in spiritual things. But if the federal theology should fall into neglect, there is reason to fear that the materials of pulpit instruction will be destitute of that compactness and connection, apart from which conscious advancement in knowledge on the part of the people is impossible. The topics handled will be disjointed and isolated. Progressive instruction will cease to be realised, and perhaps cease to be aimed at. The next step will be that it will cease to be desired. The production of evanescent, sentimental impression will be the object mainly in view on the preacher's part, and mainly desired by the people. The duty of the pulpit to nourish up an intelligent Christian people in "the words of knowledge and understanding" will be forgotten. And it will be quite true *then* that the federal theology will be " old-fashioned." It is not *yet* true. On the contrary, the doctrine of the Covenant is eminently acceptable with our pious and intelligent people,—with precisely the class of people whose voice is entitled to be heard, whose edification our ministry is bound very specially to seek, and whose tastes and wishes may most legitimately and most safely be considered. *These* are the people among whom a young minister may expect to find loving, sympathising, personal friends, to encourage his heart and hold up his hands. These are they who will be ready to lighten his burdens, cheer him in his difficulties, countenance and help on his plans for usefulness, and be examples in his flock in every grace of godliness. To pretermit *their* edification—on the plea that what style of pulpit ministration edified and nourished them in earlier days is " old-fashioned " now —were suicidal; and every sensible and kindly-hearted young pastor will instinctively feel it to be so. Certain forms and phrases may indeed become old-fashioned; and a brother is not to be held in bondage in that respect. By all means let them be remodelled, wherever that is necessary, to suit the literary tastes of the day, and to fall in fittingly with whatever is truly valuable in modern refinement. If the substance is scriptural the form may be altered to suit any age: the material being in that case as solid gold, it can always be minted in any really current coin of the realm of letters. The preacher, or writer who cannot trust his powers to do that much, has no right to refer to modern culture at all. Modern culture has evidently done little for him.

The real question is this: Is the theology of the covenants a real and natural category of Divine truth? Is it Scriptural? And is it comprehensive, and permanently valuable? If not: if, as some would seem to think, it were merely a temporary development, adopted by theologians in their transition to something better, larger, more vital, and more powerful: if it be "old-fashioned" in the sense of being antiquated and effete: by all means let it take its course to oblivion. There can be no great wisdom, in such a case, and there can be as little success, in attempting to arrest it. Those, however, who entertain that opinion are bound to show that the progress of theological science has really replaced the federal theology with something better, something more satisfactory and scientific. And it is because we believe it impossible to show this, that we would earnestly advocate its continued culture and promulgation.

It will not be supposed that we would advocate the use, from age to age, of any stereotyped phraseology. On the contrary, we believe the federal theology to be a scheme of thought so instinct with vitality as to be independent of particular phrases and formulas, and thoroughly adaptable to the utmost of variety and elasticity that truly free Christian thought can demand. Had we not this deep conviction, we would not think it worth our while to detain on it the attention of our readers or ourselves. The key-note of the federal theology, as we take it, is UNION WITH CHRIST. Though it took shape, as a formal scheme of doctrine or exposition, later than the days of Calvin, it is virtually—through the great predominence and ruling power in the "Institutes" of the idea of "union with Christ"—the leading thought in Calvin's theology; far more so than any or even all of the "five" celebrated "points." And if this is true; if the heart and soul of this theology is found in the union and communion of Christ and His people; then is it so full of vital power that it will adopt into its service all fresh forms of literary effort and all valid products of literary culture, and will go on to create more for itself when these are done. We advocate no tame reproduction of old and worn-out forms of speech. It is the solid riches of Divine truth we would conserve, and the highest attainments of the Church of God as the heir and expositor thereof. And we are very sure that one of these very highest attainments has been the great scheme of thought which is known as the doctrine of the Covenant of Grace.

Part First.

Doctrine of the Covenant directly Scriptural.

It may seem unnecessary to say that this is a doctrine which has express verbal warrant in Holy Scripture. We have been led to this topic in connection with the doctrine of the Atonement; and, it may be in point, therefore, to call to mind the significant phrase, "The blood of the everlasting covenant" (Heb. xiii. 20). Surely that single Divine form of speech is sufficient to set forth an organic connection between the Covenant of Grace and the sacrifice of Jesus. Take again the memorable promise: "As for thee also, by the blood of thy covenant I have sent forth thy prisoners out of the pit wherein is no water" (Zech. ix. 11); and our Lord's own affecting utterance in instituting the sacrament of the Supper: "This cup is the new covenant in my blood." Surely these Divine expressions are very express; and they are sufficient to show that no man discusses the doctrine of Christ's death who severs it from the considerations presented by the Covenant of Grace. It is the "blood" that maketh "atonement;" but in this case the "blood" is the "blood of the Covenant." Men may therefore discuss as long as they please an abstract theory, of an abstract atonement; but if they give not heed to *this* atonement which the Covenant of Grace conditions and explains, they are not any more dealing with true theology, than men should deal with real astronomy who should speculate on central forces in the abstract and pretermit the actual law of gravitation —the law of the inverse square of the distance—which rules in the starry heavens.

It is scarcely necessary to refer to the express assertion of the covenant between the Father and the Son in the proposition: "The counsel of peace shall be between them both" (Zech. vi. 13). Our Lord is designated at once the "Mediator of the Covenant" (Heb. viii. 6; xii. 24), and the "Surety of the Covenant" (Heb. vii. 22). Nay, He is represented as the *substance* of the Covenant: "I the Lord have called Thee in righteousness, and will hold thine hand, and will keep Thee, and give Thee for a covenant of the people, for a light to the Gentiles" (Isa. xlii. 6; xlix. 8). The work of Christ is thus in express terms affirmed to be a covenant work—

a work having immediate respect to a covenant. The work of the Spirit is spoken of in similar connection with a covenant: "As for me, this is my covenant with them, saith the Lord; My Spirit that is upon thee, and my words that are in thy mouth, shall not depart out of thy mouth, nor out of the mouth of thy seed, nor out of the mouth of thy seed's seed, saith the Lord, from henceforth and for ever" (Isa. lix. 21). When the Lord invites lost sinners to Himself, it is in terms like these: "Incline your ear, and come unto me: hear, and your souls shall live, and I will make with you an everlasting covenant, even the sure mercies of David" (Isa. lv. 3). When, moved by such entreaties, sinners ask the way to Zion, with their faces thitherward, it is with the mutual exhortation: "Come, and let us join ourselves to the Lord in a perpetual covenant that shall not be forgotten" (Jer. i. 5). When, after entering on this blessed relation with God, they would express their full satisfaction with it in the midst of all life's troubles and afflictions, they are wont to say: "Though my house be not so with God; yet He hath made with me an everlasting covenant, ordered in all things and sure: this is all my salvation, and all my desire" (2 Sam. xxiii. 5). For in the midst of all troubles by which their sins are chastised and their spirit chastened, the Lord sustains their faith by the gracious declaration: "My covenant will I not break, nor alter the word that hath gone out of my mouth" (Ps. lxxxix. 34). And when grieved in the view of the "cruelty" that obtains in the "dark places of the earth," the Church's strongest appeal to God on their behalf is this : "Have respect unto Thy covenant " (Ps. lxxiv. 20).

These are some of the more express verbal assertions of the reality and fact of a Covenant of Grace. Intelligent piety is familiar with them as with household words; and we quote them simply to show that the federal theology is no product of mere human ingenuity—no merely artificial structure—but a Scriptural theme, the terminology of which is directly furnished by Scripture itself. It is no roundabout result of mere theologising, but one of the immediate *data* of Divine nspiration.

Part Second.

Doctrine of the Covenant Scriptural by Large Induction.

But apart even from such direct verbal sanction from the Divine word, the federal theology may be justified as the inevitable result of a large and complete induction of particulars from Scripture. It is impossible to systematise accurately concerning the work of Christ and of His Spirit, in the redemption and salvation of men, without landing in substantially the doctrine of the Covenant of Grace. Even although Holy Scripture did not lead the way so expressly and verbally as we have seen that it does, scientific or Baconian induction of particulars would bring us substantially to the great scheme of the federal theology. The many instances which Scripture gives of intercommunion between the Father and the Son, are found, when combined, to carry in them all the elements and characteristics of a covenant.

The closing chapters of the "Gospel according to Isaiah" are peculiarly rich in passages which cannot be intelligently appreciated without leading to this conclusion. The authority of the Father appoints certain duties to the Son: the Father's love and faithfulness guarantee to the Son certain promises of support, countenance, comfort, victory. The Son undertakes the duties assigned, and appeals to the promises relating to them. The Father re-stipulates to bestow certain rewards in return for the obedient and faithful discharge of the duties enjoined: and "for the joy therein set before Him, the Son endures the cross, despising the shame." What could be more definite in this light than the closing verses of the memorable fifty-third chapter of Isaiah? "When thou shalt make his soul an offering for sin, he shall see his seed, he shall prolong his days, and the pleasure of the Lord shall prosper in his hand. He shall see of the travail of his soul, and shall be satisfied: by his knowledge shall my righteous servant justify many; for he shall bear their iniquities. Therefore will I divide him a portion with the great, and he shall divide the spoil with the strong; because he hath poured out his soul unto death: and he was numbered with the transgressors; and he bare the sin of many, and made intercession for the transgressors."

It is not possible to read passages like these without seeing that there are far more abundant Scriptural elements from which to conclude the existence of a Covenant of Grace between the Father and the Son, than even of a covenant of works between God and Adam. In fact it is more from what is partly the analogy and partly the antithesis of the two covenants, when set forth in the mutual light which they reflect on each other, that the covenant of works becomes manifest, than in any very express or abundant evidence of its own alone. So certain is this, that it will uniformly be found that the theology which is meagre in reference to the Covenant of Grace, is still more so as to the covenant of works. The first Adam was but "the type of him that was to come," the shadow of the "last Adam." And where the "last Adam" is little recognised as a covenant head, there can be little reason or inducement to recognise the "first" in that light either. It is in Christ pre-eminently that the doctrine of covenant takes fullest shape; and apart even from express verbal affirmations of it, we find that it is continually subsumed in Holy Scripture's descriptions of His work in the days of His flesh, and of His reward in His risen glory.

On no scheme whatever that shall be true to the leading contents of Scripture, concerning the work of the incarnate Redeemer, can we possibly avoid coming to the conclusion that He acts according to a covenant with the Father. Whatever Christ did, He designed to do; and whatever He designed to do, He designed because

He had been *designated* to do it. He had been "sanctified," and "sealed," and "sent" into the world. He continually averred, in this view, that He "did *nothing* of Himself." He was acting by commission; and that not merely in general, but by commission reaching to every detail of speech and action alike. He did the "works of His Father." He spake his "Father's words." "*Whatsoever* He spake, and *whatsoever* He did," it was "as the Father had given Him commandment." He had been designated therefore by no isolated decree, by no individual or separate oracle, but by regular, full, complete covenant. Under no other category or instrument than that of compact, *fœdus*, covenant, is it possible to bring all the fulness, circumstance, detail, history, order, and fruit of His work. We are simply shut up to the theory of an "everlasting covenant." Such a covenant is, indeed, in terms averred; and that is a great satisfaction to the reverential theological mind. But even if it had not been averred, we are, on principles of induction precisely analagous to those of true Baconian philosophy, simply shut up to the theory of the federal theology.

Nor does this result fail with us in subsequent application. Whether we make use of it analytically or synthetically, we find it to be the largest category of Christology that is either necessary or possible. We find it embracing all Christ's work, and all inspired expositions of it. It accounts for all the phenomena which it professes to explain. It explains all Christ's history, as the incarnate Son of God; all His interposition, as the Saviour of men. It embraces alike the impetration of redemption and the application of it. It expounds Christ's complete office, and the office and work of the Spirit. It gives doctrinal significance to what were otherwise mere external history; for it places the outward movements of Christ's career on earth in their true relations with the eternal purpose of the Godhead, and the eternal destinies of men. And in its completeness—involving, as it does, its aspects and bearing towards the covenant clients, as well as towards the covenant head—it is the formal, definite, tangible instrument and charter by means of which faith comes into sure and pleadable possession of Christ himself, and of all the benefits of His redemption.

Alike in reference, therefore, to doctrine and to spiritual life, it is suicidal to sever the Atonement of Christ from the Covenant of Grace. The demands alike of theology and of faith require a different treatment. Against an Atonement isolated from the Covenant, endless objections may be brought, and endless work laid to the hands of theology in answering them. The abstract doctrine of an abstract atonement, it may be found difficult, perhaps impossible, to defend against the keen-witted opponents with whom we have in these days to deal. But it is a most instructive fact that the vast multitude of these objections derive their plausibility, if not their power, just from overlooking those characteristics of the actual atonement which the Covenant of

Grace attributes to it; and the defenders of the truth should learn from this the lesson, to decline, as a matter which in no respect concerns them, the defence of any doctrine of atonement, save the Atonement of the Son's Covenant with the Father. The presentation of it in this, its own true light, will carry it clear, without a conflict, of the greater number of the assaults that are made upon it, and will immediately reveal, without an argument, the hollowness and shallowness of the many pitiful theories of Christ's death which *litterateurs* would substitute in its room.

Part Third.

Doctrine of the Covenant necessary if we would Formulate the Relation between Christ and His People.

How are we to formulate and establish the relation subsisting between Christ and His people, as Redeemer and redeemed, unless we fall back upon the doctrine of the Covenant? *Some* relation, it is evident, must be acknowledged as subsisting between Christ and those on whose behalf He dies, else we do not even come within sight of the idea of a vicarious sacrifice. The possibility of real atonement absolutely postulates and demands a conjunction between Him who atones and those for whom His atonement is available. This is beyond the need of proof. And as there is an absolute and obvious necessity for *some* conjunction or relation, so in searching for *the* conjunction or relation which actually subsists, our search cannot terminate satisfactorily till we reach and recognise the covenant oneness. The same reason that demands *a* relation, remains unsatisfied till it meets with *this* relation.

(1.) For, in the *first* place, it will not meet the necessities of the case to refer to the union between Christ and His people which is effected in their regeneration by the agency of the Holy Spirit and the instrumentality of that faith which is His gift. This, no doubt, is all-important in its own place. The Divine scheme is, that all fulness dwells in Christ: that all the treasures of knowledge and of wisdom are hid in Him: that all spiritual blessings for the Church of God are treasured up in Him: that no saving gift or grace or blessing is given, so to speak, *past* Him, or out of Him: all are given *in* Him. Hence an actual conjunction with Him, by the indwelling of His own Spirit and the embracing action of our faith, is indispensable to our enjoying "the redemption which is *in* Christ," or any of the blessings of His purchase.

But the question is not, What conjunction between Christ and a sinner is requisite in order to that sinner obtaining the benefits of His redeeming work? The question is, What conjunction between Christ and the sinner is requisite in order to that redeeming work being undertaken and achieved by Christ on his behalf? We are not in search of a relation that shall justify the *application* of Christ's redemption, but of one that shall justify the *impetration* of it. And *that* evidently must be a relation anterior to the actual, personal, spiritual conjunction that is established in regeneration.

(2.) Nor, in the *second* place, are the necessities of the case met by a reference to the Incarnation. No doubt this also is an invaluable relation—an indispensable element of conjunction—between the Redeemer and the redeemed. That a union should subsist between Christ and His people, such as is implied in their possession of a common nature, is of vital moment. "Forasmuch then as the children are partakers of flesh and blood, He also himself likewise took part in the same, that through death He might destroy him that had the power of death, and deliver them who through fear of death were all their lifetime subject to bondage. . . . In all things it behoved Him to be made like unto His brethren, that He might be a merciful and faithful high priest in things pertaining to God, to make reconciliation for the sins of the people. For in that He himself hath suffered, being tempted, He is able to succour them that are tempted" (Heb. ii. 14–18). Yet, vitally important as this is, unless we are to be satisfied with a relation which Christ holds alike to the saved and the unsaved, we cannot rest satisfied with the Incarnation as fully answering the kind of conjunction which we are seeking between those who are actually redeemed and Christ as specifically their Redeemer. Even in the very heart of the passage last quoted a very significant phrase occurs, as if expressly designed to guide us past so erroneous an idea. "For verily He took the seed of Abraham." He took the seed of "Abraham,"—not of Adam. In His own person He is to be regarded as "the Seed of the woman,"—not the seed of the man. And in His work—in the whole work of which His Incarnation is the foundation and commencement—"He taketh hold," not of Adam's, but Abraham's seed. There is, therefore, a conjunction between Him and His people, which His possession, along with them, of a common nature does not exhaust nor express. There must be some other relation, anterior even to the Incarnation, constituting, indeed, a ground and reason even for it also.

For we are in search of a relation that shall constitute a justifying ground for Christ's whole work. But His Incarnation is part of His work. That He should "humble Himself, and take upon Him the form of a servant, and be found in fashion as a man,"—this is a part, and a great part, of what the Son of God undertook on our behalf. To assign *this*, therefore, as that conjunction between Christ and His people which we are in search of, is to assign a part of Christ's work as a ground or justifying reason of the rest of it, or rather of the whole of it. And that obviously overthrows the initial terms of our inquiry. For if the Incarnation is part of the work He undertook on His people's behalf, the question returns, What relation or conjunction subsists between Christ and His people which renders it fit and congruous and righteous that He should accomplish for them the work for which He became incarnate, and should for them become incarnate in order to accomplish it?

(3.) Nor is it sufficient to say, in the *third* place, that the relation is that of suretyship and substitution. This undoubtedly is a great step in advance. Only let the ground thus taken up be secured. Let the inquiry be pressed to the uttermost; let it be exhausted. All truly scientific investigation searches on and on, till it arrives at somewhat of which no further explanation can be given or is required. Theology as a science meets this canon, and then claims a right to rest. Let us then still inquire.

Christ undertakes the work of Calvary, the death of the cross, for His people, because He stands towards them in the relation of a surety—a surety on their behalf to the offended Lawgiver and Judge. Be it so: but what shall justify His occupying that relation? What renders it fit, proper, righteous, that He should be accepted as standing in that relation towards them, and in that relation suffering for them? To this also it is not difficult to reply. He is their surety, because He is their substitute. He acts *on their behalf*, because He stands *in their room*. One only question now remains; and there can be no possibility, as there should be no inducement, to evade it. The relation of a substitute justifies the suretyship; what shall justify the substitution?

It is to this at last that the question must really be narrowed. The exact hinge and whole stress of the inquiry is here. And we can attain no satisfaction on this point, no sufficient answer to this question, and therefore no satisfactory conclusion to our whole line of investigation, till the doctrine of the everlasting Covenant oneness comes into view. That is the great underlying relation. That is the grand primary conjunction between the Redeemer and the redeemed, which alone bears up, and justifies, and accounts for all else in respect of relation which can be predicated as true concerning them. "Both He that sanctifieth and they that are sanctified are ALL OF ONE: for WHICH cause He is not ashamed to call them brethren" (Heb. ii. 11). His substitution is a good reason for His suretyship. Covenant oneness is, if possible, a still better reason for His substitution. For now is the *vicariousness* of His sacrifice not merely brought to light, but vindicated. It is not merely true that He suffers for us; it is also true that we suffer in Him. And the latter of these propositions justifies the truth and righteousness of the former. He is substituted *for us*, because He is one *with us*—identified with us, and we with Him.

Moreover, the especial aspect of this oneness as a *Covenant* oneness must be apprehended and kept in view. In contemplating the oneness, we must contemplate it as covenanted. For, in order to complete our exclusion of unsatisfactory solutions of the problem, we must observe,—

(4.) In the *fourth* place, that it is not enough to consider this oneness as decreed; we must consider it as specially and expressly covenanted: not merely as decreed by the sovereign authority of the Godhead, but covenanted between the eternal Father and the eternal Son.

To trace the oneness between Christ and His people to a Divine decree may honour the Godhead: but does it honour the Trinity in Godhead? On the contrary, it refuses recognition of the Trinity, precisely in that grand manifestation in which the doctrine of the Trinity—the truth of the distinct personalities of the Divine persons—is most especially to be recognised. There is no revelation of the Trinity in Godhead comparable to that which is afforded by the Covenant of Grace. To "us men, and" in "our salvation," the doctrine of the Trinity is commended, as at once revealed and precious, as placed in clearest evidence in the distinct actings of the persons of the Godhead in that Divine compact which is the spring and fountainhead of our eternal hopes. And even "to the principalities and powers in heavenly places," it is probable, "there is made known by the Church" and her covenanted salvation, in the most eminent possible demonstration, the subsistence of three persons in the one Divine Being. To be satisfied, therefore, with regarding Christ's oneness with His people as simply decreed and not covenanted, would be a very grave mistake; a mistake for which indeed there can be no excuse, as there can surely be no intelligible temptation. Moreover, it were to pretermit the due recognition of the voluntariness of Christ's susception and entire accomplishment of the work given Him to do. And still further, it were to overlook the splendid evidence of *love* as the great originating principle and motive of His redemption. There is a certain aspect of coldness about a mere decree. Practically, in the mind's view, it comes too closely to be identified, in point of impression, with the idea of cold, dead, impersonal fate. Unitarianism is ever doomed to have this practical outgoing. It is in Trinity that provision is seen for the vivid warmth of personality and personal love; and especially in the covenant of Trinity for man's redemption. There are distinct personal actings of the Father, and of the Son, and of the Spirit, in the Covenant. There are distinct actings of the will of the Father, and of the will of the Son in that oneness that is constituted between Christ and His people, and which justifies and bears up all that is achieved for their salvation. And these actings of will are actings of love. Hear the overflowings of love from Christ's heart, as His achievements for His people are by Himself referred back upon the loving deed by which the Father made them over to Him to be His own:—"O righteous Father, Thine they were, and Thou gavest them Me, and I have kept them." He means to say: *Therefore*, for that reason, have I kept them; even as I would keep that love-gift of Thine, which I did so willingly and lovingly receive. Identified, by loving covenant between Himself and the Father, with the people given unto Him; truly representing them, because identified in covenanted oneness with them; He becomes their competent and acceptable substitute and surety,—His substitution in every light most justifiable in the eye of law most stringent and of righteousness inexpugnable. And the vindication of His vicarious sacrifice of Himself for their salvation, is set on high in the intelligent and joyful convictions of the poor and needy, beyond the possibility of any sinister and false philosophy endangering it.

While the Divine Head of the Church has, in His great goodness, long kept these views before men's minds in Scotland, we cannot but cherish a deep sympathy— we would say *pity*, but that the word might be considered invidious, while no such feeling is in our heart—towards many earnest and noble minds in Germany, evidently inquiring with the greatest ardour after the truth as it is in Jesus Christ, but baffled because the covenant oneness between Redeemer and redeemed has not yet come into their field of vision. It is the doctrine of the Covenant that they need. No wonder that, in ignorance of this great guiding principle, to a beautiful and so love-worthy spirit as that of ULLMANN, "substitution" should seem an arbitrary and capricious thing; and that to many others "imputation" should be obnoxious, as a mere make-believe and legal fiction, with which they cannot accredit the God of truth. Moral instinct, the dictates of pious feeling, and Holy Scripture all combine to convince them that "the judgment of God must be according to truth." That moral axiom—that sacred spiritual postulate—they feel they must at all hazards conserve. And they are right. Any doctrine of Atonement or of justification that should impugn it, is thereby necessarily demonstrated to be false. But let Christ and His people be federally one, by the sovereign authority and love of the Father, and by the voluntary covenanted acceptation of the Son. In that case, legal fiction, make-believe, arbitrariness and caprice, are at the furthest possible remove from the Divine Covenant transaction of our redemption,—alike from the basis of it, and from all the fruits of it. "Christ bears the sins of many," because, in His covenanted indentification with these "many," their sins are sinlessly and truly His sins. And unto the same "many sons and daughters" of the Covenant, the Father imputes the righteousness of the Son, because, in their covenant oneness with the Son, His righteousness is undeservedly but truly their own righteousness. And all throughout, "the judgment of God is according to truth."

But we must bring this train of thought to a close. We have proved that the doctrine of the Covenant is a directly Scriptural category: that it is the result of a large induction of particulars, conducted on the same canon as that to which all true science must be amenable: and that it is at once a most searching and indeed conclusively satisfactory instrument of investigation, and a most powerful instrument alike of exposition and defence. We should have been glad to show how the doctrine of the Covenant bears on spiritual life, as well as theological accuracy; how it touches the interests of spiritual life at every point; how it is absolutely indispensable to give validity—to give any real trustworthiness—to what, in modern phrase, is called the "Christian consciousness," being indeed the Divine and perfect charter or standard to which "Christian consciousness" must perpetually refer itself, alike for its existence, and its verification, and its utterances, if it is to have any right to speak at all. But we must pause. May the doctrine of the Covenant of Grace—of the federal oneness of Christ and His people—long remain enshrined in the heart's core of Scottish piety! In the noble *Vaterland*, too, may it soon become widely known and acceptable! "I will sing of the mercies of the Lord for ever: with my mouth will I make known thy faithfulness to all generations. For I have said, Mercy shall be built up for ever: thy faithfulness shalt thou establish in the very heavens. I have made a Covenant with my Chosen, I have sworn unto David my servant, Thy seed will I establish for ever, and build up thy throne to all generations."

CHAPTER III.

ATONEMENT AND CHRIST'S PRIESTLY OFFICE.

THE doctrine of the Covenant of Grace is an impregnable wall of circumvallation round the scriptural theory of the Atonement. So, likewise, is the doctrine of Christ's Priesthood. And to her divinely constructed defences Zion's attention is divinely called.

"Let Mount Zion rejoice. Walk about Zion, and *go round about her:* tell the towers thereof. Set your heart to her bulwarks" (Ps. xlviii. 11–13, *marg.*). Carry not her interests and crown jewels outside these bulwarks, but let your defence be carried on *within.* "Great is the Lord, and greatly to be praised *in* the city of our God" (ver. 1). Those who praise Him there—within the city, within the bulwarks—need not be afraid, whosoever may "assemble;" for lo! they shall "pass by together." Show them Zion's bulwarks, till they "marvel and are troubled and haste away." And adventure not the ark down amongst the Philistines outside.

It is on this principle that, in explaining and defending the doctrine of the Atonement, we would affirm and maintain a proposition bearing on the Priesthood of

Christ analogous to that which we have already illustrated in reference to the Covenant of Grace, namely,—

That the Doctrine of the Atonement ought on no account to be discussed apart from, or outside the category of, Christ's Priestly Office.

Men may discuss, as long as they please, arbitrary philosophies of the abstract idea of atonement; but if it be professed to investigate the scriptural doctrine of the Atonement of Christ—of the death of the Son of God—we must demand, as essential to the *status questionis*, that it be set forth as embraced within the category of His Priesthood. So clearly does Holy Scripture, on the very face of it, bear out the reasonableness of this demand, that no conceivable objection can be taken to it, save such as would resolve into a refusal to make Scripture the supreme arbiter in the discussion: and with those who should take that position, we have of course in this matter nothing to do,—except, indeed, to move the previous question.

Now, in handling the topic of Christ's Priesthood, with the view of showing what light it casts on the *status questionis*, and on the argument concerning the Atonement, there are, in the *first* place, some preliminary considerations to be attended to. In the *second* place, the intrinsic idea of the nature of the office has to be kept in view. And in the *third* place, the immediate and inevitable characteristics which the very nature of the office must impart to Christ's death will be seen to be such as greatly to relieve the argument on the Atonement from the necessity of dealing at any great length,—or indeed with any very great degree of respectfulness,—with the false views and objections which are being paraded in opposition to it.

Part First.

Preliminaries concerning Priesthood.

As to what is merely preliminary, we lay it down,—

I. In the first place, that the Priesthood is a *real* office —a real office, definite and specific. This is of some importance,—more so, indeed, than may at first appear. For the noble word "Priesthood" has been misappropriated and misapplied, even so as greatly to deface it of its intrinsic and peculiar import. There is a certain literary slang abroad—we must be pardoned for our inability to find any better designation for it—which talks of the "priests of literature ;" of the " priests of science ;" of man as the "interpreter and priest of nature:" and we have even some recollection of hearing those who meant no harm talking in the pulpit concerning Adam, in his unfallen state, as the " priest of Eden." If men, for the purpose of giving factitious force and grandeur to their language, will persist in translating words from a region of thought in which they are in their proper place, into another into which they cannot be imported without being thereby stripped of all their specific and intrinsic meaning, it may be difficult to hinder them. But it becomes necessary at least to see to it that these abused and misappropriated symbols of exact, and definite, and important thought be not in their own native realm attenuated into the meaninglessness to which they degenerate when made to figure in a region of themes altogether alien to their import. The idea of priesthood—if priesthood is to have any real and definite meaning at all—can have no place whatever in science, or literature, or nature, or any such realm. It belongs to the realm of grace, presupposing sin and the Divine design to overcome and remove sin. And for my part, I would as soon think of transferring the language of Geometry and Algebra to Botany, and talk of the hypotenuse of a flower, or the *square root* of a tree, or the differential cöefficient of a convolvulus, as speak of the priesthood of nature or of letters.

Nor is it merely on the score of incongruity and paralogism that this ought to be avoided. The great evil is, that it tends to reduce the idea of priesthood to the utmost vagueness, and to impress men with the notion that they have some intelligent apprehension of what they are talking of, while they have none. The word becomes a mere figure of speech, a free and easy use of which is to be made without any definite inquiry into what, even *as* a figure of speech, it means. Accordingly, there are those who affirm that, though Christ is no doubt in Scripture called a priest, yet it is only figuratively. Among the many memorable utterances of the elder Marcus Dods, few are more memorable than the answer which he gives to this absurd affirmation. "If the great 'High Priest of our profession' was only figuratively a priest, assuredly those priests who only exercised those delegated powers which they received from Him could be no more; and consequently, there never was a real priest in existence. The very word, upon this supposition, stands in the unprecedented situation of having a figurative application without ever having had a real literal meaning."

Priesthood is an office—a real office, very definite and peculiar. It is an office embracing very definite and specific duties, demanding special and peculiar qualifications, and not to be entered on save at the special call and appointment of God. "No man taketh this honour unto himself, but he that is called of God, as was Aaron. Even so Christ glorified not himself to be made an high priest; but He [glorified him] who said unto him, Thou art my Son, this day have I begotten Thee. As he saith also in another place, Thou art a priest for ever, after the order of Melchisedec" (Heb. v. 4–6).

II. But, secondly: It is not enough to maintain that Christ's Priesthood is a real and veritable office; it must be regarded and set forth as pre-eminently *the* office—the foundation office—which Christ as a Redeemer executes. Besides being a Priest, our Lord is a Prophet and a King; and He is both these, not incidentally, occasionally, or by the way, but by office. He is officially the Prophet, and officially the King, of Zion. Nevertheless, His Priesthood is a more fundamental office than these—its necessity, its duties, and the discharge of these duties lying closer to the heart of His interposition for our salvation than aught that pertains to either of the other offices which He fulfils. The Divine Spirit does not affirm that His appointment either to His prophetic or His kingly office " glorified " Him. But the affirmation is expressly made of His appointment to the sacerdotal office: " God glorified Him to be made an high priest" (Heb. v. 5). To inaugurate Him into the office of prophet or of king, we read not that the dread solemnity of the Divine oath was had recourse to. " But the Lord hath sworn and will not repent, Thou art a priest for ever, after the order of Melchisedec " (Ps. cx. 4). Four times is this remarkable oracle quoted in terms in the New Testament (Heb. v. 6, xi. 20, vii. 17, vii. 21). And four times is the unique peculiarity of the interposal of the oath commented and reasoned on, and made a fountain of precious and irrefragable inference. It is with great emphasis, and with strong argument of consolation to the heirs of promise that Paul avers how " God interposed Himself by an oath" (Heb. vi. 17, *marg.*). And it is with great frequency, and with resistless demonstration of the perpetuity, the intransferableness, and the perfection of Christ's Priesthood, that he points to the oath as conferring unparalleled and unapproachable glory upon that blessed office of our Mediator. " Not without an oath was He made priest" (Heb. vii.

20). "Those priests without an oath, but *this* with an oath" (ver. 21). "The law made them; but the word of the oath maketh the Son" (ver. 28). Surely we may well "conclude," with Calvin, "that the Priesthood of Christ is invested with great importance, seeing that it is ratified by the oath of God. And in fact it is the very turning-point on which our salvation depends."

To assign the position of primacy among Christ's offices to His Priesthood, is not to disparage the other offices. On the contrary, it is to honour them, and to prepare the way for the display of their real import and bearings.

For, as a Prophet, it is Christ's duty and office to reveal to the Church precisely the import and glory of His Priesthood—to reveal His Priesthood in its presuppositions, its actings, and its fruits. The character of God, His sovereignty, His holiness and justice, His law, His claims—these on the one hand: and on the other hand, man's sin, his guilt, his liability to eternal death, and his utter impotence under the sentence thereof, and under the bondage of spiritual death: such are the presuppositions of the Priesthood. God's long-suffering; His grace, and love, and loving purpose, and loving choice of an elect number as His own; His reconcilableness: a true and proper propitiation achieved; sin expiated; an actual reconciliation effected; free access to God's throne opened up: these are partly the immediate causes, and partly the direct actings, of the Priesthood. Pardon of sin; justification in righteousness; peace with God; the Holy Ghost as the Spirit of regeneration and of adoption, with every gift and grace of love Divine, even all spiritual blessings in heavenly places: these are the fruits of Priesthood. But all that is contained in these various enumerations, it is Christ's duty as a Prophet to unfold by His word and Spirit to the Church. They are, however, as we have said, just the presuppositions, causes, actings, and fruits of His Priesthood. The Priesthood, therefore, is at once the foundation, and provides the subject-matter of Christ's office as a Prophet.

It holds the same place of priority and importance relatively to the kingly office. The sceptre which He wields as a King, He earned as a Priest. The throne on which He now sits is the reward of His so acceptable discharge of His priestly office. And He shall bear the glory, and shall sit and rule upon His throne; and He shall be a Priest upon His throne (Zech. vi. 13). It is the throne of God and of the "Lamb."

If, then, Christ's interposition for our salvation is accomplished in the way of *office;* if the office which rules and determines all else connected with His interposition be the Priestly office; and if, moreover, the core and culmination of this interposition of Christ be His death on Calvary; could any course be imagined more extraordinary and suicidal than that, in expounding and defending the doctrine of Christ's death, we should consent to isolate it, and to discuss it apart from the doctrine of His Priesthood? Even the most distant preliminary observations that can be made upon the topic, if only relevant, must be conclusive on the question that has now been put.

This will become still more manifest when we make closer advance upon the topic, and consider the real nature and design of the priestly office.

Part Second.

The Intrinsic Nature of Priesthood.

Let us consider the intrinsic nature of the office of Priesthood.

And here we have scriptural definition to guide us, as nearly mathematically exact as the nature of the topic admits of. "Every high priest taken from among men is ordained for men in things pertaining to God, that he may offer both gifts and sacrifices for sins" (Heb. v. 1). What success can we have in discussing any theme if we neglect our definitions? And if the theme be scriptural, where shall we find reliable definitions if we neglect those which Scripture expressly provides? Looking, then, to the very full description of priesthood given in the inspired deliverance just quoted;—besides the two considerations, *first*, That the priest must possess the nature and be related to the race for whose welfare he interposes,—he must be "taken from among men;" and *secondly*, That he must possess the call and ordination of God,—" every high priest is ordained;"—there are the three following things implied in it:—

I. Priesthood rests on personal relation. He is "ordained for men."

That is a law of the office; fundamental, indeed, and essential to the nature and constituting idea of it. "*Every* high priest is ordained for men." His office is absolutely groundless, meaningless, and void, save as he is related to and acts "for men." He is an ordained agent on behalf of men—instead and on behalf of individual persons. For it cannot be a general and indefinite relation to mankind, to the race—to humanity in the mass, as some speak—that is intended. No doubt the priest must be related to humanity—to human nature generally. But whatever demand arises from the nature and design of his office in that direction, is met by the prior portion of this definition, which says that he is "taken *from among* men." That exhausts all that has to be said of his general relation to the race. Something far more express and definite—something thoroughly distinct and additional—is indicated in the affirmation that he is "ordained *for* men." Most obviously individual men, particular persons, are here indicated; and special personal relation to them. He is ordained expressly for them. He takes office for them; and he will take action for them. And his action will be complete and effectual; for, though taken from among men, the last Adam is "the Lord from heaven," and his work is perfect.

II. The action which he takes has God for its object.

Priesthood and all its direct and immediate actings are directly and immediately towards God. He is ordained "in things pertaining to God"—τὰ πρὸς τὸν Θεὸν— things towards God. The whole aspects and bearing of priesthood are towards God. It looks and it acts Godward. Its immediate object is God. While it deals with the things of God, it deals with them, not in their aspects towards man, but in their bearings on God himself,—on God's sovereignty, and character, and claims, and law. Its object, we repeat, is God. It propitiates God; it intercedes to God. It satisfies God's justice; it pacifies God's wrath; it secures God's favour; it seals God's covenant love; and gives effect to God's eternal purpose and grace. Herein it is conspicuously distinguished from the prophetic and kingly offices of our Lord. These, in their several actings, have not God for their immediate object, but mainly the souls of His people. Christ executes the office of a Prophet by revealing *to us,* by His Word and Spirit, the will of God for our salvation. Christ executes the office of a King in subduing *us* to Himself, in ruling and defending *us;* and when the kingly office takes wider action, it is in restraining and conquering all His and our enemies. There is no possible excuse, therefore, for confounding the sacerdotal office with either the prophetic or the kingly.

III. While priesthood thus acts in personal relation, in relation to and on behalf of individual persons; and while it acts directly towards God as its object; its primary and immediate acting is *offering*. To act as a priest is to offer. "He is ordained for men, in things pertaining to God, *that he may offer*" (Heb. v. 1). And again: "He ought to *offer*" (Heb. v. 3). And again: "Every high priest is ordained to *offer* gifts and sacrifices: wherefore it is *of necessity* that this man have somewhat also to *offer*" (Heb. viii. 3).

This, then, is *the* action which Christ has to take, when He takes action as a Priest. He has to "offer." He has to offer "to God;" for all priestly action is Godward. He has to offer "for men"—in personal relation to, and on behalf of, individual men personally and individually. Moreover, the offering is "for sins:" "He ought to offer for sins" (Heb. v. 2). Not for sin; but "sins:" not sin in the abstract, impersonally, unrelatedly, and in the general; but "sins," actual and individual sins. What sins? What sins, but those of the persons for whom He acts as having been ordained for them?

Combine these positions,—adding the ideas of Christ's spotless personal holiness, and of His perpetual intercession,—and we have the full doctrine of the Priesthood, and *in and under it*, the full doctrine of the Atonement, which cannot be separated from it without being shorn of its glory and left almost defenceless:—"Christ executeth the office of a priest, in His once offering Himself a sacrifice without spot to God, to be a reconciliation for the sins of His people; and in making continual intercession for them."

Part Third.

Pointing the Argument from Priesthood.

Without expanding these elements of thought on the fundamental ideas and intrinsic nature and immediate action of the Priesthood, let us now consider what immediate and inevitable characteristics they impart to the death of Christ—our object being to show how they relieve the argument on the Atonement from the necessity of dealing at any length with the various false doctrines that are in vogue. For if it be true, in the *first* place, that Priesthood rests on personal relation; in the *second* place, that its whole action is immediately towards God; and in the *third* place, that its immediate action is *real* action, not mere *suffering*, but real action, and that action *offering*: then we are prepared to take preliminary and effectual protest against a whole host of heretical ideas, to the effect that they are not even entitled to a hearing,—far less to be permitted to obstruct, or to be acknowledged as able so much as even to touch, the argument of orthodox evangelical doctrine on the Atonement.

I. Does Priesthood rest on personal relation—insomuch that apart from this idea we have formed no scriptural notion of the office? Then immediately all Socinian ideas of Example and Martyrdom; all Neo-Socinian, Maurician ideas of Self-denial, Self-sacrifice, Self-surrender, and so forth; YOUNG'S notion of Moral Influence; and BUSHNELL'S theory of a Govermental Display;—all these motley attempts at explanation of the death of Christ must disappear immediately. None of them, nor all of them put together, come within sight of the doctrine, or even the idea, of Priesthood. Let them *see* real priesthood, and like the "assembled kings" of the Psalmist, when they "see it, they pass by together; they are troubled and haste them away." In none of them can we descry the element of *office*. In none of them still less the office of *priesthood*. For in none of them is there room for personal relation, without which, to the constituting notion of priesthood there is not even an approach.

No doubt Example, Martyrdom, Moral Influence, Governmental Display, may all have bearings on persons. Personal *results* may in the end be accomplished. And hence personal relations may be said in the end to be established towards those whom Example, Influence, etc., may have beneficially affected. But it is not personal relations ultimately as the result, but personal relations *ab initio* to start with, that are the postulate of Priesthood. Moreover, such beneficial relations, as a final result, however splendidly accomplished, could not generate *office*,—office, which is desiderated not as an end but as a means, a means without whose provision and presence from the outset the end is unattainable. Far less could they generate *priestly* office. But indeed it is not requisite to insist on the specific office of priesthood in order to put the heterogeneous phalanx of heresies to flight. The barest and vaguest idea of *office* in the general is enough. Is Example an office? Is Martyrdom an office? Is Self-denial an office? Is Moral Influence an office? Is a man an office-bearer because he is exemplary, self-denying, morally influential? How the question covers these theories with confusion! "Are all apostles?" said Paul. Are all office-bearers? may we also say. Yea, truly: all at least are bound to be so, if self-sacrifice and self-denial be *ex officio*. There can be no "taking from among men" in that case. There can be no inaugurating of representatives to act "for men" in these things. Christ's office of Priesthood proposes to relieve men of the obligation to eternal death. It is an insult to a man's moral nature to propose to relieve him of the duty of being morally exemplary, or morally influential. Obligations of that nature are incumbent upon all men; and they are intransferable. In the nature of things they cannot be delegated to representatives. They carry in them nothing official, and it is impossible that their obligations or actings could be framed into an office.

But it is not only this motley crowd of miserable substitutes for the Atonement of the Lord Jesus that the first principle of priesthood is fitted to expose and overthrow. It is equally effective in setting aside the theory of universal or indefinite atonement. If the atonement of Christ falls under the category of His Priesthood, it is impossible it can be impersonal, indefinite, unlimited; for the priesthood is not. In order to its very constitution, it pre-requires personal relation; and the same must be true of the Atonement, unless the Atonement transpires outside the limits and actings and conditions of the priesthood. The priesthood is "for men," and for "sins." Not for mankind in the general, but "for *men*,"—particular men. And not for *sin* in the general, but "for *sins*,"—particular sins. The personal relation of the priest is a relation to particular persons, with especial reference to their particular sins; or, more briefly, it is a relation to these persons considered as sinners. A general reference or relation is out of the question. When indefinite and general relation is contended for, then the antithesis must be brought out between the two phrases —antithetical precisely in order to the expiscation of this very point—the two phrases, "Taken from among men," and, "Ordained for men." Whatever of general relation to humanity can be legitimately predicated, is affirmed in the first of these phrases. The fact of Christ's own humanity exhausts what is true in respect of general relation or general reference. The Priest is the man Christ Jesus: taken from among men; raised up out of the people. His office is special, not general, unlimited, and indefinite. It is "for men,"—for persons, for particular individual persons: and for every individual person on whose behalf it is not effectual unto actual and complete salvation, for him it was either not undertaken, or for him it has failed.

The pre-requisite of personal relation to particular persons is indispensable in all real priesthood whatsoever. It is true of "every" priest that is taken from among men. Any "general reference" contradictory to this, or in addition to this—except simply community of nature, secured by his being taken from among men—violates the very first principle of the office. We see the presence and action of this principle most clearly in the Levitical priesthood. The priests of Levi were chosen *for*, or in lieu of, the first-born; and they were ordained *for*, or in room and on behalf of men, even for the Israel of God collectively and individually. They acted for individuals; and besides such action, they had no priestly action whatsoever, no official duty to discharge. The introduction of a "general reference" into the theory of their office is an absurdity. The success of their priestly actings was complete, and also cognisable, just because it was for particular persons. Indefiniteness, generality, vagueness, unlimitedness, universality, are ideas with which no theory of their office can possibly cohere. To admit any such idea, is to render the action of their office impalpable, and the result of it untraceable. But its action is most palpable, and its results can be most easily traced, while they are seen to have been in every instance complete, and absolutely successful. For whomsoever a Levitical priest sacerdotally officiated, he was completely successful—completely successful in averting the evil, or procuring the privilege, which his official action contemplated. And if the same thing is not admitted concerning the priesthood of Christ, then we are logically landed, in the *first* place, in this most offensive result, That Christ's Priesthood is relatively inferior to that of Levi; and, in the *second* place, in this prodigious paralogism also,—that is, if the Levitical priesthood was typical of Christ's,— namely, That uniform and complete success in the one is, by Divine wisdom, erected into a type and symbol of extensive failure in the other!* The moment we take up with the theory of a "general reference" of the Atonement—the moment we abandon the elemental principle of individual personal relations—we close against ourselves the very gate of entrance into the scriptural doctrine of priesthood, and the glorious realm of truth into which it leads.

II. Is the action of priesthood directly and immediately towards God? Has it God for its immediate object? Then this again effectually and at once precludes even a hearing for the vast majority of false theories of the Atonement; for they do not even pretend to present God as the object of what action they acknowledge in the death of Christ. And very obviously Example, and Martyrdom, and Self-Denial, and Governmental Display, and Moral Influence, are not "towards God." Martyrdom may be *from* God; but it is towards, and upon, the sufferer. Example surely is not offered to God, but to

---

* For the directly converse but equally effective application of this same argument, as against the views of Ullmann, see CHRIST'S PRESENCE IN THE GOSPEL HISTORY, *second edition*, p. 335. "It is not the way of the Divine wisdom to set up failure as typical of success!"

men. Self-denial has not God for its object, but ungodliness and worldly lust. And Moral Influence—shall it be exerted upon God? Or shall a Display of the Principles of His own Government be given to the Almighty himself? It requires not profound study to refute theories like these. The student who has learned the first clause of his first definition, will find it a sword to cleave them lifeless, and a spade to bury their remains.

But it is often said,—You ought to deal gently with these views, erroneous though they be, seeing that there is, more or less, a measure of truth in them all.

Let us adjust this matter, or at least indicate how it ought to be adjusted. For we must take occasion, from this very common plea in mitigation, additionally to glorify the truth of God, and additionally to strip these "other gospels" of men of their plausibilities. We lay down the following positions :—

In the *first* place; there is not only no measure of truth in these theories, but they are wholly false and deadly, *when* presented, as they *are* presented, as adequate expositions of the doctrine of Atonement, explanations of the reason and design of the death of Jesus. It must not be forgotten that they are given forth, severally and all of them, as satisfactory solutions of the question, What is the intrinsic nature, the constituting conception, of Christ's sacrifice on the cross? They profess to exhibit the fundamental idea and the primary design of Atonement. And in this light they are, beyond the possibility of doubt, each of them "another gospel;" and as such, though proclaimed by the angels of heaven, they are liable to the Anathema of Inspiration.

In the *second* place; there is no measure of truth in them, even though they should be put forth as *partial* answers to the question which they profess to solve. They have no right to stand as even a *portion* of the truth concerning the doctrine of the intrinsic nature and immediate object and design of the Atonement. There is not even an element of truth in them that will co-ordinate with that doctrine as maintained by the whole Catholic Church of God. That doctrine is itself either *the* truth, or it is a baseless fabric. Assuredly it has in it no room for these theories, as forming with it parts of one whole. Claiming to rank with it in any such light,—which in point of fact they never do,— they would be seen immediately to be false.

And in the *third* place; regarded as secondary and subordinate results of the Atonement,—not entering into its intrinsic nature and explanatory of its immediate design, but as mere secondary and subordinate results,—even in this light, the contents of these theories are not truth and fact, but merely unrealised and unrealisable ideas, mere conceptions which the theories themselves can never embody as realities. And in this sense also, as in every other, there is no measure of truth in them. They never can be translated into truth and fact; they never can emerge from dream-land, from the region of the ideal and of mere conception; till they are acknowledged as not of the essence and constituting idea of atonement, but *only* as the secondary and subordinate outcome thereof. The fundamental notion and essence of atonement, as embodied in the priestly work of Christ, is the offering of Himself unto God a sacrifice and a reconciliation for the sins of His people. It is His substitutionary oblation of Himself, bearing the curse and bringing in righteousness, thereby satisfying Divine justice, and reconciling us unto God. It is from such atonement as *this*—atonement in its unique and specific meaning, in its peculiar and essential idea, and in its complete achievement by Christ, acting herein as an high priest "for men," offering "for sins"—it is from, and *only* from, such atonement as this, that these theories derive into them that measure of truth which they themselves, by attempting to supplant their own parent thought, turn into falsehood and deadly error. And this might be shown, to edification, in full detail. We can do little more than hint the line of thought.

(1.) It was by the atonement of a substitutionary sacrifice for sin, satisfying Divine justice, that Christ had scope for that unmurmuring patience by which He left us an "Example" that we should follow His steps (1 Pet. ii. 21–24).

(2.) It was by dying a substitutionary and atoning death that He underwent "Martyrdom" as a witness for the truth (John xviii. 37).

(3.) It was in setting His face as a flint to go to Jerusalem, there to fill up with antitypical reality all

Jerusalem's priestly services, by offering Himself without spot to God a curse-bearing sacrifice for sin, that He denied Himself and took up His cross, and commended " Self-denial " to His followers.

(4.) It was when He proffered Himself to the sword of offended justice, awakened against Him, according to His own covenant arrangement, by the Father, that He illustrated " Self-surrender."

(5.) With Him " Self-sacrifice " was specifically sacrifice for sin, a satisfaction and a reconciliation.

(6.) There is indeed in His Cross a " Governmental Display." It " declares the righteousness of God for the remission of sins;" but only because Christ is there " set forth a *propitiation* through faith in His blood " (Rom. iii. 25). And it declares, manifests, displays the love of God; but only in that God " sent forth His Son to be the *propitiation* for our sins" (1 John iv. 10).

(7.) A "Moral Influence," also, undoubtedly flows from the cross of Jesus. But it is a fountain of moral influence;—and moral influence without spiritual power were needlessly exerted on men dead in trespasses and sins;—it is a fountain both of Moral Influence and of regenerating energy to turn us unto righteousness, *only* because He there gave Himself in justice-satisfying substitution, "the just for the unjust, that He might bring us unto God" (1 Pet. iii. 18).

Secure the intrinsic and essential nature, and the primary and direct design, of the atoning death of

Christ, and all the secondary results—flitting otherwise as mere shades in dream-land, vainly claiming the reality of fact—become real and true, and are secured. But when *they* claim to be of the essence of atonement, they fight against their own realisation. It is the same with all secondaries in relation to their primary. Happiness, followed as a primary object of pursuit, is unattainable. Duty, followed as a primary, brings happiness in its train. And in like manner, all good in these theories—all good conception or idea in them—remains ideal and unattainable, until based on the doctrine of substitution and satisfaction which to their own ruin they would supplant. They are like the second intended row of stones for a building which is never suffered to have a first row or foundation; like the second month of a year, that shall have no first month or beginning. In the hands of those who plead them as explanations of the cross, they are at the best but "airy nothings;" "their local habitation," and only home of life—their source of truth, reality, and power—is just that same old doctrine which they malign and would subvert. As if sunbeams should revile the sun!

III. But now, *thirdly:* Is the action of Priesthood *real* action; not mere suffering or endurance, but real action; and that action, *offering?* Then, without bringing out the nature of this action more fully,—without even asking what the exact and intrinsic nature of this action is,—we may see that it bears very powerfully, though perhaps not so patently, upon all the false theories which have passed under our review. For these theories, if probed, will be found to have no room in them for the idea of *action* in the death of Christ. Their advocates contemplate Christ's death, not as action, but exclusively as suffering. It is a providential event; to which Christ is subjected; not a priestly action which Christ achieves. They recognise His passive endurance; not His priestly agency. They see that He suffered: they see not that He " offered."

I maintain that on this single ground alone they are fatally incapacitated from discussing the doctrine of Christ's atoning death, and rightfully precluded even from a hearing in the discussion. Did Christ merely *suffer* in His death? Was His own *agency* not concerned in it? Then, was He not a Priest on Calvary, but merely a Lamb? And if so, the question at once arises, Who offered up this Lamb of God, the eternal Son of God, a sacrifice upon the cross? Either the Father, or the Spirit, was the Priest; neither of whom was ever " taken from among men," or " ordained for men, to offer." Or, there was no Priest. For assuredly no creature could be admitted to the honour of offering up the Only-begotten of the Father.* And in any case, in this view, Christ's death occurs outside His Priesthood; and if that be true, His death can be nothing to us.

---

* I find that in this sentence I have unconsciously quoted Calvin almost *verbatim*, from a passage with which a good many years ago I was familiar. See INSTITUTES, Book II., Chap. xv. 6.

I refuse to believe in the cross of Christ as a mere passive endurance. And I refuse to discuss the doctrine of His death under any such restriction of its marvellous, peculiar, and transcendent glory. I deny that His God-glorifying agency was overborne before He died, leaving Him a mere victim to causes and means of death, aside from His own active will and power offering Him to God. I deny that on His cross all His duty turned at last into patience, and became negation. It was His duty to die: and He discharged His duty. It never was any other man's duty to die: therefore, do not rob Him of a glory all His own. "It is appointed unto all men once to die;" appointed as a destiny,—never, save to Him, as a duty. It is indeed our duty to endure death with faith and patience. But it is the patience, the faith, that is in our case the duty, not death. Death cannot be our duty. We do not act in dying; we are acted on, and we endure it. Christ acted in dying. It was His duty to die—His official duty. Official action was in it—priestly agency. He "dismissed His Spirit." He "gave Himself." Herein is His love: herein also is His power: herein the triumph and transcendent glory of His victory over death. He is an unquelled, unconquered, conquering agent in offering Himself up to God. It is true He suffers—suffers the just for the unjust. Men are killing Him; and Satan tempting and tormenting Him. The Father bruises Him:— "It pleased the Lord to bruise Him," and to say, "Awake, O sword, against Him." He endures the

Cross. He suffers death. He dies a sufferer. So much the more wondrous is the truth that He dies a conquering agent in dying. He trembles; but He does not faint. He does not swoon, but agonize. And "*agony*" is *action* to the uttermost. This is the glory of His triumph. Leave this out of view,—put aside His priestly agency and priestly action in His death,—suppose His agency and action to have been, ere death, exhausted, leaving room for passive sufferance and patience merely; and you cannot " glory in the Cross," nor teach the Church of God to glory in it. You leave the glory of Christ's triumph, and the evidence of Christ's love, deep buried in the shame of Calvary, and in the grave of Golgotha. And it is not any glory in the resurrection that can in that case reflect back upon the Cross, and light it up with a glory not originally and intrinsically there. If He died a mere passive victim, He did not die a victor: and no subsequent glory can in that case redeem what in that case was defeat. But He died a triumphant agent. He prevailed against death to live until He said, " 'Tis finished," and then to die, not merely voluntarily, but by positive priestly action, giving Himself to God. The Cross itself is glorious; not from the subsequent resurrection and enthronement, but glorious from itself. It is itself a chariot of triumph. There is more agency and power in Christ's cross, than in all His work as Creator of the universe. There is as much spiritual glory in the Cross of Calvary, as in the throne of the Lamb in heaven. Christ crucified is—not after, but *in* being crucified—the Power of God. And He is the Power of God, because He is the Priest of God. It is His priestly duty to die—a duty unparalleled and unapproachable. He falters not in the discharge of it. Official agency is in His sacrificial priestly death. "He *offered* Himself." "He loved the Church, and *gave* Himself for it."

Ah! these are views of Christ's glorious priestly work —very simple, yea, on the very surface of it—which will not consist with even a hearing to those many representations which really evacuate His office altogether. We commend them to the students and younger ministers and preachers among our readers. We would not presume to instruct brethren of our own or of longer standing in the ministry. But those lately entered, or entering, on the duty of preaching the gospel of a veritable Sacrifice for sins, may perhaps kindly accept a word of exhortation. Probe deep into the simplest elemental principles of Christ's priestly office. They are capable of being preached in continually fresh variety of combination, such as may often give them, in your people's view, the aspect almost of startling but safe originality. Shall it ever be said that you forsook them as old-fashioned? That you gave them up, as having at last become platitudes in your hands? What! Instinct with the power of the eternal purpose of the Father; beautiful in the hands and in the love of Messiah; and shining in the light of the Eternal Spirit; how can they ever become platitudes? Baptize them evermore afresh in the light of the throne of God and of the Lamb; and bring them back afresh to your people with somewhat of the rhythm ringing through them of the ceaseless song of the angels and of the elders,—of the ten thousand times ten thousand and thousands of thousands:— "Blessing, and honour, and glory, and power be unto Him that sitteth upon the throne, and unto the Lamb for ever and ever."

CHAPTER IV.

CHRIST'S PRIESTLY ACTION IN HIS DEATH.

IN the preceding chapter we have vindicated the position, That the defenders of the orthodox evangelical doctrine of the Atonement ought never to consent to discuss that doctrine outside of the larger category of the priesthood of Christ. Our closing train of thought in illustrating that position we feel inclined to resume and consider at somewhat greater length. We lay it down :—

That the Doctrine of the Atonement ought not to be discussed apart from the idea of Christ's Priestly ACTION *in His death.*

For we are deeply persuaded, that the refusal to discuss or contemplate the doctrine of Christ's death, except as that priestly *action* which Holy Scripture abundantly reveals it to have been,—while it is obviously the most effective method of establishing and defending the doctrine itself,—is at the same time the true way to take legitimate and conclusive preliminary objection to the vast majority of false representations of Christ's death, to the effect of their not being entitled even to a hearing. Let it simply be shown of any particular aberration from the catholic doctrine of the death of Christ, that there is no room in it for anything more than suffering, mere passive endurance; that it has no explanation to afford of the idea, and indeed no room in it for the idea, that Christ in His death, besides being acted on, was in that very transaction an agent, an offerer, a priest— an official agent, triumphantly discharging positive, official, active duty,—and we are immediately exempted at the outset from any necessity of further discussion, and entitled preliminarily to dismiss out of court all such perversions of the doctrine of the catholic Church of Christ. For they are flagrant perversions. Holy Scripture is so clear, so abundant,—so express, varied, and emphatic,—in its assertions of Christ's death being a transaction in which His own agency was concerned, that those who deny this, or make no account of it, cannot be considered as merely erring in scriptural interpretation, but must be regarded as rejecting Scripture as the rule of faith. With such, of course, we are entitled and bound to refuse to discuss the doctrine of the Atonement. The question of the "Rule of Faith" is that to which all discussion with such opponents must be relegated.

Part First.

Reasons why this truth has been much overlooked.

At the same time, while it is undoubtedly true that Scripture is most clear and abundant in its revelation of the truth that Christ's death was priestly *action*, we have a strong conviction that there are, or may be, not a few who acquiesce in the sound and scriptural doctrine of the Atonement, but have not given to the simple proposition which affirms the action of Christ in His own death that attention to which it is gloriously entitled. We are so familiar with the plain statement that Christ was at once the Sacrifice and the Priest,— " He offered up Himself,"—that we think we have fully mastered its contents, while we may have done little more than skim the surface.

That it must contain great depths of truth should be obvious from the fact that it presents a consideration absolutely unparalleled, and singular, and unique. That the man Christ Jesus should both suffer death,—and such a death, under the curse of the divine law, and with all conceivable aggravations of woe, and agony, and shame; and *also* that He should sinlessly, yea, obediently and officially, have an active hand in His death,—and such a death ; ought at once to strike us as passing all comprehension, and as entitled to that thoughtful, prolonged, and reverent contemplation which might enable us, under the teaching of the Spirit of truth, to place the fact before our understandings with the most exact accuracy of thought we can attain, and with the fullest completeness that we can grasp. There is, indeed, good reason to think that the severe mental exercise for which there is in this simple familiar truth such manifest scope, is precisely what has led many minds to pass it by without any attempt to fathom it. That "Christ died for our sins according to the Scriptures," they are content to believe. But that in this transaction of the death at Calvary He combined the two apparently antagonistic attitudes of suffering and offering ;—*suffering* unto such extent and such intensity as would have quelled all the active powers, not to say the patience, of any but a Divine person; and *offering* also in such activity, and such unquelled and excelling triumphant action, as if no suffering were making drain upon His active powers at all;—this is the apparent paradox in the death of Christ which many, we fear, have far too lightly considered. And yet, how, without profound consideration and appreciating admiration of it, they can intelligently "glory in the Cross," it is impossible to see.

That the simple but profound truth on which we are desirous of insisting should have been, at least to some extent, overlooked by many whose views of the Atonement are not incorrect, may in some measure be easily accounted for. Apart from the demand for severely accurate mental action, which the nature of the subject makes on all who would attain to exact theological knowledge of its various elements, several phrases have acquired a currency unfavourable to clearness and comprehensiveness. Among these we may notice what we have long thought the unhappy and not very intelligible expression—"Christ's active and passive obedience." No doubt, with explanations, the phrase may be allowed; and, without question, it is with these explanations that sound writers have used it. It has been employed to express the fact, that in Christ's life and death as our surety, there meet the endurance of the penalty of the law and the inbringing of a positive righteousness. But it may be safely doubted whether the phrase "passive obedience" naturally indicates anything that can be properly called obedience at all; and the use of it in well-known English history is not favourable to the probability of its suggesting very accurate ideas theologically. Moreover, if there is anything in Christ's interposition for our salvation that may be supposed to be called "passive" obedience, as in express contradiction to "active" obedience, it must be His death: and where this impression prevails, it obviously countenances, and indeed suggests, the idea that His death was exclusively passive—that His own activity or agency is not to be recognised in it.

Then the phrases, "Our Lord's Passion," and "The Passion Week," lead obviously in the same direction. Used exclusively, and used as adequate and complete expressions for the death of Christ, and for that ever-memorable period of His closing sufferings and crowning work as our Redeemer, they evidently concentrate attention disproportionately, and indeed alone, on that aspect in which Christ appears as the piacular victim, or the Lamb of Sacrifice; presenting to the mind no suggestion of the great truth that in His "passion" He was an official, and obedient, and triumphant agent.

The Paraphrase also—the forty-fourth—which represents "the pale ensigns" of death as overspreading the cheeks and the "trembling lips" of our Lord, while life *forsook* His closing eyes and His drooping head," does most manifest injustice to the condition of our Lord's person on the cross, and is clearly most injurious to the scriptural representations that " He cried with a loud voice" and "gave up the ghost"—*dismissed* His Spirit. The impression which such phrases are fitted to make upon the mind is just this, and nothing more,—that our Lord unmurmuringly *endured* inconceivable sufferings,—that He was being *subjected* to death as the penalty due to sin. All which is true. But they also suggest the idea, that whereas formerly He had been engaged in positive duty, going about doing good, the time for positive and active duty was now passed, and the time for simply suffering had come.

We must never cease to affirm that this representation of the Cross is most inadequate. It exhibits the Cross as the emblem and scene of patience merely, while it conceals those glorious and glorifying aspects of it in which it is seen to be an altar of priestly agency, a throne of powerful action, and a chariot of victory and triumph. It represents Christ's activity as subdued and overborne, or at least as in abeyance. It pretermits the grand consideration—which direct Scriptural assertions place before us, and which an adoring appreciation of the constitution of Christ's person, and the intrinsic nature of His work necessitate—that Christ's actual forthputting of power, and His official, and obedient, and positive agency, never were, and could not be, overborne and subdued; but that, on the contrary, they prevailed to put forth their energy, and their grandest energy, precisely against an inconceivable combination of agencies and instruments naturally fitted, had that been possible, to subdue and overbear them. Earth, and hell, and heaven: earth's rulers and her rabble; her kings, and priests, and soldiers, and malefactors assailing Him; her Jews and Gentiles; her dumb creatures even; earth's forests furnishing wood; earth's streams refusing water; earth's bitternesses mingled in vinegar and gall; earth's curse embodied in her thorns, in mockery and pain to crown Him; earth's "founded" steadfastness refusing to support Him, and her firmament to shine upon Him: hell's utmost force and fury gathered up against Him: heaven's sword devouring Him, and heaven's God forsaking Him: —earth, and hell, and heaven thus in conspiring action against Him, unto the uttermost of heaven's extremest justice, and earth's and hell's extremest *injustice*:— what is the glory of the Cross, if it be not *this;* that with such action conspiring to subdue *His* action, His action outlasted and outlived them all, and He did not die subdued and overborne into dying, He did not die till He *gave* Himself in death? Emmanuel a mere sufferer in His death! Ὁ λόγος ὁ τοῦ σταυροῦ ἡ δύναμις Θεοῦ. "The Logos of the Cross is the Power of God" (1 Cor. i. 18).

Part Second.

Direct scriptural evidence of this truth.

We may notice briefly some of the more obvious Scriptural assertions of this truth,—as well as some of the less obvious implications of it, which, when duly considered, are frequently even more instructive.

Among some of the more obvious testimonies to the doctrine that the death of Christ was an *action* of His priestly office, may be reckoned the assertion of Isaiah (liii. 12), that "He *poured out* His soul unto death;" the phrases frequently used by the Apostle Paul, that "He loved the Church, and *gave* Himself for it" (Eph. v. 21), and, specialising this love and loving service to the individual believer, "He loved me, and *gave* Himself for me" (Gal. ii. 20); and again, "Christ also hath loved us, and (παρέδωκεν) hath *delivered Himself* for us an *offering* and a sacrifice to God for a sweet smelling savour" (Eph. v. 2); and again, "When He had *by Himself purged* our sins" (Heb. i. 2). The doxology of John: "Unto Him that loved us and washed us from our sins in His own blood" (Rev. i. 5). The frequent expressions of the Lord himself: "The Son of Man came not to be ministered unto, but to *minister*, and to *give* His life a ransom for many" (Matt. xx. 28):—and, very specially, His ever-memorable account of Himself as the Good Shepherd, "The Good Shepherd *giveth* His life for His sheep:" So solicitous is our Lord on this point, that He repeats it again and again, in the strongest and most emphatic terms, positive and negative alike: "No one taketh it from me; I lay it down of myself." And so powerfully does He bring out the idea of His own agency being concerned in His death, that He places it on a level with the agency He should put forth in His resurrection, and represents obedient action equally in the two cases as constituting jointly what His Father's commandment had enjoined upon Him, and what His Father's love and approbation rested in so complacently: "Therefore doth my Father love me, because I *lay down* my life, that I might take it again. No one (οὐδεὶς) taketh it from me, but I lay it down of myself,—at my own instance, of my own will, by my own deed. I have power to lay it down, and I have power to take it again. This commandment received I of my Father" (John x. 11, 18).

How clearly is the forthputting of positive power implied in all these various expressions; as it is, also, with such emphatic iteration in the prophecy of Daniel, which went before concerning the "Anointed most Holy," that He should "finish transgression, and make an end of sin, and make reconciliation for iniquity, and bring in everlasting righteousness" (Dan. ix. 24). "Nor yet that He should *offer* Himself often, for then must He often have *suffered* since the foundation of the world; but now once, in the end of the world, hath He appeared to put away sin by the sacrifice of Himself" (Heb. ix. 25, 26): —an utterance of inspiration which fearlessly presents the sacrifice of the Cross as an *offering in suffering*, and as *suffering in offering*, doing justice alike to both aspects of the truth, together constituting one truth indissoluble, its unique singularity arising from a combination of what, in none but the God-man, could be combined.

For is it not thoroughly unique and singular, and altogether transcendently glorious? "I lay down my life that I might take it again: I have power to lay it down, and I have power to take it again." The death of Christ is not less glorious than His resurrection, nor is there less of His own glorious power in it. Nay, it would seem no hard thesis to maintain,—that Emmanuel hath put forth and glorified His power, *more* in dying than in rising again. For, if there be truth, as there is both truth and wondrous beauty, in Professor MACLAGAN'S figure of the empty scabbard bound upon the warrior's person, while the unsheathed sword is in his hand,—the fine conception by which that great divine illustrates that in the state of the dead, Emmanuel's body and His soul remained each in union with His Godhead: then it remains to ask;—Is there the action of greater power and prowess in the gentle ease with which that warrior, the battle being fought and won, returns the sword to its sheath; or in the prior, princely, peerless act in which, —what shall I say?—in which, having girt thy sword upon thy thigh, O Most Mighty, thy right hand, teaching terrible things, flashed it forth for victory!

How dishonourable, to imagine that the body of the Word made flesh was, in death, torn and reaved away from Him! How melancholy, even to have indistinct views of the glorious truth that it was not so! Alike *in* death and *after* death, both the soul and the body of Emmanuel were in His own power. In the very grave, His dead body was in His own power, for it was in His own person,—in union indissoluble with His Godhead. So likewise, of course, was His soul,—united still as ever, with His Godhead. And here, in death, was a check to death, such as that last enemy had never hitherto received. Here are a human soul and a human body of the self-same person, thoroughly separated from each other, precisely as in the case of a dead mere man,—verifying the assertion therefore that this Man, though not a mere man, is nevertheless a dead man,—and all death's claims are therefore satisfied: while, notwithstanding, His disembodied soul and dead body remain in a certain glorious union with each other still, through the intermedium of that Godhead with which, in the person of the Son, who is this dead Christ, they are each of them in immediate and direct union, although thoroughly severed from each other. Here is an element of victory over death to which perhaps adequate attention has not always been given. And it is reproduced in its measure, in the victory of every dying believer, every member of the body of Christ. For "the souls of believers, being at death made perfect in holiness, do immediately pass into glory, and *their bodies being still united to Christ* do rest in their graves till the resurrection." The soul and the body of the believer, separated from each other in death, remain still united indirectly, through the intervention of the person of Christ, to which each of them is directly united by the Spirit. Yet how shall these glorious mysteries be con served, if we overlook Christ's own *action* in His death?

Part Third.

Implicit scriptural evidence.

But, perhaps, the most instructive Scriptural evidences of this great truth are those which require a little thought to disclose their import and their force. Amongst such we may notice:—

I. In the first place, the remarkable saying of Paul to the Romans (v. 9), "Being now justified by His blood." What can this imply, but that in the blood or death of Christ we are to recognise, not merely such *endurance* as satisfies the penalty of the law, and procures the pardon of sin, but such *obedience* also, such positive righteousness, as secures the complete justification of the sinner's person? Without a perfect and positive objective righteousness, justification is impossible. The announcement of it would be the announcement of an unreality; and, with God, this simply could not be. And hence, if to the "blood" or death of Christ our "justification" is to be attributed, it can only be because in His blood a true obedience is couched,—in His death, the crowning activity of His sacerdotal work is to be recognised.

II. The same thing is obvious when Paul, to the Hebrews (ix. 14), says that "The blood of Christ, who, through the Eternal Spirit, offered Himself without spot to God, purges the conscience from dead works to serve the living God." In fact, there are several testimonies to the same effect in this one illustrious utterance. The activity of Christ in His death is expressly affirmed in the usual priestly phrase—"He offered Himself." Our attention is expressly called, moreover, to the great truth that it was precisely *this* which the Eternal Spirit furnished Him with grace and power to achieve, and to achieve in all the faultlessness—"without spot"—and all the moral beauty, which rendered it of sweet-smelling savour unto God. And over and above these more obvious assertions, we have the implication that *obedience* is couched in the blood of Jesus, in the fact that it "purges the conscience from dead works to *serve the living God.*" Had the Apostle's deliverance stopped short of this—attributing to Christ's blood power only to "purge the conscience," we might have regarded that atoning blood as couching in it merely a removal, because an endurance, of the curse. But when we find its action on the conscience not exhausted without embracing the communication of power and right to "serve the living

God," we see that it procures and conveys not merely deliverance from the dread and shame of guilt, but acceptance for the believer's "service," and *à fortiori*, therefore, acceptance for his person. And what is this but complete justification, such as rests, and can rest only, upon a perfect, positive righteousness—an " obedience unto death?"

III. And this reminds us to point out the true meaning of the inspired expression into the use of which the train of thought so naturally leads us:—He "became obedient unto death." Here, "death" is evidently a limit to the obedience of Christ. But is the obedience to be considered as exclusive of the limit, or inclusive of it? We doubt not that many read this saying of Paul's as if it implied that Christ was obedient *up to* the limit of His death, but not *in* death, and as including death in His "obedience." Making no allowance for the singular peculiarity of Christ's person as God-man, they read this phrase as if it could be applied, *pari passu*, to a mere man, and as if it were synonymous in import with the exhortation to the believer, "Be thou faithful unto death." But Christ was not merely positively obedient up to the point at which death's work upon His person began, but obedient up to the point at which death's utmost action on His person terminated; Himself with a loud voice, and as a conqueror, "dismissing His spirit." To have faltered in His *obedience*, or resigned His positive agency, a hair's-breadth short of this, would have been to abandon all the active obedience He had hitherto wrought; to leave it behind Him on this side of Calvary; and to fail to bring His righteousness safely through the ordeal of the Cross.

IV. Strength through the Eternal Spirit to offer Himself to God—strength to carry His righteousness safely through the ordeal of the cross to the throne within the veil, "perfecting" it in and by positive and victorious priestly agency in death—was precisely what Jesus prayed for in His agony, and obtained.

It is impossible in any other light than this, as the real tenor and issue of His prayer, to understand the Apostle's very solemn and memorable description of it: "Who in the days of His flesh, when He had offered up prayers and supplications, with strong crying and tears, unto Him that was able to save Him from death, and was heard in that He feared: though He were a Son, yet learned He obedience by the things which He suffered; and being made perfect, He became the author of eternal salvation to all them that obey Him" (Heb. v. 7–9). These three verses, it is to be feared, have been too often read apart from the verse that precedes and from the verse that follows them. Yet, by these two verses, this description of our Lord's agony of prayer is shut in between two explicit assertions of His priesthood. It is heralded with quotation of the divine oath by which Christ was called to the priestly office: "As he saith also in another place, Thou art a priest for ever, after the order of Melchisedec" (ver. 6). And it is not completed without a reiteration of the truth that this agony of prayer, and its answer, and the fruit of its answer, all belong to our Lord's priestly duty and activities: "Called of God an high priest, after the order of Melchisedec" (ver. 10). Why re-affirm so expressly, and so soon, the priestly dignity and glory of our Lord? What is the meaning of thus so solicitously guarding and hemming in, on the right hand and on the left, these prayers and supplications, and strong crying and tears of Emmanuel, with allusions, we were about to say, but rather with reiterations, of the one strongest possible assertion of Christ's priesthood which the Holy Spirit had put on record, and which is fortified even with the oath of God: "The Lord hath sworn and will not repent, Thou art a priest for ever, after the order of Melchisedec" (Ps. cx. 4)? What, but to convince us that we utterly misread and misconceive the whole design and issue of these prayers of Christ, unless we recognise them as priestly prayers, offered in the discharge of priestly duty, and contemplating and conserving the unsubdued maintenance of His priestly service and activity. In bringing His glorious priestly service to "perfection," He knew that He had to meet death—death armed with its "sting," which is "sin," and borne home with that "strength" which it derives from the "law." It is not indeed affirmed that He prayed to be saved from death. But it is implied. Why otherwise is God here designated as "Him that was able to save Him from death?" He might as well have been designated from any of His attributes, or any of His works,—as, for instance, "Him that created the stars of heaven,"—if we be not given to understand that Jesus selected this designation because He prayed for that which it sets forth God as able to give,—salvation from death. And for this unquestionably, therefore, we are to understand that Jesus did pray. And "He was heard." He did not indeed pray to be saved from dying. In the early progress of His agony in the garden He had said, "Father, if it be possible, let this cup pass from me." But the Apostle here, in writing to the Hebrews, is summing up the tenor and substance of the prayer—not, surely, excluding that in which the suppliant's soul finally rested, or giving merely the preliminary conflict through which it passed on to the subject-matter of the final supplication. And, moreover, it is expressly said by Paul, that whatever Jesus here prayed for He obtained. In the self-same petition, made to "Him that was able to save Him from death," we are told, "He was heard—heard in that He feared."

What, then, does it inevitably follow that He must have prayed for, if He prayed to be saved from death, and yet prayed not to be saved from dying? What but for strength *actively* to die; to die in the active service of His office, and not as the down-borne victim of death; to die as a Priest—"a Priest for ever"—a Priest in death itself; His priestly action uninterrupted in death, yea, triumphing in death—an offerer as well as a sufferer—an obedient official agent in the very article of death itself. In precisely this was He heard: " He was heard in that He feared: though He were a Son, yet learned He OBEDIENCE by the things He suffered." And in this inherency and forthputting of obedient offering in patient suffering—in this combination of piacular patience and priestly power—in thus prevailing to act upon His own person after death could no more act upon Him, and so to die, not by death's will, but by His own, offering Himself to God: in *this* "being made perfect"—being *thus* and hereby "made perfect, He became the *author*"—not passively the occasion and the means, but the author—" of eternal salvation to all them that obey Him."

V. Consider the final petition of Gethsemane, which constitutes the substance and whole aim of the prayer, in respect of which, therefore, He was answered when He was heard in that He feared. " Not my will, but thine, be done." Does this mean, Thy will be done upon me? Or does it not rather mean, Thy will be done by me? Can any one who knows either the scriptural doctrine or the subsequent history have any hesitation as to which of these interpretations is to be placed on our Lord's believing and obedient utterance, " Thy will be done?"

(1.) Take the *doctrine* of Scripture concerning this " will of God." " Wherefore, when he cometh into the world, he saith, Sacrifice and offering thou wouldest not, but a body hast thou prepared me: in burnt-offerings and sacrifices for sin thou hast had no pleasure. Then said I, Lo, I come (in the volume of the book it is written of me) to *do thy will*, O God" (Heb. x. 5–7). I come "to *do* thy will." It is no passive endurance of God's will to which He is in death to be subjected. It is an active performance of it. Nor is it His active performance of duty during His life on earth, as contradistinguished from His sufferings at its close, that this *doing* of God's will can indicate. It is precisely and exactly His sacrificial death to which it most clearly and immediately applies. For that "will" of God which He is to "do," is that same service by which He is to replace the offerings and sacrifices which are disparaged and set aside to make room for the sacrifice of the Son of God. To bring this out unmistakably is the design of the emphatic and otherwise unnecessary repetition in the verses which immediately follow:— "Above, when he said, Sacrifice, and offering, and burnt-offerings, and offerings for sin thou wouldest not, neither hadst pleasure therein (which are offered by the law); *then* said I"—manifestly concerning that offering in which the Lord *hath* pleasure—" Lo, I come to do thy will, O God" (ver. 8, 9). In the death of Christ, there was the action of Christ; there was the *doing* of the will of God.

But this is not the whole amount of God's "will" in the death of Christ, namely, that He should actively offer Himself. It was in the will of God also that Christ's offering of Himself should be vicarious, and should therefore absolutely and unconditionally secure the consecration and salvation of His people. "*By the which will*"—Paul therefore adds most emphatically—"by the which will we are sanctified through the offering of the body of Christ once for all" (ver. 10). That was the full, complete "will of God" which Jesus "came to do:"—to offer Himself; and, by the offering of Himself, to sanctify, or consecrate, and render acceptable unto God, those whom the Father had given to Him.

(2.) Look now—as so singularly confirmatory of the doctrine—to the *history* of what immediately followed the prayer of Gethsemane; a history in which the answer to the prayer, "Thy will be done,"—Thy will be done *by me*,—may be read as in a brilliant mirror. Immediately after the prayer in the garden, "a band of men and officers from the chief priests and Pharisees cometh thither, with lanterns, and torches, and weapons," to apprehend Him. He has to provide for the "doing" of the Father's will in both its aspects; *first*, as respects the placing in a clear light His own voluntary agency in offering Himself; and *secondly*, as it respects the deliverance of His disciples thereby. Accordingly, "He went forth and said unto them, Whom seek ye? They answered him, Jesus of Nazareth. Jesus saith unto them, I am he. And Judas also that betrayed him stood with them. As soon as he had said unto them, I am he, they went backward and fell to the ground." He is not to be captured: He is to surrender. For He is not to suffer merely, but to offer Himself in mortal woe. An emanation of His divine majesty therefore goes forth with power to fell His captors to the ground. They shall be made to feel, and Judas, who stands by, shall be made to see—is it not for that very reason that we are told that "Judas which betrayed Him stood with them?"—that the traitor's wickedness in betrayal was superfluous, and the captors' power and efforts useless against one who is "doing" the will of God, and giving Himself unto death as He will soon also give Himself *in* death. "The Good Shepherd *giveth* His life." This is the will of God concerning Him—that "will" which He came "to do."

But there is another part of the will of God to be provided for. "The Good Shepherd giveth His life *for the sheep*." If Christ is now "to do" the will of God in its completeness, He has to bring into play that other side of it which Paul doctrinally presents when he says, "By the which will we are sanctified through the offering of the body of Christ once for all." Jesus has not only to offer Himself, but to offer Himself for the sheep. Accordingly, "Then asked He them again, Whom seek ye? And they said, Jesus of Nazareth. Jesus answered, I have told you that I am he: *if therefore ye seek me, let these go their way;* that the saying might be fulfilled which He spake, Of those whom Thou hast given me I have lost none" (John xviii. 7–9).

Is not the prayer of Gethsemane answered? Has not the suppliant been heard—heard in that He feared? Is He not strengthened—"to *do* Thy will, O God?"

G

It was right that on the platform of visable events the personal will and powerful agency of Christ himself should thus far be seen in the transactions that immediately preceded His death. In His actual death itself, indeed, the same palpable representation of His spontaneous action and priestly agency could not, from the nature of the case, be given. His body was subjected to restraint—restraint from which His covenant-duty suffered Him not to free Himself, even at the taunting cry, "If Thou be the Son of God, come down from the cross: If He be the Christ, let Him save Himself." And the crowning activity of His office was spiritual and of the soul. But in the unseen spiritual world, while His body was hanging on the Cross, He was "pouring out His soul unto death," in spontaneous action of His own, as self-instigated, self-sustained, self-controlled as was that of Aaron when he brought the goat on which Jehovah's lot fell, and offered him as a sin-offering, and the goat on which the lot fell to be the scape-goat, he presented alive before the Lord to make an atonement with him, and let him go for a scape-goat into the wilderness. No priest "standing daily ministering and offering often times" was ever more free from coercion in his office, or so gloriously active in discharging it, as "this Man when He offered one sacrifice for sins." Nor did "this Man, after He had offered one sacrifice for sins, for ever sit down on the right hand of God" a more free and more powerful agent than when He offered that sacrifice which earned

Him the throne. We speak of His "doing" and His "dying." His dying *was* His grandest doing. The light and evidence of His *active* obedience, instead of paling on the Cross, shines out there most brilliantly of all,—shining down the darkness of death, and of the frown of incensed justice, till the dark frown passes off from the face of the Eternal Judge, and the light of a Father's countenance is lifted on the obedient Son in the moment of His saying, "Father, into Thy hands I commit my spirit." The Father's will is done. It is done by the Eternal Son, through the Eternal Spirit. Consentient actings of Father, Son, and Holy Ghost fill the death of Christ with action and with power unparalleled and transcendent; and the Logos of the Cross is the power of God.

And now, in all this, have we misread the Cross of Christ? Have we been unduly "glorying in the cross?" Have we attempted to surround it with a dignity and power and victory and majesty—we are weighing every word we pen: Have we attempted to surround it with a dignity and power and victory and majesty, and priestly energy, and kingly might, and brilliant revelation of unconquered eternal life from the "Prince of Life" in His obedience unto death, which do not intrinsically belong to it? If we have, let it be shown where we have erred, and let the unauthorised excess of glory be repudiated and removed. But if we have not, then may we not most warrantably say, If any man come unto you and bring not this doctrine, bid him not God speed?

Part Fourth.

Pointing the Argument from Christ's Priestly Action.

How the line of thought we have pursued may be pointed into an argument for immediately and powerfully exposing all false and defective views of the Atonement, it is scarcely necessary to indicate,—the polemic use of this great truth being so direct and obvious.

SOCINIANISM stands self-condemned by refusing it. Socinianism does not acknowledge that Christ was a priest in His death, or prior to His resurrection,—and, even then, a priest only metaphorically.

Mr ROBERTSON of Brighton, has denied all agency of Christ's own in His death, in language of such violence and horror and blasphemy, as almost silences all comment from the lips of piety for ever. He has dared to say of the everlasting Son of the Father: "He approached the whirling wheel of this world's evil, and was torn in pieces!"

Mr MAURICE denies it by affirming that Christ's death was only self-sacrifice, self-surrender, self-denial. If it was *this* sort of sacrifice, and not a propitiatory sacrifice and offering for sin, then Christ's own action cannot be recognised in it. Such sacrifice is passivity, pure and simple. Action of His own in it there could not possibly be,—save such as would resolve into suicide.

BUSHNELL makes the death of Christ a Governmental Display. Be it granted, for argument's sake. But governmental display is not action, though it may be the result of action. Of what action, in this case, is it the result? Will Bushnell find any? Will he reexamine his own book, and his own mind, and see what room he has left in his theory for the truth, that, in dying, Christ not merely suffered but *did* the will of God? It is needless to say that He *did* that will of God which appointed Him to make a display of the principles of God's moral government. What did He *do* to achieve that display? And Bushnell must simply answer, He suffered death. Yes; suffered. That is all that he can predicate. He must fall over into the theory of mere suffering, mere passivity; denial of priestly action, and *à fortiori*, of priesthood; mere passivity, which ignores the victory of the Cross, accepts defeats, and canonises the shame.

YOUNG explains Atonement by the notion of Moral Influence. Be it so again, for argument's sake. But the exercise of moral influence—was that the intrinsic nature of any agency of Christ's own, in virtue whereof it could be said, He dismissed His spirit, He poured out His soul? It might follow, as *result*, from His exemplary patience in suffering death; but it could not be identical with, nor explain, the never-to-be-reëxemplified deed by which He "gave Himself." There is neither explanation nor room in this theory for priestly agency on the Cross at all.

Others—to make the Atonement indefinite and universal, save as special grace may subsequently apply it to the elect—tell us that Christ's death, or Christ by His death, *removed legal bars*. The argument with such as speak thus might be long; but it may be short. I ask them, Was "removing of bars" the immediate and intrinsic action of Christ's person in dying on the Cross? Was this the action in and by which Emmanuel died? Did He die in and by removing bars? No, they will say: for they must reverse the terms: "He removed legal bars by dying." Precisely: they are speaking of *result*—the result of His death. But I demand a scriptural, doctrinal description of the very and immediate act of Christ in His dying, and in His *doing* the will of God in and by His death. And, with the Scripture in our hands, the demand which a searching theology will never fail thus to make, is met,—the question answered. There was immediate action of Christ in His death; and it was official and public action. Private, or personal, or individual it could not be; for in that case His holiness was at once a legal bar to divine justice smiting Him in death, and a moral bar to His unauthorised parting with His life Himself. It was public and official action. He was not merely charged with a cause, but with an *office*, and with a people in that office to personate; not merely with a cause to maintain, but with the interests of a people whom He should represent, and redeem by representing them. His action was priestly and representative action; representative of persons—

of persons definitely, numerically, individually known: —" I know my sheep." And the representative priestly action *in itself* was simply what Jesus adds:—" And I lay down my life for the sheep." That is not *result;* result never can in the nature of things express the intrinsic causal action. That is not result: it is Christ's immediate dying action itself. And it is *Redemption*— not removal of bars. The very and immediate action of Christ in dying for His people is intrinsically their *redemption.* He offers Himself to God for them a sacrifice for their sins; and herein He offers them to God with Himself. And it cannot be too emphatically affirmed, or too gratefully believed, or too resolutely contended, that this *is* their redemption—their redemption, efficacious, complete, and infallible. While mere "removal of bars" is a mockery, and the theory thereof leaves utterly unanswered the question, What did Christ *do* in dying? It recognises no action, and consequently no priestly action, in the Cross. It overthrows the Priesthood of our Lord.

CHAPTER V.

ATONEMENT AND INTERCESSION:—I. THE DIRECT ARGUMENT.

THEOLOGY is robbed of her regalia, and of her finest glories, when the positive priestly agency of Christ in His death fails to be recognised. To vindicate, in that case, the all-sufficiency of knowing Christ precisely as "Christ crucified," becomes impossible. "Glorying in the Cross" implies that we recognise it as the life-centre of redeeming action, and the life-centre of the exercise of all Christ's offices as our Redeemer. How the prophetic and kingly offices have each of them its root and rise in the priestly office we have already seen; and hence if the priestly action of our Lord in His death is denied or dishonoured, His action as a Prophet and His action as a King are *à fortiori* denied and dishonoured simultaneously. The dying Redeemer cannot be recognised as exercising in His death the offices of a Prophet and a King by those who fail to see Him acting as a Priest. If He is not acting as a Priest, He is not acting at all; and in that case, possibly, His death may become a means of instruction, and may ground a claim to a kingdom; but the dying Redeemer is not, in and by dying, fulfilling the duties of a Prophet, and a King.

But Christ crucified—Christ precisely in being crucified—is not a mere occasion of enlightenment and of instruction: He is an Instructor: and He is acting His office. He is not a revelation only, but a Revealer. He is not merely a *speculum*—to use the language of Polhill. He is not, in His death, a mere mirror, a text-book, an objective instrument of instruction. He is, and He is acting as, the Instructor and Prophet of the Church.

The Spirit, in testifying of the sufferings of Christ, hath very expressly said so. In the twenty-second Psalm,—of which Messiah's soul took infeftment, as all His own in death, by audibly exclaiming in its opening verse, "My God, my God, why hast thou forsaken me?"—we hear Him, as they part His garments and cast lots on His vesture (ver. 18), and as His "soul" gains dominion in the prayer of faith over the "sword," and His "darling" deliverance from "the power of the dog" (ver. 20), saved "from the lion's mouth, and from the horns of the unicorns" (ver. 21);—we hear Him thus in death, and in His triumph over death, and *because* thereof, asserting His discharge of His prophetic office:—"I will declare thy name unto my brethren" (ver. 22). According to His prayer "unto Him that was able to save Him from death" (Heb. v. 7), He is saved from death before He dies. He shall die, not beneath the hand of death, but in His own powerful priestly action,—in the sun-light of eternal life. And now, His Priesthood's triumphant power being vindicated, His first care, before He gives Himself in death, is to vindicate His Prophetic duty: " I will declare thy name unto my brethren," while He asserts, also, His high priestly guidance of His Father's worship, as Head and Leader of the many priests whom He is sanctifying while He sanctifies Himself: " In the midst of the Church will I sing praise unto thee " (ver. 22). Most appropriately, therefore, does Paul, to the Hebrews, quote this glorious utterance of the Cross (Ps. xxii. 21; Heb. ii. 10–12), in proof that the Captain of Salvation was "made perfect by suffering." He sees the perfect and irrefragable grounding of all Christ's office, as our Redeemer, and the triumphant action of all its function, in the Cross; while he assigns Him a title of victory— " the Captain of Salvation "—which brings into view, as His victory by death cannot fail to do, His Kingly office also very specially. For by death He destroyed him that had the power of death. By the Cross He spoiled principalities and powers, triumphing over them, and making a show of them openly (Heb. ii. 14; Col. ii. 15). He not merely suffered, so as to found a claim to a kingdom; but in active offering He triumphed as a King.

It appears, then, that the evidence and glory of all the offices of Christ are obscured, when His death is represented as what He merely suffered, instead of that which He actively achieved. Nor is the evil to be redressed by insisting, however emphatically, that He suffered voluntarily. It is not enough to say that His death was voluntary. However strongly that may be put, it can import no more than that He suffered *with* His own will. But He not merely suffered *with His will*, —" led as a lamb to the slaughter, and, as a sheep before her shearers is dumb, opening not His mouth" (Isa. liii. 7). He offered *by His will*, as a Priest "pouring out His soul unto death" (Isa. liii. 12). And to conceal this dying action of Messiah is to cloud the evidence of all His offices—to segregrate and seclude them all from the Cross—to cut them off from the very spring and life-centre of their action. How deplorable and desperate, therefore, must be the the exigencies of those views of the Atonement which necessitate conclusions or consequences such as these!

We might, at great length, in this manner investigate and expose the deranging influence of false and defective views of the Atonement on our most fundamental conceptions of all the offices of Christ. But we prefer restricting the investigation within the limits of the Priestly office. We proceed, therefore, to lay down and defend the following position, namely,—

That Theology must demand a Doctrine of Atonement that shall ground a valid and Scriptural Doctrine of the Intercession.

It will be easy to show that this most legitimate demand cannot be met, except in the view of the Catholic doctrine, that the Atonement is a definite, true, proper, and perfect propitiatory sacrifice and offering for the sins of the elect. And we are the more anxious to conduct this argument with some care and accuracy, because we are strongly convinced that, if logically and clearly put, it should have a good deal of weight with those who desire to be in accord with sound theology generally, and yet feel tempted to desiderate some aspect of universality in the Atonement inconsistent with its infallible efficaciousness for all for whom it has been offered.

Systematic theology has been accustomed to establish, *first* a Scriptural doctrine of the Atonement, and *then* pass on to the doctrine of the Intercession. Unquestionably this is the direct and natural order of the discussion. And we shall adopt it, in the first instance, to show how naturally, and with what ease, we reach a true and consistent theory of the Intercession by simply pursuing the train of thought we have been prosecuting on the Atonement, considered as priestly action on the part of our Lord. But while we are the thorough advocates of systematic theology and of its well-established methods, we would not hold ourselves in bondage to them. And, in particular, on the present theme, we think the method may be, with considerable advantage, reversed. Instead of arguing from the nature of the Atonement to the Intercession, we may argue back from the Intercession to the Atonement, to show what its nature and extent must be: not, of course, by reasoning in a circle, but by *first* establishing—apart from the doctrine of the Atonement—certain positions that must hold good in reference to the Intercession, and *then* inquiring what light the demonstration, thus far conducted, casts on the nature of the Atonement. We propose, then, to examine both the direct and the inverse arguments,—as in the light of this explanation we may be allowed to call them.

In the first place, however, there are certain preliminary considerations equally applicable and preparatory to the conduct of both these arguments, because they justify that assertion of a relation between the Atonement and the Intercession which is implied in arguing from the one to the other, in whatever order the argument is taken. To these, therefore, we must, in the first instance, briefly solicit attention.

Part First.

Atonement and Intercession Interblended.

I. First of all, we lay it down that the Intercession unquestionably pertains to the Priestly office. For it meets all the requirements of the definition or description of priesthood given by Paul in such orderly fashion when he says: "Every high priest taken from among men is ordained for men, in things pertaining to God, that he may offer both gifts and sacrifices for sins" (Heb. v. 1). The Intercession of Christ, we say, exactly meets all these requirements.

First : Our Lord is "ordained" to intercede. Christ

glorified not Himself to be made an Intercessor in particular, any more than to be made a High Priest in general. His intercession is authorised. It is official duty assigned to Him by the supreme authority of Godhead, and undertaken by Him in the Covenant or "Counsel of Peace." In a word, *He* glorified Him to be made an Intercessor, who said unto Him, in the oracle of the second Psalm: "Ask of me, and I will give thee the heathen for thine inheritance, and the uttermost parts of the earth for thy possession."

Secondly: The Intercession meets the priestly requirement of being " ordained for men." It is representative action; it is grounded on personal relation; it contemplates personal interests—the interests of persons definitely designated and known. There is scarcely a Scriptural affirmation of this function which does not speak of it as representative and founded on personal relation. " Christ is entered into heaven itself now to appear in the presence of God *for us*" (Heb. ix. 24). " He is able to save unto the uttermost *them* that come unto God by him, seeing he ever liveth to make intercession *for them*" (Heb. vii. 25). " He made intercession for the transgressors " (Isa. liii. 12). " Who shall lay anything to the charge of God's elect? It is Christ that maketh intercession for us " (Rom. viii. 34). " *We* have an advocate" (1 John ii. 1). " Thine *they* were, and thou gavest *them* me" (John xvii. 6). "Father, I will that *those* whom thou hast given me be with me" (John xvii. 24). "And another angel came and stood at the altar, having a golden censer; and there was given unto him much incense, that he should offer it with the prayers of *all saints* upon the golden altar which is before the throne" (Rev. viii. 3). The function is evidently grounded on personal relation, and its action is evidently on behalf of persons and their personal interests.

Thirdly: It is "in things pertaining to God"—$\tau\grave{a}$ $\pi\rho\grave{o}\varsigma$ $\tau\grave{o}\nu$ $\Theta\epsilon\grave{o}\nu$; things towards God. It is directed towards God; it has God for its object. Nothing can be plainer than this in the Intercession of Christ. It is directed towards the supreme Godhead; and nothing can be more plainly or more intensely priestly than that characteristic. It is the one fundamental distinction between the other offices and the sacerdotal. The Priesthood is a function "in things towards God" (Heb. ii. 17; v. 1); while the objects of His Prophetic and Kingly functions are the souls of His people whom He enlightens, governs, and protects.

Fourthly: The Intercession meets also the closing requirement of the definition of priesthood; "That He may offer both gifts and sacrifices for sins." In His intercession, as in His atonement, Christ is an offerer; His action is the action of offering. He offers or presents Himself—Himself a lamb as it had been slain—Himself in exaltation, as on Calvary He had offered Himself in suffering. The Father exclaims at His advent to the heavenly throne: "Who is this that hath engaged his heart to approach unto me? saith the Lord" (Jer. xxx. 21); and the efficacy of His approach and offering is the bond of certainty to the everlasting covenant, and its glorious all-embracing promise: "And ye shall be my people, and I will be your God" (ver. 22). For, concerning this approach, Jesus had said, "And now, O Father, I come to thee,"—I come unto Thee through sacrifice and death, to appear in the presence of God for them. And when He comes, He offers "gifts and sacrifice." For there is "*given*" unto the angel of the covenant " much incense "—the incense of His own infinite merits, given to Him, in the sense of being owned, admitted, and acknowledged by divine justice in its infinite value and meritoriousness—" that He should *offer* it with the prayers of all saints" (Rev. viii. 3).

Thus every possible requirement, to the most minute feature, is found to meet in the Intercession of our Lord, assigning to Him therefore beyond dispute a function of His sacerdotal office.

II. The Atonement and the Intercession being thus comprehended in the category of one and the same office—justifying of course some kind of argument from the one to the other—it is not wonderful that we find them constantly in juxtaposition, in distinct and various Scriptural assertions. Of these none is more remarkable than that of the apostle John: "We have an advocate with the Father, Jesus Christ, the righteous, who is also the propitiation for our sins" (1 John ii. 1, 2). The same connection—indicating how thoroughly the Intercession belongs to the category of the priestly, the representative, the judicial, and the "things towards God"—is evident in the answer to the challenge, "Who shall lay anything to the charge of God's elect? Who shall condemn?" The answer, drawn first from the Atonement, is not held to be complete till the Intercession is brought into view: "It is Christ that died; yea, rather, that is risen again; who is even at the right hand of God: who also maketh intercession for us." Then, nothing can be finer in this view than to see how the fifty-third chapter of Isaiah—the very rubric, so to speak, of vicarious offering—culminates in the Intercession, riveting therein the great propitiatory offering to the throne of God on high: "Therefore will I divide him a portion with the great, and he shall divide the spoil with the strong; because he hath poured out his soul unto death; and he was numbered with the transgressors; and he bare the sins of many, and made intercession for the transgressors." Well may the next utterance of the Spirit of inspiration be: "Sing, O barren, thou that didst not bear; break forth into singing, and cry aloud" (Isa. liv. 1).

The same intimate connection between the Atonement and Intercession is seen by considering how and by what Christ entered into heaven as an intercessor; for if *we* enter into the holiest and draw near by the blood of Jesus, and by a new and living way through the veil, that is to say, His flesh, it is because He hath consecrated or initiated this way for us (Heb. x. 19, 20). By His body and by His blood, separated in His atoning sacrifice, in His own act of offering Himself,—*thereby* did He go unto God, as an Intercessor. For "Christ being come, an high priest of good things to come, *first*, by a greater and a more perfect tabernacle, not made with hands, that is to say, not of this building [but by His own *body*, namely]; neither by the blood of goats and calves, but, *secondly*, by His own *blood*, He entered in once into the holy place" (Heb. ix. 11, 12).

It may seem superfluous to dwell on this at such length. But if we are to argue from the nature of the Atonement to the true doctrine of the Intercession, or from the doctrine of the Intercession to the nature and extent of the Atonement, it is desirable in the first instance to place very prominently before our minds the intimate relation that subsists between them.

III. For this reason we must proceed a step further. We have seen that neither Paul, nor Isaiah, nor John, having spoken of the Atonement, imagines that he is introducing a generically new thing when he introduces a reference to the Intercession. They are, in their theology, manifestly most intimately related, and, in fact, homogeneous. But this is not all. Scripture warrants us to affirm something more than very intimate connection. That does not exhaust the Scriptural representation. And, indeed, it seems impossible to exhaust the profound truth on this point without betaking ourselves to the language of paradox. Nor need that excite surprise; for in all the more profound departments of thought, the occurrence of paradox is a *primâ facie* evidence of accuracy rather than of error. The paradox to which we seem in this case to be driven would be something like this: The essence of the Intercession *is* Atonement; and the Atonement *is* essentially an Intercession. Or, perhaps, to put the paradox more mildly: The Atonement is real,—real sacrifice and offering, and not mere passive endurance,— because it is in its very nature an active and infallible Intercession; while, on the other hand, the Intercession is real intercession,—judicial, representative, and priestly intercession, and not a mere exercise of influence,— because it is essentially an Atonement or substitutionary oblation, once perfected on Calvary, now perpetually presented and undergoing perpetual acceptance in heaven.

Now this will become evident if we can adduce one passage of Scripture which attributes the whole of our salvation to the Atonement, and another which attributes the whole of our salvation to Intercession. And such passages will easily occur to every one familiar with the Scriptures. As to the former: "By his one offering he hath for ever perfected them that are sanctified" (Heb. x. 14). As to the latter: "He is able to save unto the uttermost those that come unto God by him, seeing he ever liveth to make intercession for them" (Heb. vii. 25).

On reading these utterances of Inspiration, it is

natural, or rather inevitable to ask,—If our salvation, even unto its "perfection," is secured by the "one offering," what need of the Intercession? and, if our salvation, even "unto the uttermost," is secured by the Intercession, what need of the Atonement? How, or on what principle, can the Offering and the Intercession thus apparently mutually exclude and ignore each other? The answer is, that *apparently* they mutually exclude each other, because they do *really* mutually and reciprocally *include* each other. The offering by which alone we are perfected is not the passive endurance or suffering of the cross, but that active priestly offering of the cross which is prolonged without suffering into the function of the Intercession. And the Intercession, by which alone we are saved, even to the uttermost, is just the perpetual presentation of the "continual burnt-offering" of Calvary, which, as an active *offering* subsists in perpetuity, and belongs to eternity, while the *suffering* of the cross belongs to history and the past, and the Atonement, had it been mere suffering, would have belonged to the past too. All this seems to be too evident to require that we should insist upon it, and, even before we touch our argument, whether the direct or the inverse, it must be obvious how strong a preliminary light it is beginning to throw on the truth of the co-extensiveness of Christ's two functions as a Priest.

For as in the typical Dispensation, so in Christ the Antitype. The two altars of Sacrifice and of Incense were combined and correlative instruments of official action to the priest in the one complete office of his priesthood; and they constituted component and indispensable factors of one complete act of sacrificial worship. The same functionary, or office-bearer, transacted at both: he transacted for the self-same person or persons: the blood of the self-same sacrifice that he had slain and offered on the one altar, he sprinkled or put upon the horns of the other. To dislocate or derange this co-ordination would be to negative his official action in its intrinsic import, to annihilate the gracious results of his priestly intervention, and indeed to evert his office utterly. His action at the altar of Atonement was pre-requisite to his approach to the altar of Incense; and the successful achievement which signalised his action at the latter revealed beyond the possibility of doubt the nature and efficacy of the services which he had accomplished at the former; while only in virtue of the two, in their combination and synthesis, was Aaron's priesthood a real priesthood at all.

And what, then, shall we say of any and all of those schemes of thought on the Atonement which, ignoring the priestly action of Christ on Calvary, and taking account of His sufferings only, derange the whole doctrine of type and antitype? For on such a scheme Aaron, who was never called as a priest to suffer, could be no type of Christ, and Christ no antitype of Aaron; but Aaron's priesthood must be owned to have been real, and Christ's to be merely figurative. Aaron was no sufferer at either altar: he was an offerer at both. In respect of suffering, at the altar of sacrifice, the slain animal was the type of Christ, the Lamb of God, that beareth away the sin of the world. But at both altars Aaron was the type of Christ; and as an offerer both in sacrifice and intercession, Christ is the antitype of Aaron. As in the type, therefore, so in the antitype; the two functions of propitiation and intercession interblend and interpenetrate each other, as constituting the indispensable factors of one complete priestly redeeming transaction unto the glory of God in the highest. The propitiation transpires in the energy of intercession; and the Intercession is transacted in the merit of propitiation. In offering Himself He offered up supplications with strong crying and tears unto Him that was able to save Him from death, to sustain Him through the Eternal Spirit to offer Himself to God, and by obedience in the things which He suffered to make Him perfect, and the Author of eternal salvation. So that in the vital power of His offering in death, we see the energy of prayer; while the intercession in like manner is in the merit of the one offering in which alike the Captain of Salvation, and they also that are sanctified, were for ever perfected (Heb. ii. 10; x. 14). A more complete interblending cannot be imagined; and no doctrine of Atonement can be correct which does not provide for recognising it, or which is not amenable to the conditions and considerations which it must necessitate and enforce.

Part Second.

Transition from Atonement to Intercession.

We are now in circumstances to see how theology effects the transition from a true doctrine of Atonement to a clear and consistent conception of the Intercession. And, following in the line of thought we have been pursuing, that transition is natural and easy.

Let it be admitted that, in the death of Christ, we have not a mere infliction of the penalty of the law on an unmurmuring sufferer, but an active and vicarious oblation of Himself as a propitiatory sacrifice for the sins of those for whom, as a representative and priest, Christ is now acting; let the idea of active obedience and oblation on the cross be that on which we fasten, in contemplating the sacrifice of Calvary; and we are already in possession of the fundamental and constituting notion of the Intercession. For we have only to consider the sufferings — amidst which this active priestly service prevails to maintain its energy, and through the ordeal of which it achieves its triumph — as passing away. We have only to remove the veil of shame, the cloud of ignominy, the burden of the curse; or rather we have only to look on and see these triumphantly removed by our High Priest's quenchless power in giving Himself to God, as He exclaims, "It is finished," "Father, into thy hands I commit my spirit:" and the priestly duty which we thus perceive that death, instead of interrupting, only perfects and glorifies into a true and proper and complete propitiation, instead of being suspended by His atoning death, passes over through that death of Atonement, and is prolonged precisely into what Scripture calls the Intercession. Every active principle that was in operation in Emmanuel's soul on the Cross passes over without a break, and blends into the permanent function of Intercession. His acknowledgment of His representative relationship, and His unflinching resolution to abide by it;—His forthputting of priestly energy;—His love to His Father;—His love to His people, collectively and individually (Eph. v. 25; Gal. ii. 20);—His delight in the everlasting covenant; —His loyal recognition of the Divine law, both in the rectitude of its commandment, and in the moral necessity of its curse, as He, like none else, has by willingly enduring it, said Amen to the curse;—His love of righteousness and hatred of iniquity (Ps. xlv. 7):—in a word, as we have said, every active principle that was at work in His oblation, when through the Eternal Spirit He offered Himself without spot to God, continues uninterruptedly through death in operation still; and acting in the ever-living person of Emmanuel, the true God and Eternal Life, considered still as a Priest, a Priest for ever, after the order of Melchisedec, *this*, in the essence of it, *is* the Intercession. There is nothing intrinsically new needing to be inaugurated. No generically different function has now to be assumed. The priestly activities of His spirit have simply to be prolonged, liberated from the concealing clouds and depressing burdens of His estate of humiliation, and glorified by His resurrection, ascension, and session at the right hand of the Majesty in the heavens in His estate of exaltation and reward: and without the introduction of any fundamentally new idea, we have the essence of the Intercession in the activity of the victorious oblation of the Cross. We say in this we have the essence of the Intercession. And that being gained and conserved, the secondary aspects of the Intercession come quite naturally and easily into view.

(1.) Thus, in the first place: Introduce the idea of an accuser and an accusation. The Intercession then becomes an Advocacy: "We have an advocate with the Father." Accusation is in the category of the judicial. So is that intercession into which we have seen that a true propitiatory oblation so directly and so simply blends. And its judicial aspect is only somewhat more plainly brought out when it asserts for itself the action of advocacy.

An instance of the intercessor acting as an advocate, we have in the history of Simon Peter: "Simon, Simon, Satan has desired to have you that he may sift you as wheat; but I have prayed for thee that thy faith fail not" (Luke xxii. 31, 32); and another in the case of Joshua the high priest, "standing before the angel of the Lord, and Satan standing at his right hand to resist him. And the Lord said, The Lord rebuke thee, Satan; the Lord that hath chosen Jerusalem, rebuke thee: is not this a brand plucked out of the fire?" (Zech. iii. 1, 2.)

(2.) Again: Introduce the idea of the dangers, wants, necessities, and sorrows of His people; and the Intercession appears as a Ministry of sympathy and loving care: "For we have not an high priest which cannot be touched with the feelings of our infirmities; but was in all points tempted like as we are, yet without sin: For in that he himself hath suffered, being tempted, he is able to succour them that are tempted" (Heb. iv. 15; ii. 18). This sympathy and care of the Intercessor for His afflicted Church is represented in vision to the prophet Zechariah, as going forth in a supplication for Jerusalem in her captivity,—and Him the Father heareth alway: "The Lord answered the Angel that talked with me with good and comfortable words" (chap. i. 13).

(3.) Once more: Introduce the idea of the Church as a spirtual body organised for the worship of God; and the Intercession appears as Headship of Worship—worship conducted under the immediate and supreme responsibility of the High Priest of Zion, who hath condescended to say of himself and of his people, "We know whom we worship" (John iv. 22). In this headship and ministry of worship, "there is given unto him much incense that he should offer it with the prayers of all saints" (Rev. viii. 3). Nor does he disdain to lead the praises also of the Church, saying: "In the midst of the Church will I sing praise unto thee" (Ps. xxii. 22;

Heb. ii. 12). It is thus that the Church of God constitutes a royal priesthood, acting in the fellowship and concert of the heavenly ministry of her great High Priest within the veil. Having this great High Priest over the house of God, she draws near with a true heart. Having Jesus, the Son of God, who as a great High Priest has passed into the heavens, she comes boldly to the throne of grace. She enters Heaven by faith and prayer and song. Heaven is her only Temple now: and she worships there among the wing-veiled choirs of the Seraphim and "before the gods" (Ps. cxxxviii. 1). She is infinitely independent, therefore, of the earthly ornaments and "beggarly elements" of a ritualistic service. The King of glory, the Divine Mediator of her prayers and Leader of her songs, is "for beauty and for glory, for excellency and for comeliness" both to her and to her services too. Who is this King of glory? The Lord of hosts: He is the King of glory. Lift up your heads, O ye gates; even lift them up, ye everlasting doors!

Part Third.

Pointing the direct Argument from Intercession.

Each of these secondary aspects of the Intercession opens up trains of thought which belong, in their details, more to the field of homiletics than to that of systematic theology. But it is good to see how the true foundation of them rests in a correct apprehension of what the real essence of the Intercession is: and that, we have seen, is reached by bringing into prominence the active obedience of Christ in His propitiation for our sins.

But as to all the other theories of the Atonement—all more or less antagonistic to that which we have been attempting to vindicate—how are *they* to find their way to any consistent theory of the Intercession? We believe they must all stand condemned by the confusion and perplexity which they introduce into our conceptions of Christ's whole priestly office; and, more particularly, by the hopeless gulf of separation which they interpose between the Atonement and Intercession of our Lord. Self-denial—self-sacrifice—sacrifice as a "law of being!"—example—martyrdom—moral influence—governmental display—"removal of bars"—"opening of doors:" take any, take all the ever-shifting aspects of the chameleon phantasmagoria by which men rack their invention to evade the glory of the Cross: and by what theological alchymy, by what spiritual Rosicrucianism, will you transmute them into a ministry of Intercession? We have already classed them all together, under one common feature by which they are all alike distinguished, however in other respects they may differ: they make no account of Christ's activity in His death. The moment that that is admitted, it is seen to be inevitable that Christ must have acted as a representative of persons, and offered Himself in priestly duty an oblation and propitiation for their sins unto their unconditional and infallible salvation. There is no room for universality here, other than the universality of the Catholic Church invisible, on whose behalf Christ prolongs His oblationary priestly service into an ever-living ministry of Intercession. The Intercession, therefore, and the Atonement are on this view most manifestly co-extensive; and the whole scheme of thought is traversed by making the one more limited or unlimited than the other.

But now, take the death of Christ as mere suffering, and how is any valid idea of intercession to be developed out of that? How is the transition to be made? Considered as mere suffering, there is no continuity possible to admit of any transition. Christ's death, in that light, is a pause; and a new beginning has to be found, if any priestly intercession is to be affirmed. If He was a priest before, His priesthood by such a death meets a check—nay, is brought to an end. He dies out of His office, as Aaron did, if He does not die into a more manifestly triumphant exercise of it. And in that case His office must require to be constituted anew.

Some, indeed, would seem quite willing to accept that conclusion, and willing to regard the resurrection of our Lord as the occasion on which His office was reconstituted and resumed. But in that case they must imagine that by His resurrection His person was reconstituted as well as His priestly office—that, in rising from the dead, He resumed His body into union with His person. As if His dead body in the grave had not continued in union with His Godhead, which is the seat of His personality, as much as His disembodied spirit did!—His body and soul, each united indissolubly with His Godhead, though separated in death from each other. Was the Word made flesh a second time?

But apart from that: where is there a single syllable in Holy Scripture to indicate the inauguration, after Christ's death, of any official function whatsover, priestly, or kingly, or prophetic? Yet this is inexorably necessary if an intercession consequent upon atonement is to be acknowledged, and that atonement was a mere endurance. You cannot frame the suffering of death into a living ministry of intercession. You may look upon it as an argument, but no ingenuity can transchange it into a ministry. If suffering therefore was all, then, when it passes away, a wholly new thing must come into play, if there is to be anything called advocacy or intercession. But recognise *offering* in suffering: the suffering may pass away, but the living attitude of offering continues, yea, "ever liveth," and henceforth carrieth in it for evermore the boundless merit that was in the suffering which is past: and the priestly offerer, whose priestly activity has never for a moment been suspended, presents Himself before the throne, both "a Lamb as it had been slain"—in that attitude an objective plea—and also a high priest, the living minister who presents the plea; able to save unto the uttermost them that come unto God by Him, seeing He ever liveth to make intercession.

We have almost been betrayed already into the inverse argument—that which leads over from the only admissible conception of the Intercession to the true character and idea of the Atonement which in the order of nature must have preceded it. But that argument is so interesting and instructive, that in order to avoid such extreme condensation as would be unfavourable to clearness, we must devote a fresh chapter to the consideration of it.

CHAPTER VI.

ATONEMENT AND INTERCESSION :—II. THE INVERSE ARGUMENT.

If the transition from the Atoning Sacrifice to the Intercession is such as we have attempted to establish; if the Intercession is simply the same official action carried forward in its triumph from the field of suffering and humiliation into that of exaltation and heavenly glory,—fundamentally the same priestly activities being in operation still; what evidence is there that these priestly activities have in the moment of their triumph, and because of it, been narrowed and contracted from the wide limits, or rather the want of limits, of an indefinite and universal atonement into an intercession, which, on all hands, is admitted to concern those only who are ultimately benefited and saved by it? Surely this is a question which may well give pause to the advocates of an unlimited atonement. We may well ask them to produce from Scripture some indication of this strange result, if not some justifying reason for a restriction so curious and ungracious occurring in Christ's priestly function in the very moment of its victory. Assuredly it would be extremely strange, if exactly when the priestly work of Christ passes through its one terrible ordeal of the Cross, it should emerge with its limits enormously contracted;—if henceforth, in its dignity and triumph, it should be far narrower in its relations and actings than when it had to contend with circumstances of conflict, and shame, and woe. Strange, if,—whereas, while it was clouded and burdened with the darkening and crushing curse due to sin, it had equal regard to all who were in that same condition,—now, when it is liberated from the burden, and has emerged from the cloud, vast multitudes, to whom an interest in the conflict had been assigned, are excluded from all interest in the victory! Does this look like a triumph of grace? Does a king count a campaign glorious from which he emerges with a narrower national territory than before?—We profess ourselves unable to see wherein this simple illustration does injustice to the doctrine we are criticising.

There is, in fact, no escape from the awkward predicament in which that doctrine is thus landed, except by denying that the relation between Atonement and Intercession is such as we have represented, and by finding some other bridge of transition by which to pass over from the one to the other. What that may be, we profess ourselves incompetent to discover. The advocates of universal atonement, we are persuaded, will find it difficult alike to discover or invent; and we trust, in the meantime, to show reason to preclude all argument in any such direction. And this we hope to accomplish by inverting the argument which connects the Atonement and the Intercession, and by showing what features an intercession that is worthy of the character of God, must postulate in that atonement with which it professes to be related, and on which it professes to be based.

Resigning, then, all benefits from what we may believe we have established concerning the true nature of the Atonement; and beginning with such simple affirmation of Christ's Intercession as that of Paul, when he says, that "He maketh intercession for us;" let us see how, from this starting-point, we reach by another route the Scriptural theory of a proper and definite propitiation for sin.

The most general conception we can form of Intercession is that of an intervention, or interposition, or beneficent ministration, designed for the procurement and bestowal of advantages not otherwise to be obtained, or not otherwise so readily or so fully. If it be admitted that they are not otherwise to be obtained at all—and in the present case that ought clearly to be the assumption—the argument is rendered so much the easier. Coming nearer to the point, and seeking a more distinct and specific conception of the actual Intercession of our Lord, it would seem that there are only two alternative ideas of its exact nature possible. Either, *first*, Christ exercises influence with God; or, *secondly*, He presents a plea, which, according to God's own appointment, He has officially brought into existence as a ground or reason, in virtue of which it is consistent with righteousness for God to bestow blessings which could not otherwise be bestowed.

These seem to be the two alternatives; and they are to be considered as contrasted and mutually exclusive of each other. No doubt, in vague use of language, the presentation of such a plea as that contemplated in the second alternative might be called, in a sense, an exercise of influence. But it would be an improper use of the phrase. And, at all events, the phrase is used here as excluding a very precise predicament which is contrasted with what the vague idea of influence implies. We shall attempt to show that the first of these views of the Intercession is inadmissible, being wholly unworthy of the Divine character; that we are therefore shut up to the second alternative idea of the Intercession; and we shall then show that all the false and defective views of the Atonement have this common feature, that they fail to provide such a plea or ground as the only admissible idea of Intercession demands, and that they shut up their advocates to the inadmissible theory of mere influence.

Part First.

Intercession considered as an Exercise of Influence.

The idea that Christ's intercession is not the presentation of a righteous objective plea, but the exercise of a subjective influence, is one which we must resolutely repudiate, and which, with that view, we must relentlessly examine and expose. We would account this unnecessary, were it not that we mean to show that such a view of the Intercession is logically the inevitable landing-place of all erroneous doctrines of the Atonement. But, in order to render it plain that that alone is conclusive evidence of their erroneousness, we shall not 'consider it superfluous to follow out this false view of the Intercession to its inevitable and fatal consequences.

Those who regard Christ in His Intercession as exercising some influence with the Father are, of course, shut up to the dilemma that the Father was either antecedently willing, or antecedently unwilling, to bestow whatever this influence is exerted to procure. And it seems to matter little which horn they elect.

I. Is it said that the Father, apart from, and prior to, this exercise of influence on the part of the Son, is unwilling? Then—

(1.) Such a relation as this implies may be consistent with the nature and character of created finite beings —diverse in will, and deficient or limited in goodness, power, and wisdom; but it is destructive of our idea of Divine persons. The Father and the Son, with the Holy Spirit, are three persons in the unity of the Godhead, of one substance, power, and eternity. The Incarnation of the eternal Word is without prejudice to this, the inviolable constitution of the Godhead; so also is

His office, in all its range, and every one of its functions or actings. It is inconceivable that He should assume any office or position that could prejudice the great truth which, in the days of His flesh, and while exercising His office, He sedulously affirmed: "I and my Father are one." God is "of one mind, and who can turn Him?" But if God the Son could turn the mind of God the Father, then God is not of one mind, neither are the Son and the Father one.

(2.) Such Influence is inconsistent with the idea of office, authorisation, and appointment. It is inconceivable that the unwilling Father should appoint His Son to the office of rendering Him willing to do that which He is antecedently *unwilling* to do. Such procedure is not only inconceivable in the case of Divine persons, but in the case even of rational created beings. An intercession of mere influence, therefore, represents the Son, the man Christ Jesus, as glorifying Himself to be made an Intercessor. But this is in flagrant contradiction to the general allegation of the Holy Spirit, that "*no* man taketh this office upon him, save he that is called of God, as was Aaron," as well as the express application of that indispensable requisite to this Divine Intercessor in particular: "So Christ glorified not himself to be made an high priest, but he that said unto him, Thou art my Son, this day have I begotten thee" (Heb. v. 4, 5). Surely it is unnecessary to affirm that Christ's covenant appointment to the priesthood, proves that the Father was willing to bestow all that should be sued out by the priestly Intercessor, and required no influence, and, indeed, no intercession, to render Him willing.

(3.) Such Influence is derogatory to the Divine goodness, beneficence, and mercy. It presupposes the Divine Father as needing to be mollified, pleaded with, and prevailed upon, to entertain placable disposition and merciful designs towards His creatures. Whatever ideas of salvation, as something good and merciful, it can contemplate, it represents them as not originating with the Godhead, but as requiring to be urged upon God's notice, His acceptance, His concurrence, and His will. This is the view of the Divine character which many opponents of the doctrine of the Atonement charge that doctrine with countenancing. Against that doctrine it is groundlessly and slanderously alleged. Of *their own* views it is a necessary consequence. And we shall prove that, when we show that their views shut them up to this Influence theory of the Intercession.

(4.) Such Influence is derogatory to the Divine justice. It is a dictate of the moral sense of mankind that the action of justice is deranged when personal influence is admitted to have play in affecting its administration. It is one of the plainest and most obvious forms of the corruption of justice. It is only when justice is not traversed, and, indeed, is not concerned, that even among finite creatures personal influence is considered as admissible. There is nothing of which the Minister of Justice is more jealous to purge himself, than just the idea that he could be supposed open to such influence on the part of others, or willing to exercise it himself. When the sentence of condemnation which has been passed is sought to be cancelled, it is not by the exercise of personal influence on the Monarch, but because the interceding Minister of State urges that, since the trial, evidence of innocence has come to light, or doubt at least has been thrown upon the guilt imputed. If it be otherwise, the nation feels that the fountain of justice has been corrupted. And if this could be imagined to be possible in the administration of God, "then how should God judge the world?" (Rom. iii. 6.)

II. But suppose, now, on the other hand, that God is antecedently willing to avert the evils which this Intercession is designed to deprecate, and to bestow the blessings which it is designed to solicit and procure.

This, no doubt, conserves the Divine origination and appointment of the Intercession. For, on this supposition, it may be consistently set forth as originating in the love of God, and as appointed by the Divine authority. But if the Intercession is fundamentally an exercise of influence, the Divine willingness, though it may account for its origin and appointment, militates fatally against its necessity and real serviceableness. If the Intercession is the presentation of a righteous ground and plea which the Intercessor has brought, and was appointed to bring, into existence, and which enables the Divine Judge and Sovereign righteously to do what, without the existence of that ground or plea, He mercifully desired to do, but could not do consistently with justice: then there is no derogation from, or impeachment of, either the justice or beneficence of God, but rather the reverse; while the wisdom of God suffers no reflection on the charge of bringing forward an evolution that is superfluous and unnecessary. On such a view of the Intercession all is plain. But where is the wisdom of conceding only to the exercise of influence that which God is antecedently desirous of bestowing? and where the wisdom of appointing the exercise of an influence, the exercise of which the very supposition represents as unnecessary?

It is said that such an appointed intervention is requisite to prevent evil effects that would follow were the intervention of the Intercessor dispensed with? That is perfectly intelligible and relevant if the Intercession be of that nature which we advocate, and of that necessity which such an Intercession implies. In that case, on the supposition of no Intercession, evil effects would indeed follow,—to such extent, and of such kind, as proves that, without the Intercession, the beneficent willingness of God can take no accomplishment. Traversing of the righteousness of the Divine administration; violation of the principles of the Divine government; dishonour to the Divine law; inevitable misrepresentation of the Divine character; and disorganisation of the moral universe;—all these evil effects must follow, from sin being passed by without Atonement and Intercession, such as those we plead for. But to advocate the necessity of an Intercession of mere Influence in order to prevent evil consequences following from the fact of God bestowing blessings which it requires no new ground or plea to be brought into existence to enable Him righteously to bestow, is simply absurd.

What are the evil consequences to be dreaded on such an assumption, and which an Intercession of Influence must be brought in in order to avert? Is it that men will be in danger of taking wrong views of the Divine character? And if so, how will this Intercession rectify them?

Let us consider. As to what aspect of the Divine character, or what department of the Divine administration, will there be false views likely to arise? Will it be in reference to the Divine justice? That cannot be. At least it ought not to be; for the supposition *is*, that it is antecedently perfectly just on the part of God to act as He antecedently, in His beneficence, desires to act. And if the reality of the case, as it is thus supposed to be, does not prevent men from taking false views in this direction, the intervention of an intercession of influence will not prevent them; for as it does not profess to render God's procedure more just, so neither can it have the very slightest effect in more fully manifesting its justice.

Or again, is it in the direction of the Divine beneficence that false views are likely to arise, and an intercession of influence must intervene to prevent them? Surely such an intervention is a very awkward expedient in the case supposed. Its obvious and inevitable tendency must be the very reverse of what this theory attributes to it. The supposition is that there is a complete, antecedent, beneficent desire and will on the part of God—that there is nothing in that direction to prevent the direct and immediate bestowment of saving blessings. Surely, then, the inbringing of any ministry of influence,—the suspension, indeed, of the beneficent action of the Divine will upon any intermediate agency of any sort whatsoever, and more particularly on a ministry of influence, which must be utterly unreal, except in so far as it pleads with and prevails on God to exercise His beneficent desire and will,—cannot but cloud the evidence of precisely the Divine beneficence itself, and just promote those false views of the Divine character in reference thereto, which it is pretended to foreclose and prevent.

Perhaps it may be replied, that the design of this Intercession of Influence is to prevent men taking, in a sense, too large views of the goodness of God; to avert the danger of their confounding the Divine beneficence and placability with mere facility, and thereby putting in peril those affections of holy awe and veneration with which we ought always to contempate the Great Supreme. False views of God in that direction are indeed very dangerous, and very natural to the evil heart of unbelief; and their effectual prevention is a real problem which it concerns any holy gospel of salvation really to solve. In the case supposed, it is, however, utterly impossible to see how an Intercession of mere influence can solve it. For, on the supposition, the antecedent willingness of God to bestow forgiveness and salvation,—without any new ground or plea being brought into existence to render such forgiveness righteous, and to declare God's righteousness therein,—does either constitute and present good ground for those views of His character which the Intercession is supposed to be brought in in order to prevent, or it does not. Take then the two alternatives in their order.

If it *does* constitute and present good ground for such views, how can an intercession of influence prevent the intelligent from seeing it? or rather, how can it cause men who see it to shut their eyes to what they see? Such an intercession does not in the least alter, or pretend to alter, the ground there is for taking the view of God's character concerned. It only represents influence as being exerted with God to do exactly what it is admitted constitutes and presents good ground for men entertaining a particular view of the Divine character. And yet it is pretended that such an exercise of influence is introduced precisely to prevent men from seeing the true nature of that which it is introduced to accomplish! That is to say, It is an intercessory influence with God, intended to have a blinding influence on men! It is hardly possible to imagine illogical bewilderment going farther.

But we have the other supposition to deal with—

namely, that God's willingness to bestow forgiveness without an intercession of righteous representative priestly action, such as we plead for, constitutes and presents *no* ground for those views of the Divine goodness, which in that case are truly erroneous and false, but which men nevertheless will be in danger of adopting. If so, why introduce an intercession of influence? What possible object can it serve? It is not in things towards God—τὰ πρὸς τὸν Θεὸν—that any ministry here is necessary or can be serviceable: it is in things towards man. Men are, by the supposition, taking views of the Divine character for which there is no real ground. Let *them* be dealt in the matter. Why desiderate an Intercession to deal with God? Let those who are taking groundless and false views of God be enlightened. It is not any ministry to harmonise God's procedure with man's foolish notions that is either necessary or possible; but a ministry of instruction on the hearts and intellects of men, to harmonise their views with the realities of the case, and to deliver them from views of God, for which His procedure affords no real ground. A prophetic ministry towards man, not a priestly ministry towards God, is what is needed; not an influence exerted on Him, but an influence on those who are misunderstanding Him and His ways. An Intercession of Influence towards God is, in all the bearings of the case, an impertinence that reflects at once with dishonour on the character of God, and the scheme and idea of it with insult on the intelligence of man.

Part Second.

Intercession Considered as the Presentation of a Plea.

Turning now from the idea that the Intercession of Christ is an exercise of subjective influence with the Father, let us consider it as the presentation rather of an objective plea.

Such a plea must evidently have reference to the things pertaining to God. The Intercessor is an "ordained" office-bearer "in things pertaining to God" (Heb. v. 1); a merciful and faithful high priest "in things pertaining to God" (Heb. ii. 17). On these "things" the intercession and its plea must have direct and immediate bearing, if that intercession be embraced, as we have seen it is embraced, in the priestly office. What, then, are "the things pertaining to God"—the deep things of God which the Spirit searcheth? (1 Cor. ii. 10.) They are the Divine nature and perfections, particularly the holiness and justice of God; the Divine Sovereignty, with its purposes and designs of grace and love; the Divine law, in its subject-matter, its obligations, and its sanctions; and the Divine government, in its interests, requirements, and stability. These are the things pertaining to God; the things towards God—τὰ πρὸς τὸν Θεὸν—the things which we see when we are looking out directly towards God. And the Intercessor's plea must be to the effect, that He has, by Divine appointment, and through the accomplishment of the work given Him to do, arranged and disposed these Divine things into such order that the antecedent and gracious purposes of God's sovereign love may now be accomplished without the interests of the Divine perfections, law, or government suffering thereby; yea, and that all these interests now require the accomplishment of God's purposes of love.

It is manifest that an intercessory plea of this nature is worthy of the Divine glory, and worthy of Divine recognition, as a valid ground and justifying reason for new Divine procedure. For the Intercessor is not now resting His success on the idea of any power or influence that He may possess with the Father. Nor does this conception represent Him as soliciting the Father to give weight to considerations that existed *apart from*, and prior to, His priestly and intercessory work itself. It is the introduction and presentation of a consideration, a plea, a ground altogether new; which existed not at all prior to, or apart from, that very priesthood in which He is now acting at the right hand of the throne of the Majesty in the heavens; and it professes to be, objectively, and in itself alone, a complete and perfect ground, pleadable judicially and in court of law, and competent and entitled to carry all issues that the Intercessor craves and expects because of it,—its power and efficacy in no respect supplemented by, or requiring to draw upon, the personal influence of Him who pleads it.

I do not, of course, mean to say that the relation of infinite and ineffable love between the Eternal Father and the Eternal Son does in no respect affect or enter into this ministry of Intercession. Far from it. It is remarkable that when two Divine utterances or oracles (Ps. ii. 7, and Ps. cx. 4) are, by the inspired writer to the Hebrews (v. 5), quoted as constituting or announcing Christ's priesthood, or glorifying Him to be made an high priest, it is not that which makes mention in explicit terms of His Priesthood, but that which declares His Sonship, that is quoted first: "He glorified Him to be made an high priest who said unto Him, Thou art my Son, this day have I begotten Thee; as He saith also in another place, Thou art a priest for ever, after the order of Melchisedec." And it is also true that Jesus, in His intercessory prayer in the seventeenth chapter of John, makes explicit mention of His Father's love: "For Thou lovedst me before the foundation of the world." But in this reference to the love which His Father had for Him before the world began,—when He was "daily His delight, rejoicing always before Him, rejoicing in the habitable parts of the earth,"—Jesus is very far from seeking to supplement, by an appeal to personal influence, the force of a plea admitted to be in itself deficient, and requiring to be enforced by a consideration which it does not itself embody and contain. It does *itself* contain that consideration. It does itself shine radiantly in the glory of that relation of ineffable love between the high contracting parties in the counsel of peace. In that love the counsel or covenant between them took its rise. In the Father's love to the Son, the appointment of the Son to His priestly office originated; and in that appointment the Father's love was expressed. It was of the Father's love that the Son was designated to a work so glorious, that it should *in itself alone* carry in it perfect and all-sufficient ground for the righteous execution of purposes of love to a people whom no man can number. Here is the due place for the Son's interest with the Father, and in His Father's love—even that He should be set up from everlasting in the love that the Father had for Him from before the foundation of the world, and designated, and in due time sealed and sent into the world, on the work of establishing a perfect ground and plea for the obtaining, not by influence, but in righteous certainty and title, all saving blessing for those whom the Father's love had given to Him. Not to be put forth in the way of influence is the Son's interest with the Father, so as to dispense with an objective plea, or supplement a plea confessedly deficient; but in the very line and action of dispensing with influence, and bringing into existence a plea which is independent of influence, being in itself alone gloriously complete.

Part Third.

Element of a valid Intercessory objective Plea.

In the things, then, pertaining to God, with which the Intercessor's plea is concerned—and in reference to which He urges the relevant and valid consideration that

He has disposed them into an order or arrangement rendering the salvation of His people becoming, and righteous, and necessary—let us make a selection. Let us consider the aspect of the Divine nature and perfections towards sin,—which is the wrath of God; and the sanction of the Divine law,—which is its curse on the breakers thereof. The Intercessor presents Himself before God on our behalf, as "Jesus who hath delivered us from the wrath to come" (1 Thess. i. 10). Also He presents Himself before God as having "redeemed us from the curse of the law, being made a curse for us, that the blessing might come upon us, that we might receive the promise of the Spirit through faith" (Gal. iii. 13, 14). By these two considerations (which indeed run into one), "Christ executeth the office of a priest, in making continual intercession for us," by representing that He hath "once offered up Himself a sacrifice to satisfy Divine justice and reconcile us unto God" (Shorter Catechism, Quest. 25).

I. Consider, in the first place, the bearing of the Intercession on the removal of the Wrath of God.

The essential consideration here is, that the wrath of God to be set forth as the *necessary* aspect or expression of the Divine nature and perfections towards sin. It originates not in the will of God; for, in that case, the same will of God might set it aside or depart from it without satisfaction or pacification—without appeasement or atonement at all. But it originates from the

Divine nature, and that necessarily. On the supposition of sin, the Divine nature, and particularly the Divine holiness, assumes necessarily the aspect of wrath.—There are some recent evasions of this position.

(1.) MR MAURICE represents the wrath of God as the aspect which Divine Love assumes towards iniquity. But it may be safely left to the moral sense of mankind to say whether the Divine Love, act how it may, is the proper recompense of iniquity. And it may be safely left to the common sense of all who understand human language, to say whether those are treasuring up for themselves any conceivable aspect and action of Love, who are declared to be "treasuring up wrath against the day of wrath and revelation of the righteous judgment of God;" and whether Love, under any possible form or modification, can be understood as threatening to "render indignation and wrath, tribulation and anguish, to every soul of man that doeth evil" (Rom. ii. 3–9). Wrath is not beneficence; it is justice. It would be frightful to imagine wrath acting in the freeness of free beneficence, and not in the stringency of stringent justice. The universe were one vast hell of suspense and horror, if God's wrath could alight elsewhere than where it is *deserved*. "They that do such things are *worthy* of death" (Rom. i. 32). Wrath is vengeance—righteous vengeance, and recompense. "For we know Him that hath said, Vengeance belongeth unto me, I will recompense, saith the Lord." (Heb. x. 30). Hence substitution, atonement, satisfaction are conceivable.

INTERCESSION :—II. THE INVERSE ARGUMENT. 147

If wrath is love, they are inconceivable,—except as calamities. If the wrath of God is Divine love "burning on" against the unholy for their purification, a Substitute bearing it in my stead is no Saviour, no friend. He is a foe,—fraudulently interposing to intercept, and to deprive me of, my only possible and real salvation. Most intelligible and most natural, in this light, is the outcry against the doctrine of substitution.

(2.) It is thought by some that a transition may be effected from the Divine love to the Divine wrath, by help of the term "Jealousy." And that there is something in this may, perhaps, be granted, if the idea of the Divine jealousy be used carefully as a *transition*, and no attempt be made to employ it as an *equivalent* or explanation. We cannot enter fully into the line of thought which opens up to us here; but one or two guiding principles may be laid down.*

In the *first* place; it is to be remembered that in such references to the jealousy of God, as that in Exod. xx. 5, "I the Lord thy God am a jealous God, visiting the iniquity of the fathers upon the children

* I have reason to believe that my friend, the Rev. Stewart Salmond of Barry, has in view to subject this line of thought to a very careful examination. He has given sufficient evidence of his great qualifications for undertaking such a task. And if he will resist the temptation to hasty authorship in this hasty age; subject to careful criticism all the utterances of the Old Testament on this theme; sift, as his admirable learning qualifies him to sift, the writings of the best German theologians; and bring out the bearings of the subject alike in its ethical and theological aspects, in ripe completeness: he will do valuable service to the Church in a department where such service is eminently called for.

unto the third and fourth generation;"—He is speaking to a redeemed, and covenant people. The recognition of the covenant is in the very preface to the law as thus given at Sinai: "I am the Lord *thy God*, that hath brought thee out of the land of Egypt, and out of the house of bondage." Nor is this lost sight of, or set aside to make room for the introduction of the idea of jealousy. It is re-affirmed in the very sentence which affirms the jealousy; "I the Lord *thy God* am a jealous God." The jealousy—whatever it may imply—is introduced in vindication of the Divine glory among a people whom, as a people, God hath loved and chosen as His own. And for this reason it seems to follow that it cannot throw much light on the aspect which the Divine nature and perfections assume towards those who have no interest in the covenant. For it raises a question which it does not answer; "If these things be done in the green tree, what shall be done in the dry?"

In the *second* place; it is to be borne in mind that in its plain and unsophisticated meaning, jealousy is love vindicating its right in the beloved, by the help of anger. Anger shall be called in, in last resort, rather than that right be resigned. In this view, jealousy, even while it is "the rage of a man" (Prov. vi. 34), is "cruel as the grave," just because, and so long as, and only so long as—"love is strong as death" (Cant. viii. 6). It is, in short, a special manifestation of love; and the strength of love is the measure of the strength of jealousy. Jealousy, so to speak, is,—when purged at least from elements of base suspiciousness,—a powerful compliment to the object beloved. In the nature of the case, jealousy is compelled to deal with *primâ facie* grounds of suspicion; but when it is the honourable passion we have spoken of, it deals with these grounds not with the view and hope of proving them, but of explaining, dissipating, and *dis*proving them. It is in that view a noble passion; and shallow natures are incapable of manifesting it, and incapable of appreciating or appeasing it. They have not enough of love to do so.

And now, in the *third* place; if Jealousy is thus Love itself, vindicating its right in the beloved by the aid even of anger, so long as retention of the beloved and regaining of reciprocal love is conceived to be possible; it remains to ask whether it must not utterly expire when despair of success supervenes? The compliment, as we have ventured to call it, will then be paid no more. An entirely different passion or emotion takes place. Jealousy is designed to be restorative and recuperative; and is therefore a means to an end. But, the end despaired of, the reason for jealousy is gone. The desire now is for redress or retribution—which is itself of the nature of an end, and not a means to an end.*

* While this is passing through the press, I have lighted on the following remarkable passage—which I have read with intense interest—in the Translation of Schwegler's "History of Philosophy," by my distinguished friend, Dr James Hutchison Stirling. It occurs in the representation of the views of Hegel on "The Objective Spirit," *i.e.*, the Free Will. and it

And it is an end of an entirely distinct character from that which the entertainment and expression of jealousy aims at securing. It implies the entire resignation of love, and of love's beneficent desires. It is wrath: and the Christian is forbidden to cherish it.

But, in the *fourth* place, is he forbidden to cherish it, because in its own nature it is evil, and averse from

seems to me to indicate profound intuition into the nature of Moral Law, and the foundation of moral obligation. Speaking of "the possibility of the subjective will individualising itself against right in itself or the Universal Will," —a possibility that seems to be implied in the very nature of responsibility and free will, Hegel is represented as saying:—

"The division of the two wills is Wrong—delinquency, fraud, crime. This division demands a reconciliation, a restoration of right or of the universal will as against its temporary sublation or negation occasioned by the particular will. The right that thus restores itself as against the particular will, the negation of wrong, is penalty. Theories that found the right of penalty on purposes to prevent, deter, intimidate, or correct, mistake the nature of penalty. Prevention, intimidation, etc., are finite ends, *i.e.*, mere means, and these too, uncertain means. But an act of justice cannot be degraded into a mere means: justice is not exercised, in order that anything but itself be attained and realised. The fulfilment and self-manifestation of justice is an absolute end, an end unto its own self."

How directly these most admirable and profound statements bear upon the doctrine of this volume, the intelligent theological student will not fail to see. I do not profess to be a Hegelian,—any more than Dr Hutchison Stirling does (*Trans. of Schwegler*, p. 445): I have not even mastered the Secret of Hegel. But I rejoice to write down, under the sanction of that great metaphysician's name, in this volume on the Atonement of the Lord Jesus, remarkable utterances like these, so powerfully corroborative of those views of *penalty*, which lie at the foundation of all that we say of the Atonement as a real endurance of the penalty or curse of the Divine law, and a true and proper satisfaction to Divine justice. And I cannot but humbly express my admiration of the services which Dr Stirling is rendering to the higher philosophy and the Christian faith. To labour, however thanklessly, to expose the false philosophies—whose *role* seems to be mainly to provide vindication and classic utterance for the clamorous voices of Matter and Pleasure: and to give transcendent and supplanting prominence to the claims of Spirit, of Duty, and of God: is an industry that cannot be in vain in the Lord.

the nature of God? Far otherwise. It is incompetent to man, just *because* it is competent to God, and to God alone. "Dearly beloved, avenge not yourselves, but rather give place unto wrath; for it is written, Vengeance is mine; I will repay, saith the Lord" (Rom. xii. 19). The quotation here,—"it is written"—is from the song of Moses, where God is introduced as speaking *not* concerning His covenant people, but concerning His enemies and theirs. "To me belongeth vengeance and recompense; their foot shall slide in due time" (Deut. xxxii. 35). And the reason given for vengeance against them, is such as to prove that vengeance is entirely different from jealousy. Rather, jealousy, in respect to His people, is given as the reason for vengeance on their enemies,—so entirely different are the two attributions. "*For* the Lord shall judge his people and repent himself for his servants, when he seeth that their power is gone" (ver. 36). The quotation, therefore, by the Apostle in writing to the Romans is admirably in point. He admonishes to abstinence from wrath and self-redress, because the Judge Supreme hath given special promise to interpose and Himself effect what righteousness requires. The passage is again quoted to the Hebrews in confirmation of the terrible truth that, as there remaineth no more sacrifice for sin when the blood of the covenant has been counted an unholy thing, so there remaineth nothing but "a certain fearful looking for of judgment and fiery indignation, that shall devour the adversaries"

(Heb. x. 27). "For we know Him that hath said, Vengeance is mine; I will recompense, saith the Lord" (ver. 30).

However, therefore, the idea of Jealousy may be serviceable as a transition from the idea of love to that of wrath or vengeance, it is obvious that it cannot be employed as an explanation of wrath or vengeance, far less as an equivalent; unless, indeed, it be used in a sense entirely different from that which renders a special word—the word "jealousy"—necessary; in a sense, that is, which substantially identifies it with the word "wrath." And, of course, in that case, the ethical and theological investigation is in no respect expedited; but left precisely as it was, or rather left in greater darkness than before. Refusing on this legitimate ground, to identify jealousy and wrath; and leaving the question of the relations between them, and the transition from the one to the other, open for investigation, we are in circumstances to reiterate that—

(3.) Wrath is the aspect of the Divine Holiness towards sin. It is not therefore under the origination of the Divine will, as aspects and actings of love, in their very nature free, must be; but the *necessary* aspect which the Divine nature and perfections cannot but assume. Of course the actings or forthputtings of Divine wrath are at the *disposal* of the Divine will; for the Divine will and the Divine nature are ever in harmony. And the necessity of the Divine wrath against sin is moral, not physical; its action not being like that of gravitation and physical forces, but ever, as we have said, under the disposal or executive of the Divine will; else, in that case again, long-suffering and forbearance, and therefore salvation, would be impossible. Still, it is originally in the nature of God, and not in the will of God, that the seat and spring of wrath in its various actings must be found; and it is essentially necessary to attend to this, if we would be in circumstances to vindicate the very attribute of Love itself.

For, strange as it may at first sight appear, it is nevertheless true that the moral necessity of wrath, which the doctrine of priesthood presupposes, is the indispensable and valid vindication of the love of God. To some, this may seem a hazardous, as it may be an unexpected, affirmation. But it is of easy demonstration. For suppose the wrath of God against sin were voluntary, in the sense of not being morally necessary and inevitable. Conceive of an infinite Being entertaining and cherishing *unnecessary* anger—anger which no inherent and unchangeable perfection of his nature, and no demands arising from his moral relation to the creatures of his hand and power, render it absolutely inevitable that he should entertain and cherish; but he could, on the contrary, lay it aside, simply if he pleased. Consider him as needing to be pleaded with and prevailed upon to resile from it, and to refrain from the expression and action of it to which it tends. Conceive him as still further refusing so to resile from it, and to refrain from giving expression to it, till it has been appeased by something called atonement or satisfaction. Is it conceivable that this could consist with Love? Is not such unnecessary anger identical with that pleasure in the death of the sinner, which God has condescended to repudiate with abhorence, and by an oath: "As I live, saith the Lord, I have *no* pleasure in the death of the sinner?" Is not such a view of God's character precisely that which the heathen attribute to a supposed divinity, when in reality "they sacrifice to devils and not to God?" And—even in the most mitigated view of this huge misrepresentation of the wrath of God—if it were anything less than morally absolutely necessary, how is it possible to account for a Divine appointment of an intercessor to avert it? It is precisely because God absolutely cannot avert it from the sinner, without its being borne by a substitute, who, to every effect concerned, becomes judicially one with the sinner, and shall, in due time, make the sinner consciously, spiritually, by faith, and of choice truly one with Him, as his living vine, or living head;—precisely for this very reason it is that there is scope, and there is seen to be scope, in God's glorious nature for that Love in which the substitution, and the intercession grounded on it, take their rise. "God commendeth his love to us;" decketh it out in beauty, and arrayeth it in evidence overwhelming; "in that while we were yet sinners, Christ died for us." And "herein is love, not that we have loved God, but that he hath loved us, and sent his Son to be the propitiation for our sins."

So intimately are the two doctrines of Divine wrath and Divine love bound up together. Together they stand or fall. The Intercessor pleads that He has been able to make them stand,—able to illustrate and glorify them both. And His plea is to this effect: That in prosecution of His Father's and His own eternal purpose of love, He has, as the substitute of His people, and in a oneness with them which meets every requirement of unsearchable wisdom, borne the wrath which their iniquities had entailed as recompense inevitable; and now He claims to be recognised of God as "Jesus who delivers them from the wrath to come." Him the Father therefore heareth. And the decree goeth forth to deliver them: "Save from going down to the pit, for I have found a ransom."

II. Consider now the bearing of the Intercession on the removal of the Curse of the Law.

The curse differs from the wrath, not fundamentally, but formally. It is indeed the same thing regarded from another point of view. When the relation of acknowledged sovereignty and subjection between the Lawgiver and His responsible creature has been deranged by the entrance of sin, the Divine nature, which presented the aspect of complacency and approbation towards the creature while holy, presents now the aspect of displacency and wrath towards the sinner; and simultaneously, and as an equivalent reading of this now changed relation on the side of the other party concerned, the creature appears in the attitude of a curse,—for it is originally the concrete, the *Herem* of the Old Testament,—a devoted thing, devoted to destruction. Or, more particularly, and still more formally exact. The Divine nature, has expressed itself in the Divine law, which is the reflection of God's nature, and the formal expression of His authority. The relation has been formulated in moral law, and the curse is formally its penalty or sanction. Transferring, therefore, the substance and spirit of what has been already said concerning the wrath of God to this side of the relation, and clothing the same considerations in the formal expressions which this simply altered point of view and judicially formulated expression of it may render necessary, we should have substantially the same train of thought to follow out as before. And that, of course, it is unnecessary to repeat.

In a word or two, however, it may be shown that fundamentally the same principles re-appear; and more especially, we may briefly indicate how the same consideration of moral necessity attaches to the curse of the law, as to the wrath of God. For absolute moral necessity is the all-explaining and all-justifying consideration which must be attended to in contemplating the curse of the law, and seeking to understand the nature of the Intercession as it bears upon it. The whole inquiry into the nature of the Intercession and Atonement, or in other words, the Priesthood of Christ, is immediately deranged and perplexed, unless it be clearly apprehended that on the pre-supposition of sin, the Divine curse becomes absolutely certain and inevitable. A correct idea of sin *as* sin,—that is, as transgression of the law, —and a correct idea of that law of which sin is the transgression, will at once deliver the mind from all vague ideas of the possibility of God's curse being contingent or arbitrary, or optional. Any such notion is utterly inconsistent with—immediately and completely fatal to —the fundamental conception of moral law and moral obligation. Heaven and earth may pass away. The Creator of heaven and earth, clothed in created nature, and standing in the room of sinful creatures, may tremble as the curse of the law approaches to claim Him in His responsibility for the guilty. The omnipotent God, in the person of the beloved Son, beloved before the foundation of the world, may exclaim, "Father, if it be possible, let this cup pass from me." But not one jot or tittle of the law, either on the side of its curse or its commandment, can pass away till all be fulfilled. For neither on the one side nor on the other—neither on the side of its requirement nor of its sanction—is there the slightest element of the optional and arbitrary in that law of God which is holy and just and good. It is the expression of God's nature, which cannot change; and of God's authority, which must ever vindicate the inviolability of His nature. Nor can the possibility of its being suspended, or varied or abrogated, on the side of the curse be imagined, any more than on the side of the commandment. The Moral Law is the balance of the moral universe; and it matters not whether the right arm or the left be tampered with. In either case the result is the same: the moral balance is destroyed. And how then shall God weigh the actions of men? "How shall God judge the world?"

It is one of the shallowest imaginable thoughts, that the obligation of the curse of the law could be relaxed, and the obligation of its commandment still retained. These are not in reality two obligations, but one. A balance—to use again that simple figure—has two arms: it has but one equilibrium. Even so the moral law has a commandment for our observance, and a curse for our disobedience. But it has not two obligations, that one might be tampered with and the other nevertheless remain intact. He who, disobedient, should plead off from liability to the curse, is, whether he is conscious of it or not, pleading off from the authority of the commandment. It is the one indivisible obligation of the law which he is seeking to cast off: and his success would be nothing less than the dethronement of the Moral Ruler of the universe.

To see this, look at the exculpating pleas which our first parents put forward to shield them from the curse of death which their disobedience had entailed: "The serpent beguiled me, and I did eat:" "The woman whom thou gavest to be with me, she gave me, and I did eat." Against what do these pleas in extenuation really strike? Against what side of the Divine law are they consciously and intentionally directed? Against the law on the side of its penalty or sanction. They are designed to insinuate the element of possible contingency into the obligation of the law on the side of its curse, without affecting explicitly to tamper with the obligation of its commandment. The guilty pair mean to deny the absolute and unconditional moral necessity of the curse, and to admit its righteousness only conditionally; the condition being that disobedience shall have been perpetrated in the absence of temptation. Temptation—in effect they say—shall bar the infliction of the curse. Had we fallen untempted: had the serpent not beguiled me: had the woman not given to me: had we disobeyed under no temptation to disobey: our punishment would have been righteous; our mouth would have been stopped, and we ourselves brought in guilty before God. But, as it is, our mouth is not stopped. We plead temptation in bar of sentence from the Judge.— And is this an attempt to shake the stability of the Divine law only on one side? As soon move one arm of the balance and think the other will remain at rest. This is an attempt to overthrow *moral obligation*,—the obligation of the law in its precept, just as much as in its penalty.

To convince us of this, if indeed it be not intuitively obvious, let those pleas of exculpation which the fallen pair put forward *after* their fall be transferred in imagination to the period preceding it. They are precisely as much in point *there*, clothed with precisely the same relevancy and force *there*, before their disobedience, as after it. They tamper with the obligation of the law *there* exactly to the same effect, to provide for a possible disobedience still contemplated, as for an actual disobedience that has arisen. Simply change their form to suit the altered supposition: but do you change their spirit, or drift, or real design? I will obey, says Eve, provided the serpent do not beguile me. And I will obey, says Adam, provided the woman whom Thou gavest to be with me do not give unto me. The admission of relevancy in these pleas in this form would not be more detrimental to the law than in the form and at the time they were actually urged. The reason is, that in both cases alike they overthrow the one indivisible obligation of the law itself. For to plead a bar against the moral necessity of the curse, is to plead a bar against the authority of the commandment. It is really to dethrone the Lawgiver, and to say, "Who is the Lord that he should reign over us?"

The plea, therefore, of a righteous and effectual Intercessor must contain in it at least *this* element; namely, a practical admission of the holy, moral necessity of the curse, and that in a representation of the fact that the Intercessor has endured and exhausted the curse in His own person, and in His clients' stead, having been made a curse for them; that He hath not made void but established the law,—made of a woman, made under the law, and having now redeemed them that were under it. An objective plea like that, is independent of influence to give it power. It is perfect in itself; and with Divine justice it has in itself power to prevail. It is relevant;

and it is complete. The triumphant cry of the Cross may with confidence be uttered over it and applied to it—"It is finished." By His one offering Christ has for ever perfected them that are sanctified. The plea, in its own power, carries all that the Intercessor claims.

III. And now we must here also prominently insist again on the truth with which we have already become familiar; namely, that Christ was actively an office-bearer, and priest, and offerer of Himself in His death; actively, in the inconceivable baptism of fire and final ordeal of death—His wrath enduring, curse-bearing death—fulfilling the whole law of God which is love; love, in His case, to God forsaking Him; love to men while crucifying Him. This brings into view, as the completing element of His one perfect plea, that perfectly tested, positive and complete righteousness in which He urges that His people shall now be held justified in His person—in Him their priest and representative and head.

And,—if in the minds of any of my readers the idea still remains, that in denying for Christ's intercession the conception that it acts in the way of personal influence with the Father, I have done injustice to the relation of love and loving interest, and ineffable acceptability that subsists between the Father and the Son of His love,—here is the place in which, and the consideration by which, this idea may be finally obviated. Far from doing injustice to the interest and acceptability which the beloved Son must be supposed to have with the

Father, we are now in circumstances to insist that it all enters into the objective plea, and is in no respect required to be put forth as subjective influence. For when we say that Christ's righteousness—and the Father is well pleased for His righteousness' sake, for He hath magnified the law and made it honourable—when we say that Christ's righteousness enters as an element into the intercessory plea; or, rather, that as a righteousness perfected in the ordeal of His wrath-enduring, curse-bearing death and offering on the Cross, it *is* the one complete and indivisable plea which, as Intercessor, He urges at His Father's throne; we are not surely to dissociate His acceptable righteousness from His acceptable person. That may not and cannot be. It is Christ's person as God-man,—" ordained for men," and as having perfectly fulfilled all righteousness,—which is the righteousness of saints. "Christ" it is, that "is of God made unto us righteousness" (1 Cor. i. 30). "Christ" it is, that "is the end of the law for righteousness" (Rom. x. 4). "Thou lovest righteousness, and hatest iniquity; therefore God, thy God,"—thy God in that covenant which thou hast established and fulfilled —"hath anointed thee with the oil of gladness above thy fellows" (Ps. xlv. 7). Christ needed no work assigned Him to give Him love-interest, or love-influence, with the eternal Father. " The Father loveth the Son, and hath given all things into His hand" (John iii. 35). His love-interest with the Father is the source and origin of the covenant given Him to fulfil, and the honourable and glorious work given Him to do. But it needed a covenant of peace and a work of redemption, if He was to embody all His love-interest, all His acceptability in the Father's sight, in an objective plea which should need no influence to give it prevalence with the Father. And this He achieved in His obedience unto death, in His fulfilment of all righteousness in His people's room: and this He now pleads in His Intercession that He has achieved. The righteousness of Christ is the righteous Christ himself. There enters into the plea which He presents, all the righteousness, all the well-pleasingness, all the acceptability that is in His person. He himself as God-man: His Divine and human natures in perfect harmony with each other—His entire person, therefore, in inconceivably glorious conformity with the nature of God—for the nature of God is the very seat of His personality, and His human nature subsists in His one Divine person, as the most glorious image of that Divine nature which it has been given to any created nature to express, and to it alone to enshrine: this glorious and gloriously constituted person, having offered Himself bearing the Divine wrath and burdened with the Divine curse—now lightened of the last rack of both, by righteous and complete endurance of them; beloved of the Father because He fulfilled the commandment to lay down His life and take it again: this matchless person of God-man, in all the moral worth of all His doings in the flesh, and of all His sufferings, and of all His graces, and all His gracious thoughts, and all His holy virtues;

in the full assemblage of all His spiritual excellencies and aspects of loveliness and love-worthiness in the Father's sight: *this* is the righteousness of saints. And *this* is the Intercessor's plea.

It is independent of Influence: for all that could, consistently with the unity of Godhead, and the glory of Divine persons, be imagined under the conception of Influence, is already engrossed and embodied in it.

Part Fourth.

Pointing the Inverse Argument from Intercession.

Though it be like coming down from Pisgah to do superfluous and inglorious battle in the plains, we must pass in brief review, beneath the light of such an Intercession as we have now been considering, the various schemes of thought on the Atonement which we have often already seen to be so untenable.

And yet it seems almost like relentless controversial persecution of them to ask,—What foundation do *they* lay for an intercession? what work do *they* assign to Christ, as, in Scriptural language, He maketh intercession for us? Since not one of them professes to read in the death of Christ an atonement made for definite and designated persons; and since, nevertheless, Christ's intercession is for particular persons particularly, even for those who are ultimately saved,—for Him the Father heareth always, and He prays not for the world, but for those who have been given to Him out of the world;

how can these atonements, when urged as pleas, become specificated or pointed to bear upon the individual persons concerned? To present a plea is not to alter it. It cannot be changed by the mere circumstance of urging it. If it do not in itself carry the conclusion pretended, and that in reference to the particular person or persons indicated, the mere urging of it cannot infuse into it a relevancy and force that were not there before. The theory inexorably indispensable in such a case, is the theory of Influence. Christ exerts His influence to enforce the plea, and by influence *He* carries what the plea itself does not pretend to carry or conclude. In this light it is really, so far as our argument is concerned, a matter of no moment what the particular defective or false view of the Atonement we are examining may be. Nor does it matter how truly it may be able to plead that it provides for *some* intercession which is not merely and exclusively one of influence. That may or may not be true; it boots not. Does it provide for an Intercession wholly distinct from, and independent of, Influence? Does it provide for an Intercession that is wholly representative, judicial, priestly, and which rests for its success and prevalence wholly on the objective plea, as in and by itself alone concluding for and carrying all that the Intercessor craves, and the Intercession is designed to procure? If not: if it provides merely some semblance or some fraction of a plea; a ground or consideration which falls short of moral and judicial perfection, and falls short therefore, of absolutely perfect power or prevalence; if, after all, the personal influence of the Intercessor must come in to render it prevalent and effective: then it is on personal influence that this intercession really turns and hinges. It must take its character from—its essence must consist in—that which renders it successful, which alone renders it of any real worth. And, therefore, it is in reality an intercession of mere influence. And that we have shown to be utterly indefensible and inadmissible.

We need scarcely particularise.

What imaginable connection is there between Atonement and Intercession on the theory of Example or of Martyrdom? "I have shown them an Example, and ratified the evidence of truth by Martyrdom. *Therefore* keep, through thine own name, those whom thou hast given me!"

Or on the theory of MAURICE? "I have submitted to Self-sacrifice,—to a death of Self-denial. *Therefore* forgive and sanctify the particular persons whom now I designate and point out!"

Or on the wild dream of ROBERTSON? "I have fallen a prey to that 'law of being,' vicarious sacrifice, —'approaching the whirling wheel till I was torn in pieces.' *Therefore*———!" Therefore—what? Abrogate the *law of being?* Or?—Stop the wheel!

Or what connection is there on the scheme of BUSHNELL? "I have given a Display of the principles of thy Government, suitable and applicable to every human being. *Therefore* on some men, on certain persons, let thy Government bear in leniency and mercy!"

Or on that of Young? "I have finished a work fitted and designed to exert a Moral Influence on sinners. *Therefore* let me have influence with God!"

Or what connection is there on the scheme of Dr Balmer? "I have achieved an undertaking which bears on the welfare of each and every one of the human race precisely and exactly as it bears on any. *Therefore* I plead that it shall be made to have a wholly different bearing on some from that which it shall have on others!"

Are these such reasonings as men will dare to put into the lips of the Wisdom and Logos of God? If not,—then let them own that the Atonement of the Everlasting Son of the Father, who through the Eternal Spirit offered Himself without spot to God, is no vague, indefinite, impersonal, haphazard redeemability, preparatory merely to redemption; but very and efficacious redemption itself, even "in *His* blood who is the image of the invisible God, the first-born of every creature:" and that His Atonement being definite and perfect, and final and infallible,—for "It is finished," —His intercession is the perpetual presentation of it before the throne of the Majesty in the heavens, and the presentation therein of a plea most relevant and efficacious, infallibly securing all grace for those whom God hath given to Him, even so that "none of them is lost." Let us all own this, with personal and appropriating faith; for "whosoever will, let him come, and take of the water of life freely." Let us then hold fast the confidence and the rejoicing of the hope firm unto the end. And let us, with the spirits of the blest on high, fall down in faith and gratitude before the throne of God and of the Lamb, saying: "Thou art worthy, O LAMB, to receive power, and riches, and wisdom, and strength, and honour, and glory, and blessing: for Thou wast slain, and hast REDEEMED us to God by Thy blood."

CHAPTER VIII.

ATONEMENT AND REMISSION.

WE lay down another proposition in reference to the conditions under which the subject of this volume should be studied.

The Doctrine of the Atonement ought not to be discussed apart from a correct view of the exact immediate Object or Design of the Atonement, to secure, namely, the Remission of sins.

This is not the only object or design of the Atonement of Christ. There are other objects accomplished by it, and, of course, designedly accomplished. Some of these are less immediate than the remission of sins, —of the nature, that is, of a more ultimate end: the great last end, of course, namely, the advancement of the glory of God; as also the "gathering together in one of all things in Christ, both of which are in heaven, and which are on earth" (Eph. i. 10). There are less immediate ends also, not in the sense of their being more ultimate, but more subordinate: very specially, for instance, the removal of the middle wall of partition between Jews and Gentiles, the "abolition in His flesh of the law of commandments in ordinances, that He might reconcile both [the commonwealth of Israel and the aliens therefrom] unto God in one body by the Cross" (Eph. iii. 11–17). Moreover, there are objects or designs of Christ's death, more exactly co-ordinate with the Remission of sins, such as Redemption and Reconciliation: "He gave Himself for us that He might *redeem* us" (Titus ii. 14); and "Christ hath once suffered for sins, the just for the unjust, that He might bring us unto God" (1 Peter iii. 18), so that "when we were enemies, we were *reconciled* unto God by the death of His Son" (Rom. v. 10). So that a complete investigation of the more immediate and exact design of the Atonement would require us to prosecute the lines of thought opened up by each of the words, Remission, Reconciliation, and Redemption. In making a selection, however, we fasten on the idea of Remission. And in doing so, we cannot imagine that our choice is fitted either to derange or limit the question, when we bear in mind that in the blessed ordinance of the Supper, our Lord took the cup and gave thanks and gave it to the disciples, saying, "This is My blood of the new testament, which is shed for many for the remission of sins."

There is not one of those manifestly most reasonable canons or conditions of discussion of this subject which we have already laid down, that the opponents of the Westminster doctrine of the Atonement will not be found habitually violating. And the same thing is true in the present instance also. They will not face consideration of the exact immediate design of the Atonement. They take up with the most general term that they can find in Scripture as descriptive of the design of Christ's death—the term "salvation;" and not examining and explaining it in the light of the more definite and precise ideas which the terms remission, redemption, reconciliation, suggest, they give to the idea of salvation a vagueness for which they themselves, and not the Scriptures of God, are responsible; and many of them are found in the end making it equivalent to mere *salvability*. Indeed, they cannot possibly escape from the overwhelming temptation thus to attenuate its meaning, if their purpose is to render the Atonement impersonal and indefinite and universal, unless they are prepared to accept the doctrine of universal salvation. This has been demonstrated by so many writers on this subject, that I can add nothing to the demonstration. Piety will always maintain, without an argument, that when our Lord is called our "Saviour," it is not meant that He is the author of salvability, but the "Author of eternal Salvation" (Heb. v. 9). And logic will maintain, by an argument the simplest possible, that if the redemption purchased by Christ is merely salvability; and if we are made partakers of the redemption purchased by Christ by the effectual application of *it* to us by His Holy Spirit; then we are thereby made par takers merely of salvability: and so, after all that

Father, Son, and Holy Ghost have done for us, we are only salvable still!

The Nature of the Atonement, its Necessity, and its Object, are topics which, when logically treated, are found to run very much into one. For, if we can come to a clear understanding, in the first instance, of the Object which the Atonement is primarily designed to accomplish, the Nature of it will inevitably come into view, on the plain principle that it must be fitted and adapted to the attainment of the Object contemplated; while its Necessity will become obvious on the equally plain principle, that to the production of an effect the suitable casual efficiency is indispensible.

Now, the question has frequently been asked, and will probably continue to be asked so long as the world standeth, and men are thoughtful as to their prospects for a world to come,—Why should not God remit the sins of men without an Atonement?

It seems to us that a good deal of satisfaction on this question may be obtained from the remarkable and unqualified proposition laid down by the writer to the Hebrews: "Without shedding of blood is no remission" (chap. ix. 22). No doubt, at first sight, this seems merely to allege a fact, without assigning a reason. It seems to intimate nothing more than the historical truth, that in point of fact God never has remitted the sins of men without shedding of blood. But if emphasis is placed on the word *Remission*, and if a true idea is entertained of the transaction which that word represents, the proposition, "without shedding of blood is no remission," will be found not merely to allege a fact, but also to assign a reason for that fact—to embody not only the historical verity, but the underlying principle which justifies it, and which only needs to be carefully investigated and apprehended to furnish a satisfactory answer to the question,—Why should not God remit the sins of men without an Atonement?

For, when the inspired writer affirms that without shedding of blood is no remission, it is as if he had said:—You may imagine a forgiveness without shedding of blood, if you will; you may conjecture, or conjure up, some other scheme or principle of pardon; you may conceive of God as dealing with the sinner, and delivering him from the punishment due to his iniquities, without these iniquities being expiated,—without the penalty incurred by them being exacted,—without the law of which they are transgressions being relieved from the stain of dishonour which they had cast upon it,—without any costly sacrifice, any solemn propitiation, any priceless ransom. But whatever this transaction concerning sin might be, it would not be *remission*. Granting that it were quite possible for God to let the sinner off; to wipe out, by a mere arbitrary decree, and without any satisfaction to divine justice, the debt which the sinner had contracted; to cease from His anger towards His enemies, and return to a state of friendship; to say, Your sins be forgiven you, you have nothing now to fear;—all this, "without shedding of blood," without any sacrifice, or atonement, or expiation: still, all this, whatever it might amount to, does not amount to *remission*. Call it what you please; be it what it may; it is not remission. It may be held up as an equivalent for it; it may be in room and lieu of it; it may be all that multitudes care to inquire after, or have ever felt the need of, or troubled themselves to seek. But, however possible it might be on God's part, however satisfactory it might be on their part, it is not *remission*. It may look like it. It may seem to carry with it all that the unenlightened have any thought of when thinking of remission; but real remission it is not. Without shedding of blood it is not remission.

What the enlightened conscience of an anxious inquirer longs for, is remission—remission of sin. And what is that? It is removal of guilt; removal of liability to the wrath of God; removal of criminality or ill-desert. It is a sentence of "Not Guilty;" for "God will by no means clear the guilty" (Exod. xxxiv. 7). It is a recognition of blamelessness before the Holy One of Israel; a position and relation towards God, therefore, in which His wrath would be undue, unrighteous, impossible. That would be Remission. And the memorable announcement, "without shedding of blood is no remission," intimates, not so much that God will not grant *this* without shedding of blood, as that, whatever God might without shedding of blood grant, it would not be *this*, but something far short of this, something very different from this. In the very nature of the case, it would not be remission.

It is evident that this consideration opens up to us a thoroughly legitimate train of thought, at once emancipating us from all *a priori* speculations as to what is abstractly possible or impossible for Him who is past finding out, and leaving to us the far plainer task of investigating the conditions under which alone, from the nature of the case, the very definite idea of a true remission can be realised: while it is equally evident that, by attacking the problem, or approaching the question, from this point of view, we blend very much into one topic the three ideas of the Object, the Nature, and the Necessity of the Atonement. Choosing this, then, as our line of thought; renouncing, that is to say, all vague questions as to whether God could not have done some good to miserable man without the death of His Eternal Son as a propitiatory sacrifice upon the cross; and seeking a guiding light in a definite and precise idea of what is implied in *remission*, we will be in circumstances to enter on some valid investigation of the Scriptural doctrine of the nature and necessity of the Atonement.

There seem to be three aspects of the idea of Remission, conspiring to prove that it is not realisable apart from Atonement, or Satisfaction, or Propitiatory Sacrifice :—

I. Remission of sin is an act competent only to the Divine Lawgiver and Judge, and which, therefore, must quadrate with Divine justice. But without shedding of blood there is no such act of the Divine Judge.

II. Remission of sin is an act competent only to the Divine Sovereign, and is expressive of special Divine mercy and love. But without shedding of blood there is no evidence of such Divine love and mercy.

III. Remission of sin is an act competent only to the Divine Lord of the conscience acting as such, giving security, peace, and honour to the conscience. But without shedding of blood, there is no such act as that.

Let us take these three views of Remission of Sin. First, It is an act of the Divine Judge; Second, It is an act of Divine love; Third, It gives peace to the conscience, and calls forth purity and honour in the moral nature. But remove the shedding of blood: suppose sin dealt with, and pardoned without the shedding of blood, without an atoning sacrifice: and all these characteristics, or features, of true remission are gone:—no transaction of Divine justice; no gift or evidence of Divine love; nothing to pacify the conscience, or to purify and pique to holy honour the paralysed moral sense.

We proceed to show that such are the results of supposing sin forgiven without the shedding of blood.

Part First.
Remission and Law.

Remission—true, valid remission of sin—is an act of the Divine Judge, in His judicial capacity, acting in law and by rule of justice. For God to deal with sin at all, whether to punish or to pardon, is to deal with that which is "transgression of the law." When God deals with sin, His dealings, like His judgments, must be according to truth. He must deal with sin *as* sin. He must deal with it as what it is, not as what it is not. And sin is transgression of the law. But to deal with that which is transgression of the law is to act as the Lawgiver and Judge. Who can remit sin but God only? And when He remits sin, He is dealing with the sinner as his most high Lord and rightful Lawgiver, taking cognisance of his disobedience to the Divine law and dealing righteously concerning it.

There are some who would strip the Almighty God altogether of the office and function of a Lawgiver and Judge. For their part they prefer a more genial view of the relation between God and His creatures. They prefer regarding Him as a Father. And when they see Him dealing with sin in the way of punishing it, they tell us it is in fatherly affection, seeking to correct and chasten and purify His children,—not in execution of vengeance, not to satisfy justice, not to inflict a penalty. Any view of God's procedure concerning sin that would represent God as acting in the rigid justice of a Judge, whose immediate function is not to benefit the offender, but uphold the law, they represent as harsh, as attributing implacability to God, as robbing Him of the beneficence of His nature, as contradicting the heavenly declaration that "God is love."

(1.) But the human Conscience testifies that God is a Lawgiver, a Ruler, a Judge. And guilty conscience testifies that I have offended against Him, revolted from Him, injured Him in His claims, repudiated His authority, in that very office and capacity. My most plain and ordinary and commonplace sense of sin is, that I have refused God as my Lawgiver; that I have said, I will not have Him to reign over me; that I have not made His law the rule of my will. My conscience, in accusing me as a sinner, does not depone primarily that I have rejected a Father's benevolent advice; but that I have rejected a Lawgiver's rightful authority—that I have done that which God said, "Thou shalt not do." Even if it testifies that I have despised His beneficence and wronged Him as a Father, it testifies that as a Judge He is clothed with right and power to compel redress of the wrongs which, as a Father, He hath sustained. The very office of conscience is to testify of God as a Judge.

(2.) Or, turning from the dictates of Conscience to the scheme of Providence. Can any man face the facts of Providence, and maintain that God uniformly punishes sin as a Father, that He only seeks to correct and benefit His erring children, never as a Judge avenging on His enemies the insults offered to His majesty and law? Did the fire that fell from heaven on the cities of the plain chasten, purify, and sanctify their debased inhabitants? Did it not rather avenge the quarrel of the Almighty Judge, vindicate His righteousness, maintain the rigour of His law, and condemn the wicked in an overthrow, making them examples of Divine wrath till the end of time, suffering the vengeance of eternal fire? Did the exterminating waters of the deluge demonstrate the Fatherly beneficence of God? or did they not really express the righteous indignation of an insulted Lawgiver? Conscience and the course of Providence demonstrate that God is clothed with the office of a Ruler and a Judge.

(3.) And the Constitution of Society confirms the demonstration. For there is such a thing as human law —authoritative commandment among men, with penalty annexed for disobedience. There is the human judge, whose office it is to maintain the honour, and apply the action of law, where disobedience has been perpetrated. There is the solemn scene of the court-room of sacred justice,—the tribunal, the bench, the bar, the criminal, the prosecutor, the judge, the jury; the indictment read; the relative law appealed to; the fact admitted or proven; the penalty pronounced, and, at last, with all the rigour and remorselessness of fate, exacted. Law, government, condemnation, penalty,—are realities among men. And the question is, How does that come to pass? Whence came they? Are they relics of barbarism,—to be purged away before advancing civilisation? Or are they component parts of honourable institutions, to be perfected as civilisation progresses? Let the breathless interest of millions tell, as they watch some noted trial in their native country, while the outraged sense of righteousness and honour thrills from north to south, from shore to shore, and reverential expectation waits the issue, thanking God that impartial justice, with even balance, and with flashing sword, has her inviolable temple in the land! Yes; it is not one of man's corruptions, but a relic of his greatness and moral glory; it is not of human invention, it is of Divine origin, that justice and judgment, and the sacred office of the judge, have their dwelling among men. But if God is not a judge, it is impossible to account for the existence of that noble and solemn office on earth at all. God might as well create the faculties of sight and hearing in men, without Himself being possessed of ability to see and hear, as He could put it into men's hearts to maintain judgment in human government, if He were not a lawgiver and judge Himself. "He that formed the eye, shall He not see? He that formed the ear, shall He not hear?" He that clothed man with the office of the judge, and with authority to execute judgment; must not justice and judgment form the habitation of His own throne? Must He not Himself be the judge of all the earth? For what can the office be among men, or how could it ever have originated, were it not a reflection, a derivation, from the same office in God? Nor is it without a flood of light on this theme of sacrifice, as juridical, retributive, and expiatory, that when God did first delegate His function of judgment to man, it was in language which has since been consecrated to the service of the doctrine of propitiation:—"By man shall His *blood* be *shed*" (Gen. ix. 6).

And acting in this office, what can come beneath God's cognisance, waiting His decision concerning it, if not sin?—sin, which is the transgression of His law, the refusal of His Lordship over us, the rejection of His commandment and authority.

Be it observed then, that in whatever way God may deal with sin, it is as a Judge that He has to deal with it. It is as the righteous Lawgiver, the rightful Ruler of all the universe. It is in no private capacity. It is in the broad public relation in which He stands to all the universe—the great upholder of law and government. If He executes vengeance on sin, it is in this capacity that He does so. If He remit sin, it is in this capacity that He remits it,—as the administrator of eternal justice. His act in doing so will be an act of high, public, sovereign state; a judicial procedure; an act in administration of justice.

But if sin be forgiven without shedding of blood, there is not the shadow of any such act. The Divine law has been violated, yet no order taken that it be honoured. Divine justice offended, yet no procedure adopted to satisfy it: the authority of God assailed, yet no vindication of it achieved: sentence of death incurred, yet not inflicted: a curse entailed, but never executed: a fearful threatening uttered, yet braved and scorned, and proved to be worthy of contempt by its being set aside unfulfilled. It is not even pretended on this scheme, that remission of sin is an act of God, acting as a public lawgiver and judge. He is supposed, as it were, to have a private meeting with the sinner, and to tell him not to be afraid, for He means not to prosecute him for his sin at all, not to bring him into judgment, not to demand a trial. He simply lets the sinner off, and simply lets his sin pass. So benevolent is He said to be, that He seeks no satisfaction to justice, —a step declared to imply implacability and harshness. He will quash all legal and terrible procedure. He will quietly resile from His claims, and be silent considerately concerning His injuries.

But whatever this might be, it is not *Remission*. It is not the thorough, authoritative, conclusive removal of guilt; for that can be the act of the judge alone. But is *he* acting as a judge, who arbitrarily sets aside the law and all its penalty; silences the lord high prosecutor, dismisses the witnesses, disbands the jury, and declares that he has made up his mind to forgive the prisoner at the bar? Would that be an act of justice? Would it stand for a valid remission of the criminal's offence? As little would it be Remission—as little would it be a valid, judicial transaction on God's part —were He " without shedding of blood," without the introduction of a sacrifice, without demanding an atonement, without providing a propitiation, to clear the guilty, to let the sinner off, to let sin pass unpunished.

Part Second.

Remission and Love.

Remission is an act of signal and Sovereign Divine Love and Mercy,—but without shedding of blood there is no evidence of any such attributes on God's part at all.

We conceive of Remission as a transaction of Mercy even more readily than we regard it as an act of justice and judgment. Mercy to the guilty—pure and profound compassion for the miserable—matchless love even to an enemy, are what we naturally imagine to be the moving causes with God in remitting the sins of His people. And Scripture testifies that it is so— even "for His great love wherewith He loveth them" (Eph. ii. 4), even "according to His loving-kindness, and according to the multitude of His tender mercies" (Ps. li. 1). But were God to forgive the iniquities of His people without a ransom, without shedding of blood, there would be no such act of loving-kindness on His part—no evidence whatever of His mercy, compassion, and love towards them.

It is confidently affirmed, indeed, that the scheme of forgiveness without Atonement goes to magnify the Divine benevolence; while the doctrine that God forgives no sin without a full satisfaction is said to cloud and conceal that lovely attribute altogether. Nevertheless it is of easy demonstration that apart from the atonement of the cross there is no proof forthcoming that God is merciful, while it is just the atonement which proves the mercy of the Lord, and moreover proves it to be infinite.

For, if God comes to me, a guilty transgressor of His law, and tells me that He means to let me off; that He means to let my sin pass; that He cannot find it in His heart to inflict upon me the vengeance which He threatened; and so without any more ado, I pass away, free from judgment, free from terror: I soon begin to question whether I am so greatly indebted to Divine beneficence as in the first rapture of my escape I fancied. I begin to consider whether, after all, it is any great token of God's love to me that I have just obtained. And I argue that, if it was at God's option, at His mere option, to cast me into hell, or save me from it, without any expiation of my sin, or any satisfaction to His justice; if it was in His power to free me from wrath and woe, without any claim of justice interposing to object, or needing to be met; if there were no imperative call of righteousness demanding my condemnation to eternal death, but God could free me simply if He chose, and no interests of righteousness be injured by His doing so,—why, then, instead of arguing any wonderful benevolence on His part towards me, that He puts forth with infinite ease His will and power to save, the wonder would be that He should abstain from doing so. There is really no marvellous grace, no peculiar amazing compassion, no overwhelming evidence of personal distinguishing, peculiar love to me, when God stretches forth His hand to save from a fate which Divine justice was not inflexibly assigning to me, and as to which Divine justice can in no way object, though it be made to pass away from me. I cannot possibly recognise any peculiar stamp, or signature of marvellous Divine mercy, in the act which frees me from a fate which no demands of justice assigned to me. The marvel rather would be if God could have left me to be overtaken by it. It would have been, in such a case, no small ground on which to rest a charge of cruelty if He had: it is little evidence of love that He has not.

Contrast the two cases by the aid of illustration.

(1.) I see, let us say, a wretched fellow-creature about to expiate, by death, his offence against his country's laws. Ten thousand onlookers around might be my obedient vassals and retainers; and a single glance from my eye might be enough to rouse them for his instantaneous rescue. But though it might cost me but a glance or nod, I stand unmoved, and allow the fearful doom to fall. Is there any evidence in this that I am a man *destitute of compassion?* None whatever. An inflexible and righteous necessity, and moral and legal necessity interposes. Justice demands the doom, and compassion must look on inactive.

(2.) But again:—I see, let us say, a slanting tower toppling over and falling on a little child; and no call of righteousness superseding and paralysing the action of my compassion here, I rush forward and snatch the little one in safety from the threatened fate. Is there any great evidence in this that I am a man *full of compassion?*—that peculiar, marvellous, ever-flowing floods of pity swell my bosom always, and stamp my character with radiant signatures of tender loving-kindness? Surely not. It is mere humanity, the absence whereof were moral baseness. I would be ashamed to hear my action lauded as any marvel of generous and special love. I would be ashamed of my fellow-men, if I did not think that millions of them were promptly ready to emulate and equal it at any time. Above all, there is nothing in it to show that for this little one in special I entertain an intense, peculiar affection—a distinguishing, endearing love for this particular child, along with a profound and settled interest in all that bears upon its welfare: no evidence of that whatever.

Even so, if no inflexible necessity calls for the wrath of God on my iniquity;—if no claims of justice, no interests of government, no demands of law, and truth, and righteousness, are violated by my sin going unpunished, by God clearing me though I am guilty;—if He can, apart from atonement, avert eternal ruin from me without violating any of the perfections of His divine nature, or any of the provisions and requirements of His Divine government;—if He can altogether rescue me without any satisfaction to Divine justice, or any claim of Divine justice needing to be satisfied: then I cannot see how I ever can come to be convinced that His averting from me that awful, eternal, infinite ruin, in these plain and easy circumstances, evidences, to me-ward any marvellous, or special, or tender love. And when, over and above this, I am told that His whole nature is so beneficent that He recoils from the sight of suffering among His creatures; that He is too kind and merciful to visit their faults with the damnation of hell, and may be expected at last to deal leniently with every one whose case will at all admit of it; I begin to think that, with a nature so constituted,—so sensitively pained by the sight of pain in others,—it is more out of love to Himself than love to me that He forgives my sin; more that He may Himself escape the pain of seeing my pain, than out of any very marvellous, amazing, personal, peculiar love to me. So little can a forgiveness without shedding of blood demonstrate the mercy and love of God.

But view the question on the other side. I go to God as a guilty and confessed transgressor, a violator of His holy law, an acknowledged enemy to His authority and government. I go to acknowledge that I have rebelled against Him. And I find Him seated on a throne high and lifted up, and His train filleth the temple. Above it stand the seraphim, each one having six wings; with twain they cover their face, and with twain they cover their feet, and with twain they do fly. I hear them worship their God and mine, saying, "Holy, holy, holy, is the LORD of hosts, the whole earth is full of Thy glory." I look towards that throne whither the angelic beings bend to utter forth their adorations: and as I gaze into the glory that enwraps itself into the light which is inaccessible; and as I tremble before the wondrous majesty of Godhead seated in the throne of righteous and eternal administration, I become conscious of the infinite baseness of doing what this great and holy God—my Lawgiver and my Lord—hath said, "Thou shalt not do." I need no proof now that sin deserveth God's wrath and curse. In His holy glorious presence, I feel the sentence of death in myself. I feel that my settled neglect of this glorious God is an offence at which all heaven may stand aghast, and I cry, "Woe is me, for I am undone."

What a shock to all my moral nature, if in this moment of quickened moral sensibility: what a shock and outrage: what a hollow, trifling voice of levity and lies, breaking on my ear: were it now proclaimed unto me :—Do not be afraid, for God can easily clear the guilty : He can let sin pass unpunished ; He will let the sinner off! But on the other hand, how fully in accordance with all my prostrate reverence for the character and sanctity of Godhead, if, in this moment of my deep humiliation, the voice saith, " Holiness becometh Thine house, O Lord, for ever: and the wages of sin is death" (Ps. xciii. 5; Rom. vi. 23). This ratifies the dictate of my own soul within. It tells me,—what I again tell to God,—even that He is just in judging and clear in speaking (Ps. li. 4); that the punishment of sin is an absolute moral necessity; that God is righteous in taking vengeance (Rom. iii. 5).

But when justice has thus assigned to me eternal

death, as no harsh, no arbitrary, no optional decree on God's part, but the very doom which I have myself incurred, and no discretionary act on God's part can set it aside; and when the setting of it aside, without shedding of blood, could never prove that God loveth me, He hath another proof of love, which eternity will for ever celebrate, but never fully fathom. He does not propose to tolerate my sin; to let it pass; to let me off. He proposes to expiate my sin; to "make an end" of it; to execute all the vengeance due to it; and then bring me near to Himself in holy peace and fellowship for ever. Unto this end He sends forth His own Beloved Son, to link His destiny with mine, to link His person with mine; to take my nature into personal subsistence in Godhead; to take my sins as His own, and bear them in His own body on the tree, till He satisfy every demand of justice, and destroy death and him that had the power of death. If I stand and gaze again at that throne, and think that the coequal glorious Son of God who sits upon it—by whom were all things made, whether they be thrones, or dominions, or principalities, or powers—is Himself freely given by the Father to me, to be in death the ransom of my sin, my redemption, my propitiation, my bleeding sacrifice, my blessed peace; and if I turn from that throne of glory where my Saviour sat adored by angels, as when "Isaiah saw His glory and spake of Him," to yon cross of shame, where He, the same Divine Person, hung in agony and woe,—crucified by men, tempted and tried by devils, forsaken of God, weighed down by my curse, bearing my condemnation, yielding His life a ransom for my sin, a price for my salvation, answering all the claims of righteousness which made me an eternal outcast and a curse from God, achieving my liberty from death, and Satan, and sin, and this present evil world, and bringing in my eternal righteousness, my eternal life, my right and title to eternal life and blessedness from God:—then I, who erewhile did fail to see any proof of love Divine in God forgiving sin without a sacrifice, find here at last the proof of love, peculiar, matchless, infinitely generous, and unfathomable; and I say, "Herein now at last is love; not that we have loved God, but that he hath loved us, and sent his Son to be the propitiation for our sins" (1 John iv. 10).

It was no proof to me of love on God's part that He should propose to pardon what Divine justice did not inflexibly demand should be punished—avenged: for to punish where justice does not demand it, savours of cruelty; while to abstain from inflicting what justice does *not* demand is a poor proof indeed of any great benevolence. But in the shedding of blood—in the sacrifice of Christ—I see the glory of God's nature as holy, and the inflexible and righteous demand of His justice against sin. And I see, also, a love which proposes to remit an offence, an evil, so great that it deserves eternal woe. I see a love so great as to provide—what justice demands—a full satisfaction to make remission righteous. I see a love so great that for the sake of those for whom remission is to be provided, it spares not an object infinitely precious, infinitely lovely, love-worthy, and beloved. And I now say, overwhelmed with the full conviction and assurance of God's love, and the transcendency of that love—love that unto eternity never can be surpassed or equalled—I now say, "Hereby perceive we the love of God towards us, in that he laid down his life for us" (1 John iii. 16).

It is the shedding of Christ's blood which proves the love of God. For without shedding of blood there is no such transaction of marvellous, infinite, peculiar, and sovereign love as the true and valid remission of sin—remission in the gift and death of "God manifest in the flesh"—implies.

Part Third.

Remission and Conscience.

Remission of sin is a Divine act of the Lord of the conscience, giving security and peace to the conscience. But without shedding of blood there is no such act.

Put this aspect of Remission at once, not into the hands of speculative argument, but to the test of conviction and experience. Awakened, convicted, altogether restless, I go to God concerning my sin; and on the scheme that would administer pardon without propitiation, God simply lets me off; He lets my sin pass.

Does this satisfy me? Does it give me security and peace? Does it tranquillise my conscience, and give me rest? Can I, on the back of such a transaction, take up the joyful and exulting language, "Return unto thy rest, O my soul, for the Lord hath dealt bountifully with thee?" Most assuredly not. My conscience is not satisfied: my case is not met: my sin is not remitted.

For, when I am aroused in conscience to seek remission of sin, what is there in my conscience that must be met and removed? There is, *first*, a dread of wrath; and, *secondly*, a sense of ill desert. There are these two things;—a fear that wrath is coming, and a feeling that it ought to come.

(1.) And first, as to the less noble and less holy dread of wrath. Does such a scheme of pardon really, validly, wholly, and finally remove it? It is my sin which leads me to dread the wrath of God, and I go to God concerning it; and without shedding of blood, without executing the penalty my sin deserves, without an expiation or a sacrifice, God says to me, "I will clear you, though you be guilty. Your sin is true: also it is great: but let it pass."

And so my sin is allowed to pass; and I look after it as it passes; and I begin to ask, Whither will it go? and when may it not return? and how can I get on such terms of confidence with God and love to Him, as to trust Him while my sin still subsists, while my sin that was allowed to pass is still wandering, and may come back to find and claim me, or be called back at any time to confront and to condemn me? What security have

I got, what guarantee does the whole procedure afford, that God will not keep my sin in remembrance against me; keep it to be serviceable in schooling and taming me if I should prove refractory or disobedient; keep it as an engine of despotism to wield upon me if necessary; a Damocles's sword hung over me? The possibility of His doing so is not disproved by His forgiving sin without an atonement. Nay, it is by such a procedure rendered highly probable; for He that could say to-day, "The wages of sin is death," and could say to-morrow, "The wages of sin is not death; sin shall be forgiven without death, without shedding of blood," may change His mind again on the day following, and falling back on the former declaration, recall my sin and deal with it again in all the unrelentingness I originally dreaded. On such terms, I can have no real security and peace. And without absolute security,—without, at least, a ground for absolute and perfect security seen and rested on,—I can have no confidence, no full assurance of heart towards God, no peaceful liberty, no real rest. Nay, more: were God reserving in His own hand such an engine of power against me, holy honourableness between Him and me would be impossible. My intercourse with Him would be that of trembling obsequiousness and sycophancy. My great ruling motive in all my walk with Him would be to keep off from dangerous ground; to avoid waking up an unfinished controversy. Soul-inspiring adoration would never stir my spirit. At the best I would be only flattering God with my mouth, being in no steadfast covenant with Him: meanly I would be labouring to avoid provoking Him to fall back upon the power over me which, in my uncancelled, undestroyed sin, He still reserves: my religion would be a poor and pitiful calculation continually as to how I might best succeed in letting God's memory and my own slumber on a painful topic.

Nor is it at all wonderful that the demoralising dread of wrath should still torment the conscience; for,—

(2.) Its sense of ill-desert is not met by such forgiveness. The evil conscience is not merely a prophet of coming evil: it is a true declarator of rightful penalty. It predicts that evil *will* come, but only by protesting that evil *ought* to come. And hence, till some arrangement be made on God's part, and apprehended and embraced on mine, by which evil *ought no more* to come upon me,—till then, conscience is unsatisfied and restless. But a pardon without propitiation never professes or attempts to deal with this demand of the conscience. In fact, it does not deal with man's conscience or moral nature at all. It appeals to his fear of physical evil dreaded, to his sense of satisfaction in physical evil averted. But to the higher declaration of conscience, that sin *deserves* the wrath of God, such pardon has nothing whatever to say. It leaves the conscience as it found it.

Let sin pass, you say. Let sin pass; I and my God being face to face, dealing concerning it. Let it pass.

No; I reply, with all the energy of my soul, and all

the opposition of conscience; let it not pass. That will not remove my dread of evil, still less satisfy and quiet my sense of ill-desert. Let it not pass. Let God "make an end of it." Let it be "put away," "finished," "blotted out," annihilated. That alone will quell my fear of evil. Let it be ended and put away by its righteous penalty being executed—executed on my Surety and Substitute, with whom, by faith, I am united and made one. That alone will meet my sense of right. For I am a sinner; and I take guilt to myself—the guilt of sin, which is the guilt of death. No scheme which prevents me from taking guilt to myself can save me. It must demoralise me. But give me an atoning dying Substitute and Surety; and make me so thoroughly one with Him in God's esteem, and by the Spirit's work, and by my own faith, as that in taking guilt to myself, I inevitably and immediately lay it on Him; so thoroughly one with Him that I cannot possibly take guilt to Him, but by taking guilt to myself,—which conserves His rights, in that none can surreptitiously or impenitently seize the salvation wrought by Him, and conserves the rights of my moral nature too, in that my faith in my Sin-bearer is my believing confession of sin,—that truth in the inward parts which God desireth and which I also desire. Deal with my sin thus. And then, but not till then, shall my soul return unto her rest. *Then* will I meet my God with open face, and single eye, and frank and honourable brow, when I know that He keepeth no engine of secret despotism in hand against me,—which it were a devil's work to do, and a traitor's doom to dread,—but hath spoiled the principalities of darkness of all their power to concuss and terrify me, destroyed unto eternity the only bond which gave me up to evil, blotting out the handwriting of ordinances which was against me, nailing it to His cross. Then will I meet my God in holy confidence and honour. Then will I meet God's great and holy law with great and holy courage, with great and holy uprightness, seeing that I am not forgiven at the expense of its glory, but by a sacrifice that magnifies and makes it honourable. Then will I meet my great accuser with holy honourable triumph over him, and he shall no more scorn me on the ground that his own doom is more righteous, and his endurance of it more honourable to him, than is my release to me; for my sin is not quashed and compromised any more than his, but expiated in righteousness, which his will never be.

Deal thus with my sin. Extinguish it for ever. Make a holy, perfect end of it. Finish my transgression. Make reconciliation for mine iniquity. Remove my sin from me as far as the east is distant from the west. Yea, annihilate it: as when the iniquity of Israel shall be sought for, and there shall be none; and the sins of Judah, and they shall not be found. Then am I placed on terms of peace, security, liberty, and honour with my God. All my sense of right gets fullest scope; and all my sense of safety gets fullest satisfaction. I see that God is righteous; I see that God is love; and

I see that I am saved. I feel my heart sprinkled from an evil conscience; dreading nothing from His righteousness; filled with His love abundantly. This, this is Remission now. This is true redemption now, even the forgiveness of sins, through *His* blood, which is the image of the invisible God, the first-born of every creature, by whom were all things made, visible and invisible, whether they be thrones, or dominions, or principalities, or powers. Oh! marvellous shedding of blood—" His blood "—by which valid, and holy, and perfect, and eternal Remission is secured. Therefore we sing, with all the heavenly choir, a song in celebration of such Remission so obtained—" Unto Him that loved us, and that washed us from our sins in His own blood, and hath made us kings and priests unto the Father; unto Him be glory and dominion for ever and ever. Amen."

CHAPTER VIII.

THE COUNTER-IMPUTATIONS OF SIN AND RIGHTEOUSNESS.

IF the arguments by which we have attempted to establish, *That there cannot be Remission without Atonement*, are admitted to be valid, it will be seen that they establish also the converse of that proposition, namely, *That there cannot be Atonement without Remission*.

For it is not any vague and general sort of atonement that is requisite to secure remission, but such particular and definite atonement as *cannot but* secure it. The same arguments, therefore, that are good to show the necessity of atonement in order to the remission of sins, are equally good to show the necessity of the remission of sins where atonement has been made: and no man is thoroughly established in the one truth who does not see that it inevitably involves the other. Where the necessary condition has been met, the result follows necessarily. The atonement, which has been proved indispensible to remission, is of such a nature as to necessitate remission. For if it does not necessitate and secure remission,—if it does not render remission absolutely inevitable,—then it has secured or necessitated either nothing at all, or mere remissibility. But we have established nothing concerning any atonement that is necessary to remissibility; and, therefore, on this assumption, we have established nothing concerning atonement at all. He who will not accept the converse, or introverted form of the proposition, cannot logically be permitted to cling to the direct and primary form of it. He cannot be allowed to use the word remission as meaning *remission* in the first half of an argument, and as meaning *remissibility* in the second. And if he should say that *ex animo* he now substitutes "remissibility" for "remission," he must *pari passu* make an analogous substitution for "atonement,"—whether "atonability" or not, it is for himself to say. But, at all events, it is perfectly clear that if after having proved, *That there cannot be remission without atonement*, he chooses to abandon the idea of real and actual and true remission, toning it down now to mean something far less than it meant when he began to show that the *securing* of it demands atonement; if he speak of it now, *not* as something secured, but as something that is *not* secured, and that is still conditional and contingent; then he cannot possibly hold fast by that which he proved to be indispensable for *securing* it, while he himself even contends that it is *not* secured. He has cut the branch on which he might have rested peacefully, and he has provided no other to which he can safely transfer himself. If we stop short of the belief of the efficaciousness— the unconditional and absolute efficaciousness—of the Atonement, we raze to the foundations all that we had established. "We build again the things that we destroyed" (Gal. i. 18), and destroy the things which we had built. And how this bears on the *extent* of the Atonement, it is not necessary to say.

This will become evident: and at the same time it will become evident that the objection about the innocent suffering that the guilty may escape, is not an objection, but merely an unreasoned, direct denial of our doctrine: if,—before closing our series of leading propositions concerning the conditions of a correct discussion of the subject,—we show,

That, alike, the Equity and the Efficaciousness of the Atonement are safe-guarded and secured by the counter-imputations,—namely, of the sins of the Covenant-clients to their Head, and the righteousness of the Covenant-head to his Clients.

The counter-imputations—of sin to Christ, of righteousness to His people—are nowhere in Holy Scripture brought into such close juxta-position or related to each other by so firm a *nexus*, as in the celebrated and profound sentence, "He hath made Him to be sin for us, who knew no sin; that we might be made the righteousness of God in Him" (2 Cor. v. 21). It is reported that when some one, startled by the idea of Christ being "made sin," suggested to Luther that it should be rendered "made a sin-offering," Luther answered, "No; I prefer the words as they stand, for they are more intense." And he spoke shrewdly and well. Besides, there would be equal reason for altering the second clause in a similar manner; and, indeed, the exactness and point of the antithesis would require that. So that the verse would read, " God hath made Him to be a sin-offering for us, who knew no sin, that we might be the righteousness-offering of God in Him;" a violation of the proposition so great and manifest as to show that it ought not to be violated or tampered with at all. Nor is it possible to stop even here. Consistency requires the alteration, if made at all, to go the length of a reading so absurd as this: He hath made Him to be a sin-offering for us, who knew no sin-offering! For the word ἁμαρτία must have *one* rendering, else the antithesis with which this great theological saying is replenished, and the precision of the truth which it is designed to teach, are lost.

It is of course true that God hath made Christ to be a sin-offering, a sacrifice for sin; but that is not the same thing as His having made Christ to be sin. His being made sin is by no means identical with His being made a sacrifice for sin. It goes deeper and further back into the problem. It is at once the preliminary and the reason for His being made a sacrifice for sin. He is made sin, and *therefore* He is made a sin-offering. It is His being made sin which justifies His being made a sin-offering. In order that He may really and righteously, congruously and consistently, be made a sacrifice for sin, it behoves that He be first made sin. And this *locus insignis* of the Pauline theology does not state the fact that

Christ was made a sacrifice for sin; it states a truth which is the ground and reason of that fact. It lays the foundation for the sacrifice in a prior transaction.

That transaction may be viewed in this light. God is seeking out and searching for sin, that He may deal with it judicially; that He may deal with it as the holiness of the Divine nature, and the righteousness of the Divine law, and the justice of the Divine government, require that it should be dealt with. The sword of justice is seen pursuing sin, to inflict the threatened penalty of wrath and death. Meantime, in His supreme sovereignty, God puts forward His own Son manifest in the flesh to represent sin, to personate sin, to stand in the room of sin. "God sends His own Son in the likeness of sinful flesh and FOR SIN" (Rom. viii. 3); that is, in lieu or in room of sin. It is the same phrase in Heb. x. 6, though our translators have obliterated the precision of it by supplying a word that was not needed. "In burnt-offerings and *sacrifices* for sin Thou hast had no pleasure;" correctly rendered, "In burnt-offerings, and FOR SIN, Thou hast had no pleasure." Even so, God sends forth His own Son "FOR SIN," in lieu or room of sin, to represent or personate sin, so thoroughly, indeed, that Divine law and justice pursuing sin find Christ in sin's room, and take hold on Christ; for He is "FOR SIN," "made sin;" and thus "God, sending His own Son *for sin, condemns sin* in the flesh," even in the flesh of Him who is for sin, and in the likeness of sinful flesh. He condemns sin, in condemning Christ; for Christ is

"FOR SIN;" He is,—to use a common and intelligible expression,—He is what is for it. He is FOR SIN: and He is so by the authority and appointment of the sovereign Lord and Judge himself; for God hath made Him to be sin.

Divine justice and Divine wrath, then, are seen searching for sin—our sin—to execute upon it the vengeance due to sin. And in this search Divine justice and Divine wrath inevitably find Christ; for God hath made Him that knew no sin to be sin for us. In like manner, and in exact counterpart of this, Divine justice and Divine love are seen searching for righteousness— the righteousness of God—the righteousness which God requires—which His own holy nature and His own attribute of righteousness cannot but require. They are seen searching for "the righteousness which God's righteousness requires Him to require." * They are searching for it, in order to smile upon it—to lavish on it the love, and complacency, and favour, and blessing of God. And in searching for this righteousness, they find us, if we are in Christ: for we are "made the righteousness of God in him." And they own that their search has been successful. Nor was it unnecessary. Nay, it was more than ever necessary, from the moment that they recognised Christ as "made sin." From that moment the demand for the "righteousness

---

* The beautiful expression of the beloved and ever-to-be-lamented WILLIAM CUNNINGHAM,—the priceless gem we were honoured to receive from him in conversation,—his own matchless interpretation of the Divine expression, "The Righteousness of God" (Rom. iii. 21, 22).

of God" becomes imperious. The wondrous evolution by which the Son of God is "made sin," creates an absolutely imperious and new demand that the righteousness of God should be forthcoming, even as it never was before. And it is met in that which is the counterpart, and fruit, and justification of Christ "made sin," —even in us "made the righteousness of God."

The renowned *vox signata*, then, which we are considering, does not allege that Christ has been subjected to death " for us men and for our salvation,"—a ransom, a sacrifice, an offering for sin; but rather the reason for that,—its ground and justifying reason; namely, His being substituted in the room of sinners, and having their sins imputed or reckoned to Him. And it does not allege that we are justified unto life eternal in Christ; but the ground and reason of that; namely, our being substituted in the eye of God's law and justice, in the room of Christ, and our having His righteousness imputed to us. It does not declare that Christ is made a sacrifice for sin; but that, prior to that, and in order to that, He is made our sin. And it does not declare that we are reconciled to God—which would be the proper and formally exact antithesis, result, and counterpart of His being made a sacrifice for sin; for reconciliation is the natural and immediate fruit of sacrifice. But it declares that, as prior to our reconciliation, and in order thereunto, we are made the righteousness of God in Christ. In a word, it is the EXCHANGE OF PLACES that is the direct doctrine affirmed; and it goes utterly to enervate this profound theological proposition, and to empty it of the specific truth which it so clearly couches and so forcibly conveys, if we fail to read it simply as it stands. It is the two-fold exchange of places in respect of sin and righteousness severally, and the counter-imputations thereof, which undoubtedly it embodies and expresses. And it expresses this in three-fold antithesis. For each clause contains an antithesis of its own—the first in terms, the second implicitly; and the clauses, moreover, are antithetical as between themselves. It is as if it read thus:—

> He hath made Him that knew no sin
> To be Sin for us:
> That we (who knew no righteousness)
> Might be made the righteousness of God in Him.

We do not, of course, propose to investigate either of the antithetical clauses by itself—which would lead us into the *mare magnum* of the abstract, metaphysical, juridical, and ethical principles of imputation generally. We propose to take the two clauses conjointly, and to review them in the light which they reciprocally throw upon each other.

Concerning these two Divine and divinely related transactions, then:—the substitution of Christ in our room, through federal union with us—His being made sin for us: and the substitution of us in His room, through spiritual union with Him, founded on and growing out of His federal union with us,—our being made the righteousness of God in Him:—we may see, in the *first* place: That the Divine authority regulates them both; and, that the Divine power effects them both. In the *second* place: That they are strict and simple, unmingled and complete imputations; and that the wills of the parties—Christ's, namely, and ours—are in them both. In the *third* place: That they irresistibly carry their contrasted and complete effects with them; and *also*, that the latter transaction is the result, the sure and inevitable result, of the former.

Part First.

The Counter-imputations are accomplished by Divine Sovereignty and Divine Power.

I. The sovereign authority of God decrees and rules these two great transactions. "*He*," even God, "hath made him to be sin." Thus expressly is the first of them at least attributed to the Supreme. It is not indeed affirmed in the same express and explicit terms that God is the author of the second. It is somewhat more generally and impersonally expressed: "That we *might be made* the righteousness of God in Him." But even here the same thing is implicitly involved. For clearly the meaning is: God designed and decreed to make us the righteousness of God: in order to this, however, it was in God's own righteousness requisite that Christ should be made sin: in order that He might make us the righteousness of God, He did not shrink from making Christ to be sin: He accomplished the one evolution that He might bring about the other. Clearly, both are the doing of the Lord. And it is marvellous in our eyes.

The making of Christ to be sin, is a transaction of high state and sovereignty. It is a very singular event in the Divine government. It could originate with—it could be designed, proposed, carried out by—none but the Divine moral governor Himself; and by Him acting only in His prerogative as the Absolute Sovereign of the universe.

And it affords scope for exercising and glorifying His sovereignty as no other transaction in all the eternal history of His government can afford. For it illustrates the singular freedom—the high range and all-embracing sweep—of His sheer sovereign will, unto the uttermost It proves that God's sovereignty is free, in a freedom which could not have been conceived, and has full scope and play in circumstances in which it could not have been believed to be applicable. For God's holy law is absolute, and unconditional, and unchangeable. No possible circumstances can set limits to its action; for its very claim is to rule all circumstances whatsover. And, save for sin and salvation, the holy universe must have for ever believed that God's sovereign pleasure also was ruled and hemmed in by His unconditional and everlasting law. It must have for ever appeared impossible that God's will could act otherwise, in all matters ethical and juridical, than as His unchangeable law should rule. Hence, when sin entered, and death by sin, the sovereign God must have appeared, to all His intelligent and righteous creatures, as shut up to inflict death on all that sinned. The sphere of sovereignty must have appeared limited by the sphere of law.

But God designed to show His sovereignty to be absolutely unlimited,—not, indeed, in a way of violating law, or setting law aside, but of transcending law; —not as against law, but above law;—as not merely free within the sphere of law, but free in a sphere comprehending law and rising about it; compassing law about on every side with glory, and rising far above law, into a realm of higher freedom still.

The sovereign Lord is not shut up to the course which law prescribes—death eternal to the sinner. The freedom of His sovereignty—the council of His will— the sphere of His good pleasure—takes a larger range. He is not shut up to His course of procedure, even by His own holy law. He cannot indeed proceed in violation of it; for it is the very transcript of His own holy nature, and He cannot deny Himself. But His nature, while it defines His law, does not hamper or hem in His will. Honouring His law, and acting ever in accordance with His nature and perfections, His will goeth forth in most free, unconditioned, absolute sovereignty. And in the action of His sovereignty, in its most free and glorious forth-going, He makes Christ to be sin for us. No law required this: no law suggested this: no law objects to this. Against this there is no law. To prompt to this there is no law. The everlasting law is honoured by this, but never contemplated it. The sovereign pleasure of God, reigning within and without the law, rises high above it. And His counsel shall stand, and He will do all His pleasure.

Ah! well may we ask,—Why do sinful men quarrel with the sovereignty of God, the mere good pleasure of His will? Its unlimitedness, its absolute unconditionedness, is their only source of hope. And its glory is made great in their salvation.

For, let it be observed that this is exclusively the sovereignty of grace, of mercy, and of love. As high as the sovereignty of God in its absoluteness is carried up above its former apparent range, so high are the love, and grace, and mercy of God exalted, and seen to be of that infinite extent and unconditioned energy, that could have been neither manifested nor imagined apart from the redemption that is in Christ. And now as the principalities and powers of light adore before the glorious expansion which the sovereignty of heaven's high King has undergone or exhibited, they see that it is grace, and mercy, and love, that are shining bright over all former forth-shining of the glory of God: and now they say wonderingly, in mingled ecstasy and awe, as they never said or sang before,—"God is love."

And it is by the same absolute authority, the same sovereign will and mere good pleasure of the Lord, that we are made the righteousness of God in Christ. "He will have mercy on whom He will have mercy, and He will have compassion on whom He will have compassion." The imputation of righteousness to us—not against law

—must be above law. We must be "justified freely by His grace." We cannot imagine that it should be otherwise. We cannot imagine God, in the freest sovereignty of His will, making Christ to be sin for us; and coming down, coming under any constraint, or limitation, or condition, in making us to be the righteousness of God in Him. That which shall render us the righteousness of God, can, and must, be simply the onward movement, seeking its intended goal, of that same most free and sovereign will of God, which, in order to make us the righteousness of God, first made Christ to be sin for us. Nay; if we understand the exercise, the glory, the grand extension and expansion—as we have ventured to say—of divine sovereignty in making Christ to be sin, we cannot possibly desire to be made the righteousness of God, save by the exercise of this same sovereignty of God from its now loftiest throne—its highest regal seat of power most absolute. Who would wish His righteousness, in the eternal judgments, to shine in any glory of grace, less than the very uttermost of sovereign grace? Or who desire to see this sovereignty—so glorious in love's own utmost range, and love's own highest liberty —shorn and tamed down, hemmed in and limited, brought in bondage, or constrained by any conditions, just as it stretched forth its hand to grant salvation from eternal ruin? No. Let it be that very sovereignty of God—rising to the utmost height of its heavenly bent, and acting out, unto the uttermost bounds, or rather in the boundlessness of freedom, its own sweet, free, and loving will—that shall compass and convey my salvation. And even so it acts indeed; from its absolute throne—the "THRONE OF GRACE"—in the freest pleasure of its will. I may tremble, it is very true, to think that my escape from everlasting ruin is at the disposal of the mere and sovereign will of another. But it is at the disposal of the sovereign will of Love unfathomable. And it is at the disposal of the sovereign will of Power most absolute. My trembling, therefore, need be none other than the trembling of hope, succeeding the blank terror of despair. For when I tremble before sovereign love unlimited, armed with Omnipotency to bring salvation, I am gloriously exempted from trembling on any other ground. And when "the floods, O Lord, have lifted up, when they have lifted up their voice, and lifted up their waves;" when conscience, and death, and hell, are dooming me, and claiming me, I will not for one moment delay giving thanks that I have heard a voice louder than theirs, and mightier than the noise of many waters, saying from the throne of absolute power and infinite grace:—" I will have mercy on him, sovereignly and simply if I please; I will have mercy on whom I will have mercy, and I will have compassion on whom I will have compassion."—Glory to God in the highest!

II. The efficacy of Divine power is in both these transactions, as well as the authority of Divine sovereignty. This is manifestly implied in the language used to express them:—" He hath *made* Him to be sin

—that we might be *made* the righteousness of God." Divine power has effected it, as well as Divine authority appointed it. It has been powerfully accomplished in the fulness of times, as well as sovereignly decreed in the councils of eternity.

"God sends forth His own Son in the likeness of sinful flesh, and FOR SIN." The initial and decisive exercise of Divine power in making Christ to be sin, is in sending Him forth in the likeness of sinful flesh. The Word was made flesh, that He might be made sin. Made flesh; not sinful flesh: for it is He who knew no sin that is made sin, and He still remains He who knows no sin: but in the likeness of sinful flesh; the brightness of the Father's glory concealed by the resemblance of the stain only—the express image of the Father's person shrouded under the dark shadow of the likeness merely—of sinful flesh. Here is the substitution: the holy for the sinful; the just for the unjust; the innocent for the guilty; He who knew no sin made sin.

The Incarnation of the Eternal Word is not His being made sin: but it is the immediate preliminary in the order of nature; and it is the proof. The eternal covenant oneness—the federal union—grounds the representative character of Messiah and His substitution and suretyship. Each of these relations, indeed, leans for support on that which precedes it: suretyship justified by substitution; substitution, by real representation; representation, by federal union or covenant oneness. And here ultimately the series terminates and rests—rests in the unchangeable council and will of the Sacred Three. For, viewed by itself, the federal union is simply a decree of the Divine will, a judgment of the Divine mind, and a covenant agreement in the eternal Spirit between the Father and the Son. And if exegetical and inductive examination of Holy Scripture brings this to light as a truth revealed,—as we believe it does, though we cannot now pause to show that,—it remains simply to resolve it into the sovereign will of God, and to defend it by the simple and sublime affirmation: "His counsel shall stand, and He will do all His pleasure."

But this covenant oneness between the Son of God's love, and the people given to Him in the Counsel of Peace, needs no exercise of Divine power for its constitution. It is constituted in Eternity by a sovereign decision of the Divine will, and passes—in the order of nature, that is—into a judgment of the Divine mind. And this is the federal union. But then, unto the actual achievement of the design which it contemplates, exercises of Divine power are needed to constitute more than one real union, each of which must rest in and be represented by an accomplished fact. Hence the union of the Eternal Son to His people, in respect of His assumption of their nature into personal subsistence with the Divine nature in His person—which is His Incarnation. Hence, also, their union to Him, in respect of their being created again in Him by the renewing of the Holy Ghost—which is their regeneration.

And hence, as we have said, the Incarnation, which is not in itself Christ's being made sin, is the immediate preliminary and the proof thereof. If the question be asked, What shall be the sign of Christ being made sin for us? the answer is, "This shall be the sign; you shall find the babe wrapped in swaddling clothes, and lying in a manger" (Luke ii. 12). And the two things are simultaneous. In His assumption of our nature, He begins to be made sin. He is a sin-bearer from the virgin's womb to the sealed grave of Golgotha. His consciousness is a sin-bearer's consciousness during all the days of His flesh—as Dr George Smeaton, than whom no greater authority on this theme exists, has done admirable service by so copiously and variously demonstrating.* His being made in the likeness of sinful flesh was indispensible to His being "for sin;" and His being "made sin," followed inevitably on His being made in the likeness of sinful flesh. "Because the children were partakers of flesh and blood, He also Himself likewise took part in the same, that He might be a merciful and faithful High Priest in things pertaining to God" (Heb. ii. 17). His Incarnation was the indispensible preliminary. And by the grandest miracle of Divine power it was achieved.

Our being made in the likeness of the holiness of the Word made flesh, the express image of the invisible God, is as indispensible to our being made the righteousness

---

* See his invaluable work, "The Doctrine of the Atonement, as taught by Christ himself." T. & T. Clark, Edinburgh.

of God, as Christ's being made in the likeness of sinful flesh was indispensible to His being made sin. Not indeed our *consciousness* of being born again, but our *being* born again, born of the Spirit and the word of God, is as indispensible in order to our having righteousness imputed to us,* as was Christ's being born of the Spirit and the virgin to His having sin imputed to Him. His incarnation is not in itself the imputation of sin to Him. And our regeneration is not in itself the imputation of righteousness to us. His being made flesh did not cancel His well-deservingness, or make Him worthy of death and the curse. And our being made spirit— Spirit-born spirit (John iii. 6)—does not cancel our ill-deservingness, or render us worthy of the blessing and of life eternal. The imputation of righteousness can alone entitle us to favour (Gal. iii. 21). The imputation of sin could alone subject the Son of God to wrath. But the imputation of sin never could have taken effect in His case had He not been made in the likeness of men. Nor can the imputation of righteousness in our case take place if we be not made anew in the likeness of God. He was made flesh that He might be made sin. We are made spirit—spirit born of the Spirit—that we may be made righteousness. He had to be partaker of the human nature (Heb. ii. 14–17): we must be made "partakers of the Divine nature" (2 Pet. i. 4). Except God be

* More lines of thought branch out from this centre than we can here and now overtake. But the thoughtful reader will observe that the order of these things, as in the Divine procedure, is in some respects reversed, as in the believer's consciousness.—HALYBURTON is *most admirable* on this.

born, He cannot come into the kingdom of sin. Except a man be born again, he cannot see the kingdom of righteousness. And Divine power—the power of the Holy Ghost, the plenipotentiary and executant of all the will of Godhead—achieves the Incarnation of God and the regeneration of men, that the Son of God may be made sin, and the sons of men made righteousness. The efficacy of Divine power is in both these transactions.

Part Second.

The Counter-Imputations are Simple and Complete Imputations, and accepted by the Parties.

I. The two transactions are imputations,—out and out, exclusively, imputations: pure, unmingled, complete imputation of sin on the one side: pure, unmingled, complete imputation of righteousness on the other. And the first throws light upon the second.

"He who knew no sin is made sin." It is not indeed expressly said in similiar terms, We who knew no righteousness are made the righteousness of God. But it is implied. We are as destitute of personal righteousness as He of personal sin. It is simply and exclusively imputation on His side—our sin imputed to Him who is holy. It is simply and exclusively imputation on our side—His righteousness imputed to us who are sinful. And as His holiness is no bar to our sin being imputed to Him, our sinfulness is no bar to His holiness being imputed to us. No bar! That is the least of it. It is

His holiness which renders the imputation of sin to Him possible: it is our sinfulness which renders the imputation of righteousness to us necessary; while, at the same time, it is rendered possible by our sin being imputed to Him. For our sin can no longer bar the imputation of righteousness to us, or invalidate, or modify, or alleviate, or impair that imputation, seeing it has been disposed of by its imputation to Him who bears it in His own body on the tree, and is made of God unto us righteousness. His holiness, in like manner, does not alleviate the imputation of sin to Him; for the imputation is so thorough, and unreserved, and unimpaired, that He is even made sin. There is nothing confused or commingled in these imputations on either side.

Besides, as they are imputations, pure and simple, so they are complete. He is made *all* our sin, as truly as He has none of His own; we are made all His righteousness, as truly as we have none of ours. For it is *we*, wholly and completely, that are His sin; *He*, wholly and completely, that is our righteousness. For *us* He is made sin; in *Him* we are made the righteousness of God. If we are in Him, then all our sin;—the sin of our life, and heart, and nature;—our original sin and our actual sin; our sin that has been, is, and shall be; the sin that dwelleth in us;—in short, the sin that we *are;—this*, Christ is made for us. All of us that is sin; all on which the sword of justice could smite and the sting of death fasten; we ourselves thus are made over to Him as His sin. And all His righteousness;—the righteousness of His heart, and life, and nature; His original and His actual righteousness; the entire lovely moral beauty of His person, His every righteous principle of thought, affection, will, desire, and deed; the righteousness, in short, which He *is;—this*, we are made in Him. All of Him that is righteousness; all of Him on which the approbation, love, joy, and delight of the Father can rest; He himself thus is made of God unto us righteousness. For it is whole Christ that is "the end of the law for righteousness unto every one that believeth."

It takes all the wondrous definiteness, and precision, and personality out of this transaction to represent the righteousness of saints as merely something that Christ suffered, or something in which Christ served on their behalf. The temptation, in such a view, is very great, to separate His suffering and His service from His person, and to consider them as what may be contemplated and dealt with apart from His person. The beam vanishes when cut off from the sun from which it flows. And Christ is the sun of righteousness, with healing in His wings. He is the Lord our righteousness. It is He that is of God made unto us righteousness,—He himself. Christ is the end of the law for righteousness,—Christ himself, in His own person, with that infinite fund of righteousness and moral excellence, the exhaustless fountain whereof is the righteousness of saints.

The "exchange of places" carries this in it inevitably. It effects a very perfect and complete commutation and counter-imputation. And nothing less can meet our case. When we began to be, we began to be sin,—conceived in sin and shapen in iniquity. When He began to be in the likeness of sinful flesh, He who knew no sin began to be sin for us—our sin; holy, harmless, and undefiled, and separate from sinners, yet uniting Himself to us, to be our sin, He himself, from His beginning to be in the flesh, beginning also to be our righteousness. The very dawn of our existence, which was in sin, He blends with the dawn of His existence as Emmanuel, as made sin for us. The thread of our sinful state and history and ill-deserving destiny, even from our mother's womb, He hath conjoined with the thread of His own from the Virgin's womb, intertwining the two in one, Himself thus made sin for us. And keeping them conjoined in one—not dealing violently with ours, not snapping it, not even diverting it from its rightful destiny and outgoing, but following its course, He hath followed it conjointly with His own, unbroken, down into those depths of wrath, and death, and hell, in which ours had its righteous and inevitable issue. And as, purged from our sin, He rose from the dead, and ascended far above all heavens, still He brought the thread of our destiny with Him, entwined still in one with His own, and riveted it for ever to the throne of God and of the Lamb, on which throne He now sits, made of God unto us righteousness, we the righteousness of God in Him. Thus perfect and complete are these imputations.

II. The will of the parties is in these transactions, also, severally,—their full, intelligent, and joyful consent.

Christ is not made sin without His own consent; nor are we made righteousness without ours. "When He cometh into the world"—the world of sin,—made sin, "He saith, Lo, I come; in the volume of the book it is written of me: I delight to do thy will, O God: thy law also is within my heart" (Ps. xl. 6; Heb. x. 7). His Incarnation, His being made sin, is voluntary. "*He made Himself* of no reputation, and took upon Him the form of a servant," as well as "*was made* in the likeness of men" (Phil. ii. 7). His Incarnation was the Holy Spirit's work; but His own most active will was in it.

Our regeneration also is the Holy Spirit's work; but our own will is in it too. Not as the grand determining power: "By grace are ye saved; through faith; and that not of yourselves, it is the gift of God." Grace is the determining power; the omnipotent and resistless grace of God most high. "Thy people shall be willing in the day of THY POWER" (Ps. cx. 3). Still they are "willing." Their own will is in their regeneration; not supreme, but subordinate: yet not destroyed *as* will by being subordinated to the will of God, the grand original archetype of man's will, as at first made in God's image, and now renewed into it when man's is subordinated to God's will, informed by it, actuated by it, made the intelligent consentient engine and agent of carrying out the One Will which shall do all its pleasure. Even thus, then, as Christ's assumption of our sin was His own voluntary deed, so our assumption of His righteousness must be our voluntary act too. Hence the need, and the office, and the place of Faith. Both these high sovereign transactions of the good pleasure of Jehovah's will, appeal to the wills of the parties transposed mutually into each other's places. The Lord God, in the council of His will, deals with their wills. He secures the concurrence of their wills. He gains their full consent on either side.

And has He not in the fact of Christ's consent a wondrous leverage to wield in calling for our consent? Shall not the fact of Christ's consent secure ours? If *He* consent to pass over to the side of sin, shall we not consent to pass over to the side of righteousness? And have not His ambassadors a powerful screw—in a sense most blessed and beneficent—to press upon the sinner's heart and conscience in compassing the blessed work of shutting men up into the faith? And how does the true glory of a profound theology come out to view, as no dry, formal, abstract speculation; but the joyful handmaid, yea, the loving foster-mother, of spiritual life as in all the churches; when theology ransacks all her brightest treasures to turn them into arguments for charming and compelling men to come in, and frames her finest, richest theorems—refined and rich as aught that any science has to show—into powerful motives for the prisoner to come forth, and for them that sit in darkness to show themselves! Shall not the consent of God's own Son to be made sin, secure your consent to be made righteousness? His consent could involve Him in nothing but shame, and sorrow, and wrath, and death. Your consent brings glory, and joy, and blessing, and the life everlasting. Shall not His consent provoke and carry yours? Nay; shall not His consent be the model of yours? Can your consenting will express itself more beautifully than His, "Lo, I come?" Is it not to this "imitation of Christ" that first of all you are called? "Him that *cometh*." "Come unto me." "Whosoever will let him Come." Let him come, as I came, when joyfully, though death and hell were before me, I said, "Lo, I come." And by thus coming,—by thus answering the call, and imitating the consent, and twining your will into the will of Christ, will you not fall heir to all that is implied in Christ's consent, and make it more and more fully all your own, till making thereby both your calling and election sure, you be able to say, tremblingly, perhaps, but truthfully: "Lo, I come; in the volume of the book it is written of me" also?

Part Third.

The Counter-imputations are inevitably efficacious of their Results; the second, moreover, being the Result of the first.

I. Both these transactions of imputation carry inevitable and complete effects with them.

When He who knew no sin was made sin for us, condemnation, sorrow, shame, exile, desertion, the curse,

COUNTER-IMPUTATIONS OF SIN AND RIGHTEOUSNESS. 223

and death followed remorselessly. These are the consequences, most sure, treading with mighty and resistless march on the heels of the imputation of sin. No power in all the universe can interpose to arrest them; neither height nor depth, nor any creature, nor the creating God himself. "Father, if it be possible!" And the Father answered Him to never a word. For when sin is imputed, death, with its sting and woe, comes in triumphantly. Be He even the eternal God in whose person imputation takes place; be it even the Beloved of the Father; be it the man who knows no sin, who is holy, harmless, and undefiled, the chief among ten thousand and altogether lovely; sin has entered, and death enters by sin. His Godhead hinders it not; His relation to the Father—Oh! how near and blessed ineffably—hinders it not. His holy beauty, from the womb of the virgin, and as from the womb of the morning, hinders it not. His perfect love to the Father, His Father's infinite love to Him,—and neither is impaired or arrested for an instant of time,—hinders it not. His perfect wondrous love for those whose very sins are imputed to Him hinders it not. Though He be the living God manifest in the flesh; though He be the Eternal Son; yet learns He obedience by the things which He suffers. Made sin,—even though lovely in the Father's eyes because He loves those whose sin He is made, and lovely on the very ground of bearing the sin which He is made,—He is inevitably "made a curse" (Gal. iii. 13); not merely subjected to the endurance of a curse, but in

His person made a devoted thing—made *herem*, a curse —even unto His hanging accursed on the tree.

And, if against considerations so powerful—against His Godhead, His Sonship, His spotless holiness, His matchless moral beauty, resplendent in that He consents to be made sin—if imputed sin still prevails to carry all its consequences with terrific and resistless march, bringing in death and hell and the curse: shall the imputation of righteousness fail to carry all its issues? Shall they who receive abundance of grace and of the gift of righteousness fail to reign in life by Jesus Christ? (See Romans v. 12-21, specially verse 17.) If the worth of Godhead in all its assembled glories and perfections; and the love of Sonship in its ineffable, inviolable bond of grace unto the Father's heart; and perfect loveliness of moral beauty; and an enhanced argument of admiration in this very sin-bearing of the Son of God for sinners,—if all these considerations bar not the curse and death from their inevitable forthgoing on our Divine Substitute: shall any worthlessness of ours, any alienation, any guilt of past sin, or any present sin that dwelleth in us, bar from us the blessing of the life eternal, if we are made the righteousness of God? If imputation is so imperiously and absolutely triumphant and invincible on the one side, shall it be less triumphant or invincible on the other? The sin especially which dwelleth in us may seem to plead against and peril the blessed results of imputation of righteousness. But the spotless holiness which dwelt in Christ pleaded not successfully against, nor in the slightest measure perilled, paralysed, or put back the issues of imputed sin. Indwelling sin may indeed make our warfare perilous—" warring against the law of my mind " (Rom. vii. 23); but a present victory tarries on our helmet and our sword. It may give us in a measure the experience of the poor slave and captive,—" carrying me captive to the law of sin that is in my members " (*idem*); but a present freedom is ours notwithstanding, the perfect law of liberty making us free from the law of sin and death (James i. 25; Rom. viii. 2). It may give us in a measure the sense of deepest wretchedness,—" O wretched man that I am " (Rom. vii. 24): but a sure and perfect blessedness is still in Christ all our own. For precisely in triumph over this profound experience of warring, captivating, and woe-working sin that dwelleth in us; precisely in celebration of the inevitable, the resistlessly certain, issues of imputed righteousness, is Paul's blessed and ever-memorable boast,—and without seeing it in this light, we do not hear its true tone and rhythm, nor enter into half its depth: " There is therefore now no condemnation to them that are in Christ Jesus " (Rom. viii. 1).

Nor is it enough to affirm this inevitableness, notwithstanding whatsoever hindrances may arise. The inevitableness of life and the blessing, following in the train of imputed righteousness, is far more grandly seen, just in the light of hindrances, so powerful we might have thought, but so vain and ineffectual. The Sovereign Lord, if He pleased, might sanctify us into celestial perfection in the instant in which He makes us the righteousness of God in Christ. But could our confidence in the resistless, absolute, and eternal triumph of that imputation be so great, as in evergrowing experience and consciousness it ought now to be, when the presence and the great power even of sin, are found incapable of marring its perfection, or staying its marvellous and majestic issues of blessing, and favour, and life, and the loving-kindness which is better than life? " Iniquities prevail against me : as for our transgressions, thou shalt purge them away " (Ps. lxv. 3). " Blessed *is* the man to whom the Lord imputeth righteousness without works (Ps. xxxii. 42 ; Rom. iv. 6–8).

The Son of God is made sin. And though His Godhead is true and is there; though His Sonship is ineffable and inviolable; though His holiness is unspotted; and though the blood burst forth in His agony, and His cry is terrible upon the tree, and the earth reels and staggers, and the sun grows black ; death and the curse come on. Let *us* be made the righteousness of God in Him. And though sin is true and is here; though Satan stand at our right hand to resist us; though our iniquities take hold on us that we cannot look up; though the " O wretched man," be our daily cry with growing truth and sorrow ; though the dust of battle be upon us, and the damp of death be coming ; though the waters roar and are troubled, and the hills be carried into the midst of the sea; though our house be not so with God, and the fig-tree do not blossom, and our heart and our flesh fail: shall any or all of these things separate us from life and the blessing? "Nay, in all these things we are more than conquerors through Him that loved us. For I am persuaded,"—I am persuaded that that song of persuasion is the heritage of all who are made the righteousness of God.

II. But besides affirming that these two counter-imputations carry inevitable and complete effects with them, it remains to affirm also that the second of the imputations is itself an inevitable effect of the first: "God hath made Him that knew no sin to be sin for us, *that we might* be made the righteousness of God in Him." This is the design of Christ's being made sin, namely, that we might be made the righteousness of God. The similar correlative design of Christ's "being made a curse," is brought out in terms exactly analogous: "Made a curse for us, *that the blessing* of Abraham *might come upon us, that we might* receive the promise of the Spirit through faith" (Gal. iii. 13, 14). And the same thing is set forth in the more general formula "Ye know the grace of our Lord Jesus Christ, that, though He was rich, yet for your sakes He became poor, *that* ye through His poverty *might be* rich" (2 Cor. viii. 9). This, indeed,—to use the language of the geometrician,—is just the general theorem, embracing numerous special cases, of which the doctrine of the counter-imputations is perhaps the most important. For if, instead of the general term "riches," we read "righteousness," and if, instead of the general idea of "poverty," we take the special idea of "sin," then the grace of our Lord Jesus Christ stands in this, That He who was righteous was, for our sakes, made sin, that we, through His being made sin, might be made the righteousness of God. And again: if for "riches," we read the "blessing," and for "poverty," the "curse," the general theorem presents the case in Gal. iii. 13, namely, That the Blessed One is made a curse, that we might receive the blessing. And so, if by "riches" is meant "life," and by "poverty" is meant "death," then,—We know the grace of our Lord Jesus Christ, that, though He was the Living One, the True God, and Eternal Life, yet for our sakes, and in our room, He died, that we, through His death, might have life, and might have it more abundantly. Be it in the general case, or in any special aspect of it, the *design* is in this same manner uniformly set forth, and set forth as that which is surely and infallibly accomplished. Being God's design it is successful,—not the design only, but the result. For the work of the Lord is perfect, not breaking down in the middle, but reaching the goal,—that goal, or τελος, or end spoken of, when it is said, "Christ is the τελος of the law to every one that believeth" (Rom. x. 4).

For, as inevitably as when Christ is made sin He is made a curse, and wrath and death assail Him; and as inevitably as when we are made the righteousness of God, life and the blessing come upon us; so surely, intermediately between these two inevitables, there is another, namely, that they for whom Christ is made sin are infallibly made the righteousness of God. *He* denies the counter-imputations who denies that the second follows necessarily from the first. He misconceives the whole arrangement. For, in reality, the counter-imputations are not so much two transactions as one. The exchange of places is one indivisible evolution. It is not effected in the movement of one of the parties, but in their mutual transposition. It is a reciprocating movement; and when the reciprocation fails, the movement ceases utterly.

Hence it follows, that in giving our consent to be made the righteousness of God, we give our consent to the Son of God being made sin. It is impossible to break in upon this transaction in the middle of it. We must acquiesce in it as it is—one great and perfect whole. We must begin with it at the beginning. For herein is that saying true, "He that entereth not in by the door, but climbeth up some other way, the same is a thief and a robber." Now, the cross is the door—the gate of righteousness. For no other Christ is made of God unto us righteousness, than Christ made sin for us.

And hence the irrefragable guarantee for the penitence of Him that is made the righteousness of God. Blessed is he to whom the Lord imputeth no iniquity, but imputeth righteousness without works. But when I kept silence, my bones waxed old. Then I said, I will confess my transgressions. I will lay my sin on Jesus.

I will contemplate Him made sin: and by confession of sin, I will acquiesce in His being made sin, and accept Him as made sin for me. "And thou forgavest the iniquity of my sin" (Ps. xxxii.)—On any other scheme than that of covenant unity and counter-imputation, repentance and faith contradict each other.*

Hence, also, the vital and organic harmony between the justification of him who is made the righteousness of God, and his sanctification in all manner of holiness. For whether sanctification be regarded as the believer's duty or God's gift, it is placed on a footing of inviolable safety by these counter-imputations of sin and righteousness. To him for whom Christ has been made sin, and who is therefore made the righteousness of God, the appeal surely must come home with resistless force of obligation when it frames itself in terms like these: How uprightly, how gracefully, how righteously should "the righteousness of God" conduct itself, in all holiness and righteousness, before Him all the days of our lives! And when overwhelmed by a sense of inability to answer this appeal as its intrinsic force demands and prompts, how blessed to bear in mind not only that holiness is God's gift as well as our duty, but that when we stand before Him as ourselves "the righteousness of God" in Christ, God's own interest in God's own

---

* It will be evident to the thoughtful reader that a fine and fertile vein of thought opens up here, which this sentence simply strikes. See it "cropping out" also on p. 187 *antea.* I should greatly like, God willing, to follow up this volume with another of similiar size, investigating carefully the Atonement in its relation to Conscience.

righteousness acting righteously, may be heard imparting at once a guarantee of faithfulness and a thrill of power to the voice of majesty and grace that conveys the assurance: "I am the Lord thy God that doth sanctify thee" (Exod. xxxi. 13).

CHAPTER IX.

MR ROBERTSON OF BRIGHTON'S VIEWS OF VICARIOUS SACRIFICE.

As affording a specimen of Broad School theology on the Atonement, and as a warning against the dangers that arise from abandoning the Catholic doctrine of true and proper propitiation, I propose to criticise a sermon by the late Mr ROBERTSON of Brighton, on "Vicarious Sacrifice."

I need scarcely say that I disclaim everything like a wish to depreciate the character of an accomplished scholar, an amiable man, an earnest labourer according to the measure of his light. Mr Robertson was manifestly endowed with great natural gifts; and he wielded them, I doubt not, to the best of his knowledge for the benefit of his fellow-men. His writings, especially when treating of literary and moral topics, are characterised by a good deal of classic culture, singular freshness of thinking, and beautiful powers of expression. It is impossible, consistently with evidence, to compliment his memory in the same terms in regard to his theological views. But I must claim the benefit of the distinction, frankly accorded in all honourable controversy, between the charity that is due to an author's person and the charity that is due to his writings. It is a stale artifice, and a gross violation of the liberty and mental independence which Broad Churchmen loudly claim for themselves, which would forbid a free criticism, by identifying a just severity towards a man's writings, when supported by evidence, with malicious depreciation of their author. True charity will accept my necessarily discriminating tribute to Mr Robertson's memory, and grant me liberty to criticise his sermon, and show, if I can, that it indicates great ignorance of divine truth, and is utterly subversive of Christianity.

The sermon to which I allude is the ninth in the first series, and is entitled, "Caiaphas's View of Vicarious Sacrifice." The text is the high priest's unintentional prophecy and coarse appeal to Jewish terror: "Ye know nothing at all, nor consider that it is expedient for us, that one man should die for the people, and that the whole nation perish not" (John xi. 49, 50).

The author opens his theme by telling us that "the remarkable point in this judgment is, that it contained the very central doctrine of Christianity; unconsciously Caiaphas had uttered the profoundest of all truths, the necessity of the suffering of the innocent for the guilty." And so satisfied is he with the statement of this truth in the high priest's language, that he adds, "He had stated it in the very words which St John could have himself adopted." He then re-affirms that "that truth was the vicarious sacrifice of Christ." "There are," however, "two ways in which you may contemplate that sacrifice." It may be viewed from different sides; the side of Caiaphas, and the side of John; the side of the world, and the side of God. " The words of Caiaphas contain a formal falsehood and a material truth;" so that the subject "branches into two topics: I. The human form, in which the words are false. II. The divine principle or spirit, in which they are true."

One might well inquire how, in the human form of Caiaphas's statement, the words can be false, and yet be the very words which St John could have himself adopted. But let that pass.

Is the reader beguiled into the expectation of a loyal defence of the propitiatory sacrifice of the cross? It would be little wonder though he were. The author has announced as his subject *the* VICARIOUS *Sacrifice of Christ.* He has declared his belief that " the profoundest of all truths" is "the suffering of the innocent for the guilty." And he tells us correctly enough that, " when we speak of vicarious suffering, we mean that suffering which is endured in another's stead, and not as the sufferer's own desert." Good preliminaries these to a Scriptural exposition of the true substitution and atoning sacrifice of Christ. And his branching of his subject into the two proposed topics is not fitted to alarm. To set over against each other, in clear antagonism and antithesis, the idea of vicarious sacrifice entertained by such a one as John, the holy and the loving, and that of the coarse, malignant Caiaphas, is legitimate enough, and might be edifying. We accordingly anticipate with some interest the two views which are to be presented to us of the sacrifice of Christ. But will not the contrite Christian, who believes that the blood of Jesus has satisfied divine justice and reconciled him to God, be entitled to complain that he has been both insulted and deceived when he finds himself *identified with Caiaphas?* He will not make this discovery till he has made some progress into the sermon. He will find the monstrous injustice and selfishness of Caiaphas set forth very unsparingly before this discovery dawns upon him. And he will have advanced into the second branch of the discourse before he can fully believe that Caiaphas is held up as the type and spokesman of Evangelical Christendom! Such, however, is the fact. For there are only two forms or views of the doctrine indicated: Caiaphas's human form in which the words are false, and the divine view or principle in which they are true. Listen, then, to what the preacher regards as false:—

"Let no man say that Christ bore the wrath of God. Let no man say that God was angry with His Son. We are sometimes told of a mysterious anguish which Christ endured, the consequence of divine wrath, the sufferings of a heart laden with the conscience of the world's transgressions, which He was bearing as if they were His own sins. Do not add to the Bible what is not in the Bible. The Redeemer's conscience was not bewildered to feel *that* His own, which was *not* His own. He suffered no wrath of God. Twice came the voice from heaven, This is my beloved Son in whom I am *well pleased.* There was seen an angel strengthening Him. Nay, even to the last, never did the consciousness of purity and the Father's love forsake Him. 'Father, into Thy hands I commend my spirit.'"

Now, to say nothing of the ignorance or incompetency that would represent an evil conscience on our Redeemer's part as identical, or necessarily connected, with His endurance of the wrath of God; and the similar ignorance or incompetency that would represent the Father's unchangeable love to the Son as inconsistent with His exacting at His hands, as a Judge at the hands of a surety, the penalty of the violated law due to those in whose room He has been appointed and admitted to stand; to say nothing of these very glaring evidences of utter inability to deal with such themes, the paragraph just quoted denies in terms what all Evangelical Churches have ever held to be essential to a true propitiatory sacrifice, namely, that the substitute should bear the wrath of God. It is impossible more expressly to deny the true and proper atonement for sin rendered by Christ, even though one should affirm in terms his disbelief of the assertion, "Christ hath redeemed us from the curse of the law, *being made a curse for us.*" The views of this sermon, in fact, are thoroughly Socinian, *with this painful difference*, that it uses much of the language of Evangelical Churches as honest Socinianism would scorn to do.

With the light thus shed upon our author's design, let us now go back upon his two topics: the human form in which the words of Caiaphas are false, and the divine principle in which they are true. And " the first falsity in the human statement of that truth of vicarious sacrifice is its injustice." *Its* injustice. One naturally asks, The injustice of what? Of vicarious sacrifice? That cannot be; for it is about to be defended, against Caiaphas and — Christendom! The injustice of the human statement? And yet it is admitted to be the human statement of the truth. But let that pass also. The sermon goes on, under this head, to rail against the evangelical doctrine of the cross in the old fashion. "It has been represented as if the majesty of law demanded a victim."

We accept the representation. We believe that if the guilty were to be acquitted and accepted as righteous by the Lawgiver, the majesty of the law could not but demand a victim—worthy and willing. And we believe that the sovereignty of Love provided what the sovereignty of Law demanded,—a Substitute every way worthy and altogether willing; a victim, indeed, not in the sense of being dragged to the altar and *victimised* by death;—it is this sermon itself which actually accepts and teaches this view of Christ's death, as we shall see;—but a victim, in that He was the Lamb of God, who voluntarily offered Himself, through the Eternal Spirit, without spot, unto God, not victimised by death, but *victorious* over Him that had the power of death.

We accept this representation of law in its majesty demanding a victim. But we both loathe and resent the turn immediately given to this true representation of a holy demand: "And so as it glutted its insatiate thirst, one victim would do as well as another—the purer and the more innocent the better. It has been exhibited as if eternal love resolved in fury to strike, and so as He had His blow, it matters not whether it fell on the whole world, or on the precious head of His own chosen Son." Comment on this would be useless. And let not the charitable reader imagine that this is written against some fanatics who have misrepresented the evangelical doctrine of atonement, and whom all good people might willingly resign to the tender mercies of any School, however Broad. He is arguing against any infliction from the Father's own hand upon His beloved Son. His theory compels Him to do so. He sees Christ suffering in great measure, as all good men in some measure cannot but suffer, in a world constituted as this world is. But tell him of Christ standing at the bar of God in the room of the guilty, and of God as an offended Lawgiver and angry Judge, exacting from Him satisfaction to the law which they had broken, and he tells you, "It represents Him in terms which better describe the ungoverned rage of Saul, missing his stroke at David, who has offended, and in disappointed fury dashing his javelin at his own son Jonathan!" One feels inclined to ask, Have people never read out of the Scriptures, "Awake, O sword, against the man that is my fellow: smite the Shepherd, and the sheep shall be scattered, and I will turn my hand upon the little ones?"

After railing against the injustice of the Caiaphas-view, that is to say, on this scheme, the Christian view, of the atonement, the sermon goes on to speak, *secondly*, of its selfishness. "The more wrath instead of love is believed to be in the divine name, the more may a man find joy in believing that he is safe. It is the Siberian feeling: the innocent has glutted the wolves; and we may pursue our journey in safety. Christ has suffered, and I am safe. He bore the agony—I take the reward; I may live now with impunity." We accept the representation; "He bore the agony—I take the reward." It is not indeed a strictly correct representation, and it carries in it an invidious tone, which would entitle us to repudiate it as in effect a *mis*representation. We are not accustomed to say, "He bore the agony—I take the reward;" but, "He bore the agony—and *He* receives the reward." In His love and in His pity, He is pleased to consider our salvation as His reward,—as the joy set before Him, in the view whereof He endured the cross, despising the shame: and the Father's faithfulness and righteousness conspire to put Him in possession of it. "When His soul shall make an offering for sin, He shall see His seed, He shall prolong His days, and the pleasure of the Lord shall prosper in His hand: He shall see of the travail of His soul, and shall be satisfied; by His knowledge shall my righteous servant justify many; for He shall bear their iniquities." Still the representation, "He bore the agony—I take the reward," may be accepted as, in so far, a translation of expressions like these: Christ hath redeemed us from the curse of the law, being made a curse for us, that the blessing of Abraham might come upon us:—He hath made Him to be sin for us, that we might be made the righteousness of God in Him:—He who was rich, for our sakes became poor, that we through His poverty might be made rich.

But, *in the first place*, we indignantly reject the charge of believing that there is more wrath than love in the divine name. We believe, indeed, that there is wrath; for we cannot imagine a propitiation where no wrath is pre-supposed; and we are expressly warned to flee from the wrath to come. But we believe, not that God is wrath, but that God is love; and we believe and promulgate that, "Herein is love, not that we loved God, but that He loved us, and sent His Son to be the propitiation for our sins."

And, *in the second place*, we repudiate with abhorrence "the Siberian feeling," the charge of selfishness, and the calumny that would take exception to this doctrine as if it were calculated to foster selfishness. We see in it, on the contrary, the only true antagonist of selfishness; and we think we can read its effects better in the revelation of God and the experience of Paul than in the reasonings of Mr Robertson of Brighton: "For we thus judge, that if one died for all, then were all dead; and that He died for all, that they which live should NOT henceforth live UNTO THEMSELVES, but unto Him which died for them and which rose again."

And, *thirdly*, instead of accepting the inference, "I may live now with impunity,"—which is intended, of course, to mean, I may live as I list with impunity,— we are prepared to prove that it is just the doctrine of this sermon which is fitted to teach men to live as they please, provided only they can keep from too close contact with a certain "wheel" which we are to hear more about immediately.

After settling the injustice and selfishness of Caiaphas *and other evangelical Christians*, the author proceeds to give his own views of vicarious sacrifice—that is to say, he "passes to the hidden spirit in which these words are true." And having cleared away the slight incubus of Caiaphas and orthodox Christendom, he has scope for grand action at the outset. "I observe, first, that vicarious sacrifice is the law of being." A very oracular announcement! It is needless to say that we meet it with a direct denial. Vicarious sacrifice is not only not the law of being, it is not a *law* at all. It is one solitary, matchless, Divine *transaction*—never to be repeated, never to be equalled, never to be approached. It was the splendid and unexpected device of Divine wisdom, which in its disclosure flooded the minds of angels with the knowledge of God. It was the free counsel of the good pleasure of God's will. It was the sovereign appointment of His grace and love. We are robbed of the sovereign love of God by the notion that vicarious sacrifice is "the law of being." It is the special loving appointment of God, expressly introduced to meet our sin and misery, and to restore us to our Maker's favour and fellowship. And even the cross of Christ becomes no proof whatever of the love of God if the transaction there be only a case of "the law of being." It is the usual result,—

Vaunted defences of the love of God, as against evangelical doctrine, issue in obliterating all evidence of any such attribute in the Most High.

This doubtless is not intended. It is not God's love, but God's wrath, which it is intended to get rid of. But it obliterates the evidence for both. In particular, it gets rid of the idea of Christ suffering the wrath of God. For if vicarious sacrifice is a law of being, our author can quite well affirm that Christ's sacrifice was vicarious, and yet deny that the Divine hand inflicted any pain upon Him—that the Divine Judge exacted from Him any satisfaction for sin. In all that He suffered the Divine Redeemer was not dealing with an offended moral Lawgiver; He was merely subject to the action of a law of being.

The sermon goes on to say: "It is a mysterious and a fearful thing to observe how all God's universe is built upon this law (vicarious sacrifice as the law of being); how it penetrates and pervades all nature, so that, if it were to cease, nature would cease to exist." Is this anything else than solemn drivel? All the universe of God built on the law of vicarious sacrifice! It would be a very mysterious thing indeed. Is hell, or heaven, built on the law of vicarious sacrifice? Does this law penetrate and pervade the kingdom of darkness? Does it rule among the unfallen principalities of light? Are they all, time about, offering themselves a sacrifice in one another's stead? And are they always at it? And is it the law of their being? Reckless assertions of this sort, on a subject so solemn as the death of Christ, do not deserve to be treated respectfully.

Still, for this "law of being" there is a show of proof. Animals preying on each other—animals slain for human food—the anguish of the mother in giving birth to the child—the first settlers in a country dying by malaria from the swamps and forests which they clear away for their successors—the forlorn hope over whose dead bodies the assailants mount the breach and storm the fortress,—in all these he sees the law of vicarious sacrifice. These, however, are instances of the law being obeyed unconsciously and instinctively. "But in the redemption of our humanity, a moment comes when that law is recognised as the will of God adopted *consciously* and voluntarily obeyed as the law of man's existence. Then is it that man's true nobleness—his redemption begins." That is to say; till you voluntarily and consciously obey the law by which "the dove is struck down by the hawk," and "the winged fish falls into the jaws of the dolphin;" by which your table is covered with the flesh of slain animals; by which the ague kills off the first relay of colonists, while they drain its miry lair and clear the ground and cleanse the atmosphere for their successors; by which inexplicable French hilarity madly dances with joy at the prospect, or pleads with tears for the privilege, of being chosen for the forlorn hope, and, alas! " consciously and voluntarily" enough, bounds forward with delight to fill the fosse with dead: —till you voluntarily and consciously obey this law of being you are not redeemed. You are only a Caiaphas! So speaks this vaunted volume. One's patience is almost gone before there is time to read that, " The highest Man recognised this law, and joyfully embraced it as the law of His existence." And one thing, among others, becomes very plain; that there was nothing *peculiar* in the sacrifice of Christ, and that it is absurd to call Him and Him alone the Redeemer. If to offer one's self a vicarious sacrifice in this sense is to be a redeemer, every one of us must become a redeemer, or submit to be a Caiaphas! In fact, this is a simple assertion of the doctrine,—Every man his own redeemer. What purpose the death of Christ, on such a scheme, can serve, except as an example, it is impossible to see. And on the supposition of *His* innocence and *our* guilt, the circumstances are so diametrically diverse that, even as an example, it is totally inapplicable and impertinent. No wonder though the Jew " stumble " at it, and the Greek scorn it as " foolishness."

But the author " goes beyond this." Christ's death

was not merely a sacrifice, it was "a sacrifice for sin." "And in order to understand this, two ideas are necessary to be distinctly apprehended: the first, the notion of punishment; the second, the idea of the world's sin." The relative order in which these "two ideas" are put does not promise much clearness. For, surely, some true conception of the meaning and nature of sin should first be gained ere any attempt is made to define the notion of punishment for sin. But we take them as we find them. "Punishment," he goes on to say, "is of two kinds: the penalty which follows ignorant transgression, and the chastisement which ensues upon wilful disobedience. The first of these is called imputed guilt, the second is actual guilt. By imputed guilt is meant, in theological language, that a person is treated as if he were guilty: if, for example, you approach too near the whirling wheel of steam machinery, the mutilation which follows is the punishment of temerity. You have broken a law of nature, and the guilt of the infraction is imputed to you—there is penalty; but there is none of the chastisement which follows sin. Your conscience is not made miserable."

This is a very singular paragraph. It is quite obvious, in the first place, that the author is utterly ignorant of the meaning of such a plain theological term as "guilt." He tells us that the penalty which follows ignorant transgression is called "imputed guilt," and that the chastisement which ensues upon wilful disobedience is called "actual guilt." How can the penalty be the guilt? Guilt is righteous liability to punishment. How can it be the punishment to which it makes the transgressor liable? And why should guilt mean one thing when actual, and another thing when imputed? In either case it is liability to the penalty of moral law. But, alas! the moral law and its penalty are utterly unknown in this theory of sacrifice. Two kinds of punishment are recognised: "the penalty which follows ignorant transgression, and the chastisement which ensues on wilful disobedience." And the former is illustrated by the mutilation inflicted when you approach too near the whirling wheel of steam machinery; the latter is remorse of conscience. For the two are thus contrasted: When you suffer from the machinery, "there is penalty; but there is none of the chastisement which follows sin; your conscience is not made miserable." To be in conflict with the mechanical world without, and to be in conflict with the mental world within,—these are the two kinds of punishment; the one being penalty for ignorant transgression, the other chastisement for wilful disobedience. One thing, again, is very plain: there is no room, on this theory, for the wrath of God against sin. There may be the natural punitive action of physical law, and the inward wretchedness of remorse; but as to any infliction or penalty from the hand of God as a Judge, there is no room for it.

It would seem difficult on this alternative view of punishment to account for the sufferings of Christ. The author admits in terms that Christ was punished. "He bore the penalty of others' sins. He was punished." Was He punished with the penalty on ignorant transgression? Or was He punished with the chastisement of wilful disobedience? The dilemma would seem trying enough. But there is room for another move yet before the author's logic can be riveted in the checkmate into which he is so helplessly falling. It seems there is after all a third kind of punishment. "According to the constitution of this world, it is not only our own transgressions of ignorance, but besides, the faults of others which bring pain and sorrow on us." This is illustrated by the irritable and nervous temperament which a father's intemperance may entail upon his child, or the penury which one may inherit from a distant ancestor's extravagance. Then we are told that "in the language of theology these sufferings are called imputed guilt!" "There is between them, however, and the chastisement of personal iniquity an all-important distinction." In the latter, such punishments resulting from the man's own misconduct carry with them the miseries of conscious fault. When they "come as the penalty of the wrong of others, then philosophically, though you may call them punishment in the popular sense of the word, they are no punishments at all, but rather corrective discipline—nay, even richest blessings, if they are received from a father's hand, and transmuted by humbleness into the means of spiritual growth." And then, as having reached the goal in triumph, the author exclaims, "Apply all this to the sacrifice of Christ.

Let no man say that Christ bore the wrath of God. Let no man say that God was angry with His Son." And the passage follows which we quoted at the commencement of our comments.

Yes; apply all *this* to the sacrifice of Christ. Let no man explain the unexampled terrors, the special nature, the peculiar fruits of the sufferings of Christ, by regarding Him as answerable at the bar of divine justice in the room and stead of those who had incurred the wrath and curse of God. But apply *this* to the sacrifice of Christ. Call His sufferings " corrective discipline." Say the cup of Gethsemane, the agonizing cross, were not punishments, but " richest blessings," to be transmuted by Christ's humbleness into the means of His spiritual growth! And when you have said *this*—when you have "*applied all this to the sacrifice of Christ*"—judge whether you have not blasphemed the justice and love of God, impeached the moral purity and perfection of the Redeemer, and insulted the understanding and outraged the moral sense of every Christian man. The author himself cannot rest in this. He must fall back upon his own alternative view of punishment. He is compelled to choose in the dilemma,—Did Christ suffer the chastisement of wilful disobedience, or the penalty of ignorant transgression? And he chooses the latter. For penalty on ignorant transgression, he says, is imputed guilt! Hence it comes at last to this most deplorable dogma: " Christ came into collision with the world's evil, and He bore the penalty of that daring. He approached the whirling wheel, and was torn in pieces."

Most shocking! "He approached the whirling wheel, and was torn in pieces." What infinite degradation to the Redeemer! Himself He cannot save. He is torn in pieces. And what infinite triumph to the whirling wheel! For of course the wheel goes on whirling still; and that whirling wheel is "the world's evil!"

And this is the sacrifice of Christ—the offering of Himself to God! The author declaims against "the work of redemption being defended by parallels drawn from the most atrocious records and principles of heathenism." I just ask, What parallel can be found to his own view of that work more accurate than a sacrifice to Juggernaut beneath the crushing wheels of his bloody car? "If His chosen Son violates law, and throws Himself from the pinnacle, He dies. If you resist a law in its eternal march, the universe crushes you, that is all. . . . . If you approach too near the whirling wheel, the mutilation which follows is the punishment of your temerity. . . . . *He* approached the whirling wheel, and was torn in pieces." Was not this to become a victim in the coarse sense of being victimised? He gave way in "the collison with the world's evil." He bore the penalty of His daring; He was torn in pieces! Ah! how infinitely different is the doctrine of revelation :—"I have overcome the world;" "He was manifested that He might destroy the works of the devil"—that is, the world's evil; "He spoiled the god of this world, and made a show of him openly." His death was His triumph over the world's evil. It was not the triumph of—a whirling wheel! In the hour of His extremest weakness He was powerful to defy and vanquish the world's utmost evil; and powerful to offer Himself unto God a ransom for sin. He was not conflicting with a physical or social law of this evil world's constitution, and paying the penalty of His daring. He was magnifying the Moral Law and making it honourable, and gaining the eternal rewards of obedience unto death. He was not helpless in the embraces of an infernal machine. But His Cross—to which, from such insults on its work and doctrine, we turn with renewed adoring admiration—was the instrument which, in the lowest ebb of His human strength, He wielded with Almightiness, through the Eternal Spirit, as the weapon of His warfare and the means of His victory. And the shame and agony of the powers of darkness will be eternally renewed in the bitter reflection, that their defeat was achieved by an instrument so full of agony and shame to Him who nevertheless, by means of it, defeated them.

Such is a specimen of Robertson's sermons—a lamentable compost of unintentional blasphemy and theological ignorance. Its fundamental aberration from the truth is a very fatal one, being neither more nor less than the entire denial of Moral Law, strictly and properly so called. It speaks, indeed, of moral laws; but identifies them in kind and in action with those physical laws in accordance with which God rules the dead mechanism of the material world. You bring your body into conflict with the wheel of steam machinery. You suffer mutilation; wounds and bruises, and putrifying sores and broken bones. This is your penalty. But there are surgical remedies, and the *vis medicatrix naturæ*. In like manner, you place your mind in conflict with the laws of truth and righteousness; you utter falshood or commit iniquity. The law reacts upon you in remorse and self-contempt. This is your penalty here. But you bethink you of the law of vicarious sacrifice—the "great law of being!" And you begin "consciously" to obey it. You bethink you also of Christ's obedience to it— of His vicarious sacrifice; and, either from your own obedience to that law, or His, or from both, a sort of *vis medicatrix naturæ* comes into play in this department of pain and penalty too. In this way the whole matter is one of physical process; and somehow, as a broken leg becomes strong and serviceable again, an outraged conscience does the same. Such is the "healing of the hurt of the daughter of my people!"

It is very plain, on such a scheme, that the Moral Law is not an instrument by which we are brought into any closer and more direct and personal relation to God, than by the physical laws of nature. The whole universe, in this view, is fatalistic. The law of the Ten Commandments is no objective rule or code of duty, binding in any proper sense on the consciences of men, and claiming authoritatively to regulate their wills. It is a ceaseless subjective energy—a kind of law of spiritual gravitation, operating very much like the law which governs the movements of the planets and the fall of heavy bodies. Its violation also operates in very much the same manner, the law reacting injuriously on the breakers of it; though gradually admitting of a remedial process and a curative influence from the sacrifice of Christ, which, it would appear, is a sort of inevitable necessity in the history and development of the race, while at the same time it is very far from clear whether Christ in His redemption-work is to be regarded as having observed or violated the law Himself. "If His own chosen Son violates law, and throws Himself from the pinnacle, He dies," says Mr Robertson. And, it would appear, He did actually die in this way. For Mr Robertson, in this one same discourse, in professed exposition of vicarious sacrifice, says concerning the Lord Jesus Christ: "He approached the whirling wheel, and was torn in pieces!"

And yet, concerning productions such as this, we are told that no man who regards his reputation as a "thinker" can do other than admire and imitate them: nor are there wanting those who, through mingled vanity and pusillanimity, are trying it. They hear it said, and they seem partly to believe it, that to refuse to smile on variations such as these from the creeds and symbols of a bygone age, is "theological despotism." To exclude from our Scottish Churches, men of such genius, originality, and learning, is to suppress the spirit of erudite investigation, and to destroy intellectual independence and freedom of modern thought! But can any intelligent man be ignorant of the fact that, instead of the creeds and symbols of the Churches of the Reformation having proved suppressive of true learning and erudition, they have called forth, in the investigations that paved the way for them, in their construction, exposition, and defence, erudition and learning the most magnificent ever exhibited in any department of human thought; and that to this hour they afford scope, in the illustration and enforcement of their doctrines, for the highest exercises of the human mind, and for the noblest gifts with which any man has yet been found endowed? And what is to be the splendid gain to the Church of Christ from throwing loose, and unsettling, and abandoning all her attainments in the knowledge of the thoughts and the will of God? Tell our lawyers to plead in our courts on any theories of law they please, however mutually contradictory. Give medical degrees to hopeful young scholars and "thinkers" who claim the liberty of disbelieving the circulation of the blood, and who make the claim in the name of freedom of thought and independent investigation. Present us in our Universities with "the beautiful phenomenon" of one Professor teaching the Newtonian system of the universe; another the Ptolemaic theory of the immobility of the earth; and a third the free and independent, erudite and learned little pleasantry of the Egyptians, that the heavenly "bodies were carried round the heavens in chariots close on all sides but one, in which there was a round hole, and that eclipses were occasioned by the accidental turning of their dark sides towards us" (*ENCYCLOPÆDIA METROPOLITANA*, *Astronomy*, p. 485). Do all this. Do it on the plea of resisting scientific despotism, of liberating human thought, of asserting independence of investigation, of promoting learning and erudition. *Then* come to the Churches of Scotland, and ask us to embrace in our communion a Jowett, a Maurice, a Kingsley, and a Robertson.

Theological despotism! I take with the impeachment. And I retort with the analogue of Astronomical despotism. For, like many more, I have read a little in both sciences; and men who, in dealing with theology are ever and anon, without knowing it, running up their representations into paralogism, yea and blasphemy, I shall acknowledge as theologians, when I shall have learned to acknowledge *him* as an astronomer who believes that

The Moon which rose last night round as my shield

has the radius of "my shield" for its diameter.

CHAPTER X.

ATONEMENT, AND THE DISTINCTIVE PECULIARITY OF MORAL LAW.

So long as philosophy and theology shall conserve the distinctive peculiarity of Moral Law,—as the "categorical imperative" and as the objective charter and instrument of a strictly moral government,—the Westminster doctrine, which is the Catholic doctrine, of Atonement, is impregnable. And some of the Anglican *litterateurs* are aware of that. Hence they confound moral with physical law,—parading what is really an *unethical* view of moral law, apparently without being aware that the notion is self-contradictory.

It is to this issue that Dr CANDLISH has, with much penetration, run up his whole controversy with Mr MAURICE in his examination of the once celebrated Essays. And it is unnecessary to say that he has received, and will receive, no answer to his minute and masterly polemic. We have seen that ROBERTSON makes even Vicarious Sacrifice itself a "law of being;" and the same sort of language is not altogether unknown now in Scotland, in some men's expositions of the doctrine of the death of Christ. When the decease accomplished at Jerusalem can be explained, apart from everything *judicial* either in its appointment, its occurrence, or its fruits; it is natural enough, and indeed it becomes requisite, that nothing judicial should be recognised in the Moral Law, or in the moral government of the Most High. And hence Moral Law is now no longer to be regarded as a strict and proper commandment—objective authoritative commandment—but as a subjective influence, moulding the nature and doings of men, very much after the same fashion as gravitation governs the movements of a planet, or as chemical affinities affect the more hidden properties of matter. The distinction between Law Moral and Law Physical, which CHALMERS, with his own unapproachable splendours of expression and of exposition, set forth in a work* written long before it could have been supposed that professed theologians would confound things which differ so radically, is thus to be obliterated. And Kant is no longer to be allowed to stand in awe before his "categorical imperative," but shut up to his "starry heavens" alone. This is generalisation 'with a vengeance:' if, indeed, the word 'vengeance' do not offend them; but I confess I cannot bring myself, here or elsewhere, to substitute for it 'love burning on.'

The truly grand modern generalisation in physical science is the doctrine of the Correlation of Forces and the Conservation of Energy,† asserting as it does the

---

* See CHALMERS' "*Lectures on Romans*" (Rom. viii. 2).

† See "*Sketch of Thermodynamics*," the recent and remarkable work of my

ultimate identity of all physical forces whatsoever. And as force produces and is measured by motion, individual forces can be all made alternately to replace each other, even to exact numerical equivalence. Thus, "Heat" is ultimately but "a Mode of Motion;" and in a given amount is identical with a calculable intensity of gravitation that would cause a projectile to describe a specified parabola, or a planet a particular ellipse.

Now, on this generalised view of Moral Law, why not find an equivalent force, for instance, for the Fifth Commandment? We remember, on visiting a flat of spinning jennies in Manchester some years ago, being told by our conductor that these beautiful pieces of machinery performed the *duty* of so many children. Of course he understood himself as speaking figuratively. But that was before Robertson had published his Sermons, or Maurice written his Essays. Things are altered now. Why should not a disappointed parent, being one of the merchant princes of the earth, compensate for the distress of a domestic rebellion, by giving an order for the equivalent number of the jennies, and putting on the exact additional horse-power in the engine-room? And then the little rebels might equivalate too. For if they lose the reward of "the first commandment with pro-

---

distinguished friend Professor TAIT, whose labours, jointly with those of Sir WILLIAM THOMSON, in their "*Treatise on Natural Philosophy*," are illustrating at once their country and their century. See, also, GROVE'S "*Correlation of Forces;*" BALFOUR STEWART'S "*Treatise on Heat;*" FARADAY'S "*Electrical Researches;*" his "*Scientific Memoir,*" by TYNDAL; and his "*Life and Letters,*" by Dr BENCE JONES.

mise," there are equivalent medicinal as well as mechanical forces to make up for it, and all may be square again by the tabulated indemnifying number of Parr's life pills!" We are quite prepared to have this called profane. But Pascal has rebuked that charge. So that "you see, fathers, ridicule is, in some cases, a very appropriate means of reclaiming men from their errors; do not then expect to make people believe that it is unworthy of a Christian to treat error with derision" (*Provin. Lett. xi.*).

But we can treat this error seriously too, and we intend to do so.

I. The application of the term Law to the uniform sequences of phenomena in the physical world is sufficient to show that law, in its original signification, implies something more than the physical world can either embody or adequately illustrate. For, unquestionably, it is applied in such connections figuratively, or rhetorically. It is an instance of the rhetorical figure called personification. But personification is an attribution of ideal personality, where it is quite understood that real personality does not exist. In the solar system, for instance, the sun is poetically conceived of as a mighty monarch seated on his central throne, and issuing his commands to the planets and satellites that move like obedient subjects round him. But who does not see that in the attribution of personality, in any sense, to the elements of the material world, the objects of con-temptation—by an illusion to which the mind pleasurably resigns, without deceiving, itself—are regarded as belonging to a realm not natively and really their own? And the very use which we make satirically of the word *satellite*, as indicating slavish obedience, has no point or meaning, except as carrying in it the accusation that the individual has abandoned his position and prerogative as the inhabitant of a realm of personal liberty and moral power, and descended, as it were, into that mere physical world, the elements of which fancy must lift up into a kingdom higher than their own, before they can be conceived of as the subjects of liberty and law. The law of *elective* affinity in chemistry is another case in point. An active power of choice, or preference, is rhetorically attributed to the bodies or substances under consideration, while everybody understands that they are exhibiting neither intelligence nor will, but passively undergoing changes necessitated in the circumstances by the nature of the elements of which they are composed.

Now, if the application of the term Law to the uniformity of natural sequences be thus so obviously figurative, it is plain that its original signification must be something different; else we may repeat here the keen remark of Marcus Dods,—already quoted when refuting the notion that Christ was only figuratively a priest,— that "the very word, upon this supposition, stands in the unprecedented situation of having a figurative application without ever having had a real literal meaning."

And indeed, when we bear in mind that figurative meanings vanish where no primary idea is recognised,—though we did not mean to draw on Pascal's authority again,—we really see no reason why we should not indicate the parallel which exists between such a case and that of the foreigner, desirous of instruction in the English language, who, on being told that an excellent teacher was accustomed to charge a guinea for the first quarter and fifteen shillings for the second, declared on the spot that he saw his way clearly to take the second quarter immediately!

Possibly, however, those whom we have in our view may attempt to evade the force of this remark by denying that the term Law is applied in any secondary or figurative or rhetorical sense to the physical world. They may affirm that the physical world is the true, proper, and primary sphere of law; and that law, in its one only real and valid signification, is characteristic alike of all material substances, all mechanical and chemical forces, all physiological organisations, and all mental faculties; indeed, of all intelligent creatures in the whole compass of their being.

Doubtless this gets quit of all rhetorical application of the term; and prosaic sternness becomes the order of the day. Personification, on this understanding, is of course abjured. But what if it be found that PERSONALITY is sacrificed also?—the personality alike of man and of God? If the only kind of law to be recognised, in relation to man, is a generalised expression of the facts observable in the actual conduct of his mental powers,—such as the law of the association of ideas,—what argument have we for the personality of God, or what materials from which to realise any strict and proper personality of our own. When the very peculiar and unique idea of accountability is introduced: when Moral Law is recognised as an external objective code of duty,—a law not *of* man, but *for* man,—a law not *of* his faculties, but *for* his obedience,—postulating, on his part, a power of choice and a sense of responsibility, claiming to rule his will and securing the assent of his conscience: personality, both human and divine, is safe. For *personal relation* comes out now with a clearness and intensity of which there can be no evasion. Law of this nature recognises my personality and appeals to it,—probably was the means of first historically educing my personality into conscious realisation. It would be an interesting question in mental science whether the infant spirit is ever educated into consciousness by the mere play of intellect; or whether the first flash of conscious personal existence is not the result of realised moral obligation, and of the action of the will in reference thereto. And if there be reason to suppose that historically this is true, there would then be the corresponding metaphysical question, whether it must not necessarily be true. But, be this as it may, it is not essential to the point we have in hand, however it might confirm our views. What we ask attention to is,—that law physical, law as a mere subjective, operative principle, expressive simply of the uniform sequences in which change takes place, whether in the material or the mental world, neither postulates nor demonstrates any personal relation between man and God. And, with personal relation, personality must stand or fall. For it is against the personality of another, and in relation thereto, that my own personality is tested and adequately revealed and realised. To this condition even the mysterious constitution of the Godhead as Triune would appear to be subject. Solitary personality is what eternity hath never witnessed. From everlasting, personality has existed in fellowship, in personal relation.* But in such law as is identical merely with *formula of fact* there is not the slightest trace of personal relationship.

Introduce, however, the very different sort of law which is identical with *formula of obligation.* Let me not merely be dealt with as exhibiting *what is*, but let me

* " But for interfering with the continuity of the argument, I would have been strongly inclined to prosecute this line of thought,—Is a uni-personal Deity conceivable ? Is not Pantheism somewhat defensible as *versus* such a Deity? Can we conceive of a necessary and eternal consciousness of " I AM," without a necessary and eternal reason for the " I AM " saying " THOU ART ?" For if there cannot be a created consciousness of *I am,* without a causal necessary and eternal " I AM," can we conceive differently of the *Thou art ?* Will it do to introduce *it* first in time ? in reference to a created angel, let us say ? " Unto which of the angels said He at any time, THOU ART . . . . ? " Let alone the question of eternal Sonship. Take it more abstractly. Take the question of fellowship. " To which of the angels "— created beings—could God say " at any time," " THOU ART ? " But must not God "at any time," all throughout the past eternity, be competent to say " THOU ART," as well as " I AM ? " Could there be a beginning of the *Thou art,* any more than of the I AM ? Is there not an *a priori* argument for the doctrine of the Trinity, or at least a vindication of the doctrine from *a priori* considerations ?—See *Appendix.*

be appealed to as to what *ought to be*. Let my nature not merely be read as historically exhibiting necessary and inevitable facts, but as capable of choosing, within certain limits, what facts my history shall embody, myself responsible in each case for the choice I make. An appeal like this treats me as a separately subsisting individual person, and from another living person only can it come. The "categorical imperative" covers the personality both of man and of God. But if there is no "Thou shalt," what becomes of the "Thou?" If there is no "categorical imperative," where is the vocative? And if no vocative, where is the voice—the *vocans*? Moral law testifies to "thee"—and testifies from, and therefore of, "Him." "*It*" is the all of law physical. Hence if law physical alone be recognised, Pantheism is the abyss into which we are swept inexorably.

II. If, in the face of such conclusions, this abnegation of all that is specific and peculiar in Moral Law is to be persisted in, and the possibility of demonstrating the personality of God still asserted, we ask the advocates of this theory to consider its bearing on the Origin of Evil.

Of course, we do not ask them to furnish a philosophy or *rationale* on that great question. We neither offer, nor demand, a solution of the problem, Why, under the government of an almighty and beneficent Being, should evil have been suffered to exist? But no theology can refuse to face its existence as a fact; or refuse to speak out, if asked to say whether it lodges and leaves the origin of that fact with the creature or the Creator. On the unsophisticated theory of moral law—law assertative of authority in a personal God as Moral Ruler, and of obligation on personal beings as His subjects—this aspect of the question presents no difficulty. In this view, man is recognised as originally created upright;—not a being gifted with intelligence merely, capable of elaborating mathematical and scientific truth, and of observing and generalising physical facts; but endowed with personal power of choice, with the very special faculty of will. Nor is this a mere vague power of instinctive self-pleasing, a sort of personified *elective* chemical affinity; but a very definite consciousness of personal liberty and power, in which his distinct and separately subsisting personality comes out into inevitable manifestation, and that most over-awingly of all in the alternative it gives him of determining whether his personal footing with God shall be one of submission or of affected independence. Such is his faculty of will and its scope for choice,—with conscience behind to ratify or to reprove. Created thus, originally righteous,—with the Moral Law from the first the law *of*, as well as *to*, his will,—how is he now dealt with? What special act of providence does God exercise towards him in this estate wherein he is created? The answer is very remarkable, and bears with amazing precision on the point in hand. As if to prevent the "categorical imperative" from being lost sight of, or swallowed up, in the original accordance between man's holy will and the subject-matter of the law; as if expressly to prevent law moral from leaning over towards law physical, as from the circumstance of this accordancy it might seem to do; the "categorical imperative" is brought into play again, in circumstances fitted to restore the balance, or reclaim the dangerous bias,—brought into play with nothing in the subject-matter of its *new demand* priorly existing in man's nature to correspond to it, but compelling recognition of it as in its very form, apart from its matter, authoritative, juridical, morally governmental; and sheer and sharp is the Law now as *commandment:* "THOU SHALT not eat of it; for in the day thou thou eatest thereof THOU SHALT surely die."

It is impossible for man, under a commandment of this nature, to mistake his position as the personal subject of a personal Moral Ruler. He has to deal now, not merely with a law which is at once the law *of* his nature and a law *to* his will. His will is appealed to by a commandment which does not find itself already existing in his nature, as a spiritual tendency which might therefore be called the law *of* his being, or, in any sense, his own law. Sharply, directly, exclusively, is his will appealed to now by what he must see can be called nothing but "the law of his God." And his *probation*, as under law to his God, becomes manifest, simple, and conclusive. The fall of man, under these circumstances, may leave grave questions unsolved. But it clears up all questions anent *physical* evil, by resolving *it* into the result of the righteous displeasure of the Moral Ruler against the disobedience of man. It throws a flood of light most instructively on the *history* of the rise of *moral* evil. And it conclusively fastens the origin of *all* evil on the creature, and justifies the ways of God.

But take that theory of Moral Law, the bare possibility of any tendency toward which this most peculiar style of moral probation, with the categorical imperative so sharply and exclusively propounded and employed as its instrument, would appear to have been introduced expressly to forestall and prevent. Take the theory which makes no account of Moral Law, save as a kind of physical law *of* man's higher nature, and not an authoritative commandment *to* his will. And in what aspect does God in that case appear in this matter of the fall of man, if He appear in it as a personal being at all? Not as a righteous Moral Ruler, conducting the righteous procedure of a very special moral probation, giving commandment to a living personal being under His authority, endowed with liberty and capable of choice. Not thus. But as physically experimenting on His own creature to its ruin. The proper analogue to which is—Galvani torturing the nerves of a frog! Only that the fall of man was not designed for the promotion of science.

III. Let us bring this non-juridical idea of Moral Law into the light in its bearings on that confessed disharmony in human nature of which all men are in a measure conscious.

Of course, the first appeal to consciousness should be an appeal to man's sense of responsibility,—not to his consciousness of having failed concerning it. Is there *that*, in the constitution of man's spiritual nature, which enables him either to originate or to understand, with reference to any exercise of his will, the expression "you ought" or "you ought not?" If it be admitted, without sophistication, that there is, then an original and ineradicable distinction is admitted between law moral and law physical,—law of duty and law of mental states or processes. And the absolute requirements of exact discussion are at an end. Attempts may be made, however, to resolve the consciousness of responsibility into something secondary and composite,—with what success, we tarry not here to say. But take—not the mere abstract sense of accountability, but—man's conscious experience of inward disharmony in connection with it; and we shall find the testimony thus afforded to Law, as strictly and distinguishingly Moral, more varied and abundant than can possibly, with any show of reason, be evaded. We ask any thoughtful man, on any other view of Law, to explain, or account for, or even show the possibility of, any such subjective disharmony or derangement as all men are conscious of,—from the heathen who, with more or less of nonchalance, gives expression off-hand to his semi-discontented sense of it in his "*video meliora proboque, deteriora sequor,*" to the saint, agonising in his fight of faith, as his groans find utterance in the cry, "O wretched man that I am, who shall deliver me?" (Rom. vii. 24). Explain, if you can, how experiences like these can possibly be realised as facts, or conceived of ideally, under the action of any sort of law but what is objectively assertative of obligation? Refuse to go beyond the recognition of such law as is identical with causal subjective self-operating principle;—or, excluding the idea of causality, let it be such law as is identical, if not with force, yet with formula —formula of process and of result—be the process ever so uniform, or the result ever so certain, in justification of your use of this word Law in the matter at all;—how can you possibly account for the utterance, whether of the classic heathen of Rome, or the inspired writer to the Romans? A disharmony between a subjective state of mind, on the one hand,—call it a law of force or of process, or a formula, if you please,—and an objective law or code of duty, on the other hand; this is intelligible. But its intelligibility depends on the fundamental diversity in kind of the two laws thus seen and felt to be in conflict. Two subjective physical laws or forces can produce no such phenomenon. They may modify each other's action; but it is in the way of composition or of combination, effecting a *tertium quid*, distinct from the result that would flow from the action of either separately. But the new result bears no trace of disharmony or derangement in it. Even as under the two laws of impulse and of gravitation—the centrifugal and centripetal forces—the planet rolls on in its ellipse, as easily and sweetly, with as little of jolt or jagged motion, as under the one force it would fly away equably into limitless space, or under the other would fall with acceleration to the centre of the sun.

Of course we do not mean to identify the heathen and the Christian consciousness in this matter. It is by a very sharp transition that the one passes into the other. So much the more for our present argument. For the history of that transition and its moral philosophy cast a very strong and very steady light on the distinctive peculiarity of Moral Law. Assuredly, among all his schools and schoolmasters, Paul had no conscious knowledge of any subjective law that could have been his " schoolmaster to bring him to Christ;" and, had no other kind of law dealt with him, he would have known neither Christ nor sin to this hour. " I had not known sin," says he, " but by the law" (Rom. vii. 7). And it was not the law of a subjective process; but a law objective, outside and above himself; a law that could *speak* to him,—and that not merely after the fashion of an ideal divarication of his own consciousness as on two sides of a soliloquy, but as the voice of another than himself, speaking as one having authority. " For I had not known lust,"—I should have been conscious of nothing but legitimate desire,—" except the law had said, Thou shalt not covet." Not without the " categorical imperative " asserting its transcendency *objectively,* is conscience reinvigorated to reassert its supremacy, *de jure*, against a subjective law of depravity or uniform tendency to sin. Another *subjective* law, a merely diverse principle or tendency, would not meet the case. It is the proclamation of Moral Law that is needed. "I was alive without the law once; but when" —not another tendency, but—"the COMMANDMENT came, sin revived, and I died" (ver. 9). It was in its character and aspect of *commandment* that Law had any fitness to bring out to view so unmistakably this disharmony within, quickening and precipitating the crisis to a death-struggle. The introduction of an inward *tendency*, diametrically opposite to that of sin would silently have quickened *me*, and proportionally sopited *sin*. But by the introduction of *commandment*, "sin revived and I died." Instead of losing, sin gained ground by the *commandment*. "For, sin taking occasion by the COMMANDMENT, deceived me, and by it slew me," "working death in me by that which is good, that sin by the COMMANDMENT might become exceeding sinful" (verses 11 and 13). "Wherefore the law is holy;" I speak of it as *commandment*; for of no holy *tendency*, alas! as yet, at this stage, had I any consciousness to claim. I am carnal, sold under sin; I speak of a law that is commandment, compelling recognition from without. "The law is holy, and the *commandment* is holy, and just, and good" (ver. 12). As an authoritative code of duty, it is so. Take it as subjective principle, and how will you negative the supposed conclusions,—groundless enough on Paul's theology,—the conclusions which he anticipates in the questions, "What shall we say then? Is the law sin? Was that which is good made death unto me?" (verses 7 and 13). They are irresistible on the theory of Law being identical with subjective tendency. It is the interchangeableness of "Law" and "Commandment" which rebuts them.

Surely one may almost say, "The Scripture, foreseeing" this attempt to obliterate a vital distinction, "preached before" that distinction with emphasis and iteration most solicitous. For in a single short paragraph (Rom. vii. 7–13), in twelve references to Moral Law, six times it is called LAW, and six times COMMANDMENT.

No doubt, in the transition from what is practically the heathen to what is distinguishingly the Christian consciousness, the objective moral commandment is, in the matter of it, translated subjectively into the inner man, and reappears now as a holy tendency as well as a righteous code. That this takes place, or rather that this has taken place, is manifested in that first forthgoing and action of the renewed will of which Paul speaks when he says, "I consent unto the law that it is good." (ver. 16). But even now, not as the holy tendency of his will, although it is all that now—"the law of my mind." (ver. 23)—yet not as in any sense a law of his own, even of his inward man, does he delight in it; but after the inward man he delights in it as specifically the law of his God: "I delight *in the law of God* after the inward man" (ver. 22). And clinging to it now, identifying all his desire and all his interest with it,—still as the authoritative instrument of his reconciled, righteous Ruler's government of and over him,—he can divaricate *now* in his own consciousness, alike with good ground, with precious practical design, and with great effectiveness and great effect: "Now, then, if I do that I would not, it is no more I that do it, but sin that dwelleth in me" (ver. 17). And the righteous Lord ratifies this protest, and gives His loyal subject the benefit thereof; for it is in behalf of His own divine commandment and its unappellable authority that the protest is entered.

It is not to break the thread of this argument, which we intend immediately to resume and complete, if we pause for a moment to inquire,—

IV. What bearing this non-authoritative view of Law may be found to have on the doctrine and fact of the Incarnation. For, in point of argument or of exposition, as also in point of fact, the Incarnation must come in here to account for the possibility of Paul, or those likeminded with him, reaching that particular stage of spiritual experience which we have been considering. Paul himself is not negligent to put us in remembrance of this. For these wonderful readings or revelations that he is giving of his own intense consciousness in connection with Sin and Law, are all professedly explanatory of his assertion that he had " become dead to the law by the body of Christ" (Rom. vii. 4). Not without the interveniency of the Incarnation; not apart from some determining influence from "the body of Christ;" has he realised, or can he now explain, his own marvellous consciousness, as he here makes it patent to the intelligence and sympathy of the church for ever.

What this interveniency of the Incarnation may import, and how it operates, it is not, on the Westminster doctrine of the Atonement, difficult to explain. Accepting the fundamental beliefs of all Christian theology, we recognise the Incarnation of the Eternal Word as exhibiting the union of the divine and human natures in the one divine person of the Son of God; and the immediate design of this great mystery of godliness, God manifest in the flesh, we believe to have been accomplished by this God-man putting Himself in the room of those whom the Father hath given Him, under an authoritative and unchangeable, but by them violated Moral Law, to fulfil, as their representative, all its commandments, and endure, as their substitute, all its curse. And hence, when His clients intelligently and cordially appropriate this interposition on their behalf, it is not difficult to see how,—the Law having no longer any such claims against them as those to which it was till now necessarily and remorselessly alive,—"*that* becomes dead wherein they were held" (Rom. vii. 6); and they, alive no more in terror to claims that have been legally and fully met, become "dead to the law," and that "by the body of Christ," even "by the body of His flesh through death" (Col. i. 22).

But what instrumentality or efficiency towards anything like this can possibly be ascribed to the Incarnation of God's Son, if there be no strictly moral and authoritative juridical law? That He most expressly felt Himself to be the subject of such Law, we must most firmly hold, if the testimony of Scripture or the depositions of His own consciousness are to be believed. He felt Himself, no doubt, to be possessed of a created nature, having, impressed upon it, certain laws of operation,—laws of intelligence and holiness alike, if you will,—and by reason whereof nothing abnormal, whether in respect of wisdom or of holy rectitude, could ever manifest itself in any department of His person as "the Word made flesh." In this sense, Love may be said to be the law of His divine nature, and Love the law of His human nature also. And, in this respect, a spontaneous development of Love as the Law of His human nature, as well as His Divine, would have been exhibited, whatever object His Incarnation might have been designed to achieve, or in whatever circumstances He might have been placed. But was this the *only* kind of dealing with Law which His history exhibits? Or was this the only kind of Law dealing with *Him*, to which the averments of His own consciousness testify? Is He not, on the other hand, most solicitous to own that, in another and a very different sense, He is under Law; not merely that His character presents a phenomenon of law, however high and holy, but that He Himself is the obedient servant and subject of law,—

that He is under law to His Father? What else mean those emphatic acknowledgments of obligation and responsibility: "I *must* work the works of Him that sent me;" "I *must* be about my Father's business;" "Other sheep I have, them also *must* I bring?" And again; not merely, "I do always those things that please my Father,"—fair as a beauteous flower, developing its leaves and loveliness with fragrance acceptable to the God of love, though with no form nor comeliness in the eyes of those of whose nature, alas! love is far enough from being the law; not this merely, as if exhibiting the action only of an inward subjective holy law of His nature; it is not this merely that Jesus means when He says, "I do always those things which please my Father,"—as if one should gratify a friend by exhibiting tastes and tendencies, predilections or dispositions, similar to his own. His meaning is explained when He says elsewhere: "As my Father gave me *commandment*, so I do." And "My Father gave me a *commandment*" defining all my ministry or service, reaching to every word and every deed, "a commandment what I should say and what I should do." And, if "I lay down my life for the sheep and take it again," it is not merely because prompted by an inward law of love, whether towards Him or towards them, but because " this commandment received I of my Father."

Regard the Lord Jesus thus, as not only "made of a woman," but "made under the" objective authoritative "law" of God; and the whole ground is clear, on to the doctrines of representative probation and of true and proper priestly sacrifice, inviolably redemptive of all for whom this last Adam ministers in His redeeming office.

But on the other hand, if we recognise in His character and history nothing but the operation of a subjective law or principle of holiness, what possibility is there for the in-bringing of anything approaching to the idea of redemption, or what excuse for introducing the language that expresses it? With love, the law of His divine nature, operating now, no doubt, in His altered circumstances somewhat differently, because operating now in His human nature as well as His divine; yet He himself not any more now a servant *for* men, or a subject *under* God, than He was from all eternity; what purpose can His Incarnation be designed to serve? An Example, is it said? Be it so. But it is an example which we are not under *obligation* to follow; for the idea of obligation has been banished; and if it be recalled to serve a purpose and to bind us now, what example to us can *He* be who is Himself under no obligation, and begins to exemplify our position by placing *us* under obligation, thereby rendering it entirely dissimilar to His own? The example—let it carefully be noted also—of an inward subjective law or principle of love, with no co-existing inward principle or tendency of evil in His case, set forth for the encouragement of fallen beings, all whose subjective tendencies and principles are "only evil, and that continually!" Oh most encouraging example?—brimful of hope, as the cup of Tantalus;

beckoning men to heaven, but giving not a drop of water to cool the tongue!

But perhaps Sympathy is the secret that shall solve the problem of the Incarnation. And sympathy, it would appear, is the word in this new theologism,—warmer, confessedly, and more seductive in sentiment, while proportionally less tangible and definite in its statements, than the old Socinianism. What else, in fact, but something in the line of sympathy have they left any room for recognising in the Person and work of the Incarnate Word,—though Dean STANLEY, in his catalogue of subject-matters of his "Nineteenth Century Theology,"* makes mention, indeed, neither of Christ's *person* nor His *work*, and speaks of His "nature" as if He had either the divine or the human, but not both; or, as if the two had been compounded into a third. But letting that pass. What can that sympathy for man be worth which is dissociated from all service or subjection to God? Or what can it achieve? Or how does it operate? The Holy One in human nature, dwells with men upon the earth. And He comes for purposes of sympathy,—He comes to acquire and manifest sympathy. But as to law *objective* and authoritative, He is not placed under it, any more than they are under it. There is no ground for sympathy then in that respect; for there is nothing concerning which to sympathise. As to law *subjective*,—that is, inward operating principle, —in the case of the God-man, the law of both His

* See *Fraser's Magazine*, 1865.

natures is holy love, even "all that is of the Father;" and it operates in the unlimited fulness of the one nature, and in all the compass of the other. As to law subjective in fallen man, why all that is *in* the world is *of* the world, even "the lust of the flesh, and the lust of the eyes, and the pride of life." There is, therefore, as little ground or material of sympathy here. Antipathy, rather, would seem to be only more sharply defined, with no higher reconciling efficiency or instrumentality provided; for, in fact, reconciliation of any kind, or in any sense, is utterly excluded from this whole scheme of theological opinion. Still, sympathy is pleaded for tenaciously; as well it may, seeing it is the last refuge, if an explanation of the Incarnation has, in any sort, to be supplied. But what sort of explanation does it afford? The Son of God places Himself amidst the sorrows of men,—although not sharing with them any position, as under broken law, such as would afford an explanation of suffering and sorrow being either their lot or His; and, from the parallelism thus far between His case now and theirs, an assimilating virtue goes forth from Him which exerts a beneficial influence on them. And so, having sympathised with them in a law of their nature by which "man that is born of a woman is of few days and full of trouble," He somehow,—as by a fortunate contagion, converse to the law of infection in bodily disease,—carries them over into sympathy with the law of His natures, which is the Law of Love; so that the will of man, like the will of the God-man, is brought to vibrate harmoniously with the will of God, but not any further *in subjection* to it than it was before, or than Christ's will ever was or will be.

It is hard enough to understand, surely, how this is brought to pass. But if this is the object of the Incarnation, it is still harder to imagine why it should be described as our " becoming *dead* to the law "—the law of love—" by the *body* of Christ." One would rather say that we were made *alive* to the law by this assimilating, quickening influence. And while our sympathy with the *mind* that is in Christ might be held to account for it, what can His " *body* " be supposed to have to do with it?

At all events, if this is the kind of regeneration which, apart from all idea of redemption proper, is to be substituted alike for the redemption that is in Christ and the regeneration that is by the Spirit of Christ,

V. It may be well to consider what the real Regeneration of God's kingdom is, and how it stands connected with the contrasted kinds of law which we have been discriminating.

Resuming, then, our analysis of the experience of Paul in his quickened consciousness concerning Law, let us solicit attention to the exact point of transition where he finds himself able to assert a vital change in his consciousness and able to vindicate for himself a new relation to Law. For that transition, we see, is very sharply defined, when, realising a new subjective tendency or bias in his will,—and realising it all the more clearly and keenly from the fact of finding a thwarting influence steadily operating against it,—he finds himself not merely *as*senting by enforced conviction, but cordially *con*senting to the law. "For that which I do (οὐ γινώσκω), I allow not,—I know not, I acknowledge not, I repudiate or disown; for (ὁ θέλω) what I would, that do I not; but what I hate, that do I. If then I do that which I would not, I consent unto the law that it is good." —καλός, beautiful, worthy of, and now securing my cordial admiration (Rom. vii. 15, 16). And this "consent unto the law" is not an isolated or occasional volition. It is habitual; even as the discrepancy between "what I would," and "what I do" is habitual—that discrepancy in the light of which I read my "consent unto the law" even more clearly than if it took easy, and unhindered, and uniform complete effect.

This habitual consent of the will, indicating or implying a new subjective tendency in the inward man, Paul is now justified in calling a "law *of* his mind" (ver. 23). But manifestly he is still dealing with something different from subjective laws, as this very consent itself most clearly verifies. For if this new law of his mind, however holy and good, is identical with the "consent," it has to be discriminated from that to which the consent is given. The law to which his consent, in every *act* of volition, is given, cannot be identified with the law which his consent, as a *habit* of volition, *constitutes*. He consents unto the objective law of God, as an authoritative law *to* his will; and when, because of his *habitual* consent, he feels warranted now in speaking of "the law *of* his will or *of* his mind," whereas hitherto it had been enough to speak of "*the* law" (though even then he called it also "the commandment"), now he is careful to call it "*the law of God*" (ver. 22), as if on very purpose to anticipate and prevent misconstruction of the new phrase he was about to employ. Nor,—having thus paved the way beforehand for the adoption of that phrase,—is he less careful thereafter to exemplify the right use of it; for he does not represent himself as henceforth serving "the *law of his mind*," but tells us that "with the *mind* he himself serves the *law of God*" (ver. 25).

A most accurate moral philosopher and psychologist, as well as theologian, was this old tent-maker of Tarsus! And it would do some of our moral philosophers good to attend a little more to his writings.

The notion of subjective law may, indeed, on a superficial view, seem to fit in very nicely with the doctrine of regeneration; and may be represented as in fact harmonising admirably with the true idea of subjective grace, or, more properly, as being a philosophical expression for it. But it is very far from giving a full or accurate account of the renewal of the will; and it is a very defective reading of what we find in the will when renewed. Regeneration, the work of God's Holy Spirit, is the reversal of that depraved state of soul spoken of in Scripture when it is said, "The carnal mind is not subject to the law of God, neither indeed can be." It is not a mere plastic operation, in virtue of which a new tendency is impressed on the affections. It is a direct and personal dealing with the will, powerfully bringing it into distinctly recognised and conscious subjection to the will of God. In popular expression, it is the transfer of the Moral Law from the tables of stone to the fleshly tables of the heart. Or, allowing the Lord himself to describe His own work: "I will put my laws into their hearts, and in their minds will I write them." That is: I will secure their intelligent acquaintance with my law, and their cordial acquiescence in it, dealing alike with their minds and with their hearts. But this transfer is not of such a nature as that the law is no more to be found outside and above the will of man. It is not as if, in searching for it now, we should find that it had disappeared as an authoritative code of duty, to present itself henceforth only as a formulated expression of the facts of man's will, no longer assertative of the requirements of God's will. On the contrary, the specifically new thing which the Holy Ghost has secured, and indeed created, is just a life which, so to speak, lives in the recognition of the authoritative will of God; its own consciousness as uttered in the words, "Thy law, O God, is within my heart," being explained by the unmistakable periphrasis, "I delight to do thy will, O my God." The renewed will recognises its own renewal, precisely in this very element of its subjection to the objective authority of the Most High. A sense of that subjection was ineradicably inlaid in the conscience before; it is now accepted and welcomed by the heart. And it is this transference of the objective law, —as expressive, in the *matter* of it, of the *nature* of God, —into the inward parts subjectively; while the same law still abides outside and above the will,—continuing in the *form* of it, assertative of the *authority* of God: this it is which is the grand reconciliation of obedience most stringent, with liberty most sweet and perfect. So far as regeneration has proceeded,—and it is perfected only in death,—the subjective law *of* the will, in its renewed estate, is in exact accordance with the objective law of God *to* the will. But this reconciliation is disturbed by intromitting with either of the two factors; and it is annihilated by making one of them do duty for both. Exactly as the constituting idea of a sacrament is destroyed by transubstantiating the sign into the thing signified—the sacramental tie or bond, and therefore the sacramental idea, vanishing at the introduction of identity.

It is in vain to plead that the subjective view of Moral Law presents a higher ideal of spiritual Liberty than what we have now been pleading for. The reverse is the fact. For the withdrawment of objective law is really the denial of responsibility. And liberty is infringed, when responsibility is infringed; for liberty and responsibility are correlatives. When a man is regenerated, he is made "willing" (Ps. cx. 3,) to be under law to God, and this correlation is thereby beautifully preserved. His obedience now is not that of a slave; for the law of his God is within his heart in the character of a holy tendency, as well as standing over him with its commandment. And his obedience is not the operation of a *mere* mental tendency or spiritual mechanism working out its own bias or its own law—as the soft lulling motion of a vessel languidly drifting with the stream, though that stream were even "the river of the water of life." It is the obedience of a loving, loyal subject, adoring his Lord and King, and saying, "Lord, what wilt thou have me to do?" And this is the highest ideal of Liberty that can be framed.

It is equally vain to affirm that the subjective view of law presents a higher ideal of Grace. For if man did not fall as under a probation, of which law objective was the instrument and safe-guarding charter; if he fell as the victim of a kind of physical experiment; his restoration can carry in it nothing of the nature of grace. It must appear rather as a reparation which he had some ground to expect, if not indeed to claim. It is in the light only of righteous authoritative Law, that Grace can actually appear, or even the very idea of grace be conceived at all; and the antithesis which Paul so constantly presents between Grace and Law becomes utterly unintelligible, if by Law we are to understand the formulised expression merely of a subjective state of soul.

Moreover, on this view, regeneration makes its appearance as a phenomenon utterly dissociated from any intelligible, personal transaction between God and His people,—any transaction of the nature of a reconciliation; not to speak of the still more obnoxious transaction of a legal or forensic justification. God appears more as an influence than as a personal being; and man is represented as at best a kind of animal, high in instincts intellectual, sentimental, and emotional. For it becomes difficult to conceive of God as personal, if the assertion of His authority be suppressed; and difficult to conceive of man as personal, if distinct submission to objective authority on God's part is not also insisted on. For our idea of personality is so intertwined with implicit, if not explicit, recognition of ethical capacity and ethical relation, that, if that element be subtracted, it is very questionable whether the idea thereafter carries in it any self-constituting notion at all.

In thus representing regeneration as the unifying of the desires and tendencies of an inward law in the heart with the demands of the outward law of God, it is possible we may be charged with forgetting that, at an earlier stage of this brief discussion, we indicated a certain risk or danger, in man's original state, that might arise from this very accordance,—a kind of possible tendency towards trusting to the law of the heart, as if it would operate spontaneously and render careful consideration of Moral Law, as expressing God's authority, unnecessary. It is true, we spoke of this possible tendency as accounting for the necessity of such probation as that of Eden, in which the "categorical imperative" is introduced as clothing the subject-matter of a requirement which could appeal to nothing corresponding to it pre-existing in man's spiritual constitution. And assuredly if any danger existed of law moral lapsing, in man's regard, into the aspect of law physical, such probation was adapted with singular precision to meet the case. But it cannot be asserted that this danger can arise in that re-instated harmony of objective and subjective law which it is the very function of regeneration to establish; nor, when that harmony is complete, can subsequent probation be required, on the ground, as in the former case, that danger arises from its very completeness. For there is a mighty difference between a harmony that has undergone no ordeal, like that of Eden, and one that has been established as the very result of an ordeal exactly similar in kind but immeasurably more intense in degree. This difference, of course, cannot appear in a scheme which presents a regeneration that is dissociated from whatever is specific in redemption and reconciliation, in the strict meaning of these terms. But it *does* appear very strikingly in the regeneration which the Covenant of Grace recognises and provides. For the absolute sovereignty of God is brought out in redemption, in the terrible and matchless probation of the second Adam; and absolute subjection to God as Sovereign is secured, in the reconciliation of men to God individually, by the imperative

demand for faith in Christ and submission in Him to
"the righteousness of God." It is in indissoluble connection with *this* crucial instance and culminating display of God's sovereignty on the one hand, and this
conclusively testing demand for man's submission on
the other, that regeneration is righteously granted on
God's part, and intelligently reached and realised on
the part of him that believeth. The unifying of the
inward subjective law of the will, in its renewed state,
with the objective authoritative "commandment" under
which the regenerated soul delights to live, takes place
with no risk to the recognition of the "categorical
imperative" in this second creation. Nor is any subsequent institute of probation needed to prevent the
possibility of law moral lapsing into the likeness of law
physical now. "The darkness is past; and the true
light now shineth." The sovereignty of Law has been
recognised and established in the probation and
righteousness of that Eternal Son of God, who received from His Father a commandment to lay down
His life for the sheep, and who, though He were a Son,
yet learned obedience by the things which He suffered;
the whole import of His Incarnation and its object
being given by Himself when He says, "I came not to
do mine own will, but the will of Him that sent me."
Nor is His representative probation, when viewed as
the heritage of His people, to be considered as *their*
probation by *proxy* merely. It becomes their *own* probation most truly; as truly theirs as the first Adam's

was his own, and it is immeasurably more intense and satisfactory.

For—in bringing these discussions on the Atonement of our Lord Jesus Christ to a close,—let it be carefully observed in conclusion, That it is impossible that Christ's righteousness can be imputed on God's part, or on man's part appropriated, on any principle, or scheme, or understanding that should dispense with the real probation of men individually, in their entrance into the favour and kingdom of God. The commandment to "kiss the Son, lest His wrath should burn, and we perish from the way:" the commandment to "believe on the Lord Jesus Christ," and submit in Him to the righteousness of God; carrying in it, as that commandment evidently does, the imperative obligation to acknowledge the absolute righteousness of eternal death as the wages due to sin, to look to sovereign grace as the only source of exemption from it, and to own that grace as reigning through righteousness by the substitution of God's dear Son under the inflicting stroke of God's awakened and avenging sword:—this is the highest and most conclusive possible probation. It is far keener and deeper than the probation of Eden. When successfully endured, it opens to us the way to the true Tree of Life. And this is that ordeal, under whose all-testing fires, Law Moral from God and law subjective in the heart are, in regeneration, welded into a harmony which the eventualities of even eternity itself will never prevail to disturb. The living faith of the regenerated spirit, appropriating "the righteousness of God," carries in its heart an oath of allegiance to the sovereignty of God Most High: an oath which is at once the echo and the offspring of God's own oath of sovereignty—sovereignty alike in Law and in Grace. And the oath of faith shall never fail unto eternity, any more than the Divine oath original from which it springs and to which it answers:—" I have sworn by myself, the word is gone out of my mouth in righteousness, and shall not return, That unto me every knee shall bow, every tongue shall swear. Surely, shall one say, in the Lord have I righteousness and strength" (Isa. xlv. 23, 24).

APPENDIX.

[I am tempted to reproduce here a discourse prepared not altogether without some careful thought,—because it brings out somewhat more fully both the peculiar nature of Moral Law, and the *a priori* argument for the doctrine of the Trinity, as presented in the closing chapter of this volume.]

GOD'S BLESSEDNESS AND HIS STATUTES.

"Blessed art thou, O Lord; teach me thy statutes."—Ps. cxix. 12.

THE blessedness of God; subjection to His statutes; and the relation between these topics;—such are the threefold materials of thought furnished by this verse. Depending on the blessed God himself to teach us, we take the three topics in their order.

Part First.

The Blessedness of God.

The blessedness of God! It is a great deep, it is a dazzling bright abyss. We can look into it only as with shaded eyes; we can speak of it only as with lisping tongue, like children. Yet if with childlike spirit we look, and listen, and meditate, our exercise may neither be unacceptable to the "blessed God" nor destitute of blessing to ourselves.

The blessedness of God! It is the result of His possession of all perfections, natural and moral. "God is light;" "God is love." Infinitely wise to devise the best conceptions, to entertain the infinitely true and good and grand ideals, and infinitely powerful to carry them out into accomplishment, His intelligent nature cannot but be characterised by that combination of inviolable repose and unhindered activity which constitutes a great element in our worthiest ideas of blessedness. His moral nature also in its glorious attributes severally, as also in the unison of their fulness and in the harmony alike of their indwelling in His being and of their outgoing into action, is at once suggestive of the highest conception we can form of blessedness. Speaking even negatively—which to our feeble intellects is often the best means of grasping truth and guiding our own intelligence—speaking even negatively of God's moral nature, it must be very apparent that He is "the blessed God." In Him is no darkness, no gloom, no shadow; no variableness, or shadow of turning. In Him is no malevolence; no pleasure even in the death of the vilest or most wicked of the wicked. In Him is no unrighteousness, no inequality. His nature and His ways are "equal." Beautiful is that word "equal," as applied to God's nature and His ways; and blessed is that which it implies. There is nothing unequal in Him; there is no inequality; no excess; no defect; no incongruity. no conflicting element, no discord; no stain, no blemish, no shade, no spot, nor wrinkle, nor any such thing. In all the boundless fulness of His being He is right, and only right—right, righteous, upright; even as one of His adoring servants hath sung: "To show that the Lord is upright: "He is my rock, and there is no unrighteousness in Him" (Ps. xcii. 15). How then can we think of Him as other than the "blessed God?"

But again: the blessedness of God is intimately connected not only with the absolute perfections of His being, but with His absolute natural supremacy and moral sovereignty. These may be distinguished. His natural supremacy is His necessary and absolute independence and superiority over all that exists; His moral sovereignty is His kingly rule over intelligent, responsible beings. And in each of these relations Scripture assigns to Him the attribution of "blessedness." For in one passage He is designated as "God over all"—that is, the Supreme—"blessed for evermore" (Rom. ix. 5); and in another, "The blessed and only Potentate" (1 Tim. vi. 16)—the Sovereign; King of kings, and Lord of lords. As the Supreme He is blessed: "God over all, blessed for evermore." As the sovereign God He is blessed: "the blessed and only Potentate."

Nor is it difficult to see the grounds of these glorious assertions. He is in the fullest, the deepest sense, "God over all," and therefore blessed. He is independent—absolutely so. He has relations to that which is without His own being; but He is independent of all that is outside His own being. All except Godhead exists by His will and at His pleasure: "Of Him, and through Him, and to Him are all things." "For His pleasure they are, and they were created."

His is the uncreated, self-existent, independent Being; infinite, eternal, unchangeable, inviolable. In virtue thereof, the heaven of heavens cannot contain Him, and He dwelleth in light that is inaccessible. Language fails to tell, and thought fails to body forth unto itself, the secret dwelling-place of the Most High, where the omnipotent and self-sufficient Godhead sits enthroned above all being beside, in His supreme and absolute, yet not self-secluding independence; exalted above all circumstances, above all creatures, above all changes, above all influences; "God over all," in blessedness which no contingencies can invade, affect, control; which no creature-will can cross, no alien influence overshadow or approach; which no voice of querulousness or questioning can even penetrate or ruffle, even though a million of apostate creations should unite to cry, "What doest thou?"

For God is not only naturally, necessarily, and, so to speak, physically, the Supreme; He is morally and judicially the absolute Sovereign of the universe: and herein also He is blessed. "Blessed art thou, O LORD." Thou art the *Lord;* the Master; the Ruler. God is Judge, Lawgiver, King. The Church welcomes and glorifies Him very specially in this relation, with emphatic reiterated, rejoicing recognitions; and perilling and binding in her salvation with her recognition of it: "The Lord is our Judge; the Lord is our Lawgiver; the Lord is our King: He will save us:" as such—in this capacity in which we give Him threefold recognition; as Judge, Lawgiver, King—Sovereign Lord Most High—as such, "He will save us."

And in this moral sovereignty God is blessed. For it is the outcome of His moral nature which is blessed;

and is therefore a high exercise, expression, enjoyment of conscious blessedness. For His kingly rule is at once the outgoing of His blessed nature and the fitting action of His blessed supremacy, when He deals with intelligent and moral beings: and if His nature and His supremacy are blessed, then blessed is He also in that sovereignty which is the adequate expression alike of His nature with its perfections, and of His supremacy with its rights and claims. And the more pure and simple we perceive this sovereignty to be—the more absolute, independent, uncontrolled; the more we see it to be the pure and simple expression of His sheer and absolute will; so much the more will we see that it is blessed, and be disposed to acquiesce and rejoice in it. For if His will cannot contradict His nature, which is light and love, beneficence and righteousness; and if it vindicate to moral beings His supremacy and independence; why should it not be sheer and absolute—the mere good pleasure of His will? Shall we plead for its being brought down beneath His natural supremacy, as He is God over all, blessed for ever? Shall we plead for its being taken outside the boundless glory of His blessed nature as light and love—the only wise, the only good; in whom is nothing tortuous, perplexed, unequal, unright, unrighteous? Would we not thereby impair His blessedness as our Sovereign? or rather would we not impair and destroy our own perceptions of His blessedness? And would we rather serve a sovereign whose blessedness we could not recognise, than one whom we cannot but perceive to be the blessed and the only Potentate, the King of kings and Lord of lords, absolute and uncontrolled? Nay; it concerns me much, if I am to be His subject and His servant, to see His sovereignty as ruled by nothing but His nature,—His will controlled by nothing but His perfections,—His reign worthy of His absolute supremacy, and unimpaired by influences that must be of infinite inferiority. Let Him do what seemeth good in His own sight alone. Let me rejoice that He taketh counsel with none—whose counsel would be infinitely beneath His own, incongruous with His own, degrading to His own. "Even so, Father; for so it seemed good in Thy sight." Thy sovereign rule is blessed as Thy nature is blessed. Thou art the blessed and only Potentate. Thy kingdom come: Thy will be done on earth as it is done in heaven!

But further: the blessedness of God subsists in fellowship—fellowship worthy of His eternal being and Godhead; worthy of His glorious nature and its infinite perfections; worthy of His absolute supremacy and uncreated independence—fellowship in the everlasting relations of the ever-blessed Three in One.

As far as I can see, after much and frequent thought, the doctrine of the Trinity enters indispensably into the blessedness of God.

For it provides the element of fellowship—fellowship fully worthy of God's nature, and alone adequate to God's infinite capabilities of fellowship; and without fellowship, I confess, I cannot conceive of "blessedness" either in the creature or the Creator. I cannot conceive of a Unitarian's God as a blessed being. A uni-personal Deity inhabiting a past eternity, absolutely without all relations, without converse, without reciprocations, without all love or aught to love; in solitariness, solitude, silence;—such a past eternity inhabited by absolutely one only unrelated Person, contemplating naught and in naught conversing, alike unloving and unloved, seems to me to add only the element of infinity to the idea of all that is blank, and cold, and terribly repulsive,—to add the character of boundlessness—of illimitable magnitude—to that of the very grave itself;—the most unchristian idea even of the grave, "the cold grave to which we haste, where everlasting silence reigns."

I cannot imagine a uni-personal Deity blessed in contemplating Himself—contemplating His own nature in His own only person, however replete with all possible perfections that nature might be. I doubt whether it is even possible to imagine Him as self-conscious at all, or capable of saying from eternity, "I am;" and I do not wonder at the particular Oriental heathen doctrine which represents a uni-personal deity, Brahm, as asleep from all eternity, until He wakens up in the act of creating. And, as far as I can see, the profoundest modern doctrine of what is called the absolute Being faints and fails because it proudly shuns to borrow light from revelation, and draw upon the glorious revealed truth that Godhead subsists as Three in One. I do not say that reason may discover that truth; but I do say that that truth being from any quarter suggested, reason cannot fail to justify it more fully than has, as far as I can see, been generally admitted. For how an absolutely unrelated unity—and God must assuredly be One—how an absolutely and eternally unrelated unity should ever begin to enter on relations, I utterly fail to understand; and, I think, as against such a notion of a personal God—a uni-personal Deity —Pantheism, which affirms that God is all and all things are God, is not without something reasonable to say on its own behalf. How such a God, subsisting in one eternal Person alone, ever should begin to create, I cannot possibly imagine; more especially how He ever could call persons—personal beings—intelligent, moral persons into being. A personal God, self-conscious, can utter from all eternity the great word, "I AM." A dependent intelligent being created by Him, conscious of his own being, gives forth a created reflection of that utterance; and being in the image of God, self-conscious though dependent, expresses the essential dignity of highest created being by also saying, "I am." It is a result of the uncreated "I AM." That any creature in the universe can say, "I am," demonstrates that there must be One who from all eternity could say, "I AM,"—in His case, "I AM THAT I AM," Jehovah. But then, besides the great word "I am," there is another which seems to me as great—yea, it would appear, the necessary reciprocal and complement —"Thou art." A created intelligence can say, "I am," but that is not the first time that great word has been uttered; Jehovah was from everlasting the eternal utterance of it,—"I am;" "I AM THAT I AM." A created intelligence looking to his Creator can, in the instant following first consciousness, exclaim, "THOU ART;" and his Creator, looking to His intelligent creature, can say, "Thou art." Is this the first time that this great word has been uttered or utterable? Is it right that the great word "THOU ART," expressing relation, expressing recognition, expressing reciprocation, expressing fellowship, should begin to be uttered in time, and should have no place in eternity—should have no eternal root to grow upon, no eternal fountain to flow from, no eternal rock to lean and rest upon? I cannot think so. Is it right, is it fitting, is it conceivable, that God and His first intelligent creature should be on equal terms, in that each of them should, for the first time, begin reciprocally in recognising each other to say, each unto the other, "Thou art?" They are not on equal terms in saying "I am." God has from everlasting been the "I AM;" "I AM THAT I AM." There was no beginning of circumstances to enable Him to say, "I AM." Shall there be a beginning of circumstances to enable Him to say, "Thou art?" Is it right and fitting that this self-existent God, who has no beginning of being, should have beginning of fellowship, the very crown jewel and diadem of being? that He should begin in time, and only on the poor frail platform of created things, to say, "Thou art?" Nay. "To which of the angels said He at any time, Thou art—thou art my son; this day have I begotten thee?" But to His eternal Son He has eternally—in the unbeginning, unending now—the day that knows no morning and no evening—been saying, "THOU ART." All along the eternal line of His having said, "I AM," to His own Son He has been saying, "THOU ART—thou art my Son; this day have I begotten thee." And not reflecting merely on self, the Father hath seen, and been the blessed God in seeing, the brightness of His glory and the express image of His person in His Son: and in Him hath He also seen, and hath admired—in no self-seclusion, self-hood, or exclusiveness, but in fellowship, He hath seen and hath admired—and been blessed in admiring, Godhead's sovereignty; and *unto the Son* He saith, "Thy throne, O God, is for ever and ever; a sceptre of righteousness is the sceptre of thy kingdom."

Yes; I cannot imagine a uni-personal God as a Creator at all. I cannot imagine God beginning to say "Thou art" to a creature, if He has not been eternally saying "THOU ART" to one altogether worthy to say "I AM"—to say "I AM" in all the same exhaustless fulness of meaning in which Jehovah says, "I AM THAT I AM." Without an eternal "THOU ART," we search in vain for a beginning of creation: we meet with nothing but an eternal gulf between a uni-personal Deity and contingent created being. Reason fails to find a possibility of a beginning till she hear it said of a second Person in the Godhead, that "*He* is the beginning of the creation of God;" "The eternal Son;" the indispensible divine Mediator of creation—afterwards the divinely congruous divine Mediator of redemption. I repeat, I cannot possibly imagine a uni-personal eternal God, having in His own being no relations, no fellowship, no "THOU ART;" no one, therefore, to whom to say even, "I AM;" and therefore no voice, no word—no word at all. I cannot imagine a beginning to creation from such a God. But there has been a "beginning," for there has been a "Word" —the eternal Word; and I adore the wisdom that links that Word and that beginning thus: "In the beginning was the Word, and the Word was with God"—there was fellowship: "and the Word was God"—it was fellowship adequate for Godhead—fellowship of God with God: yea, fully adequate, for the "same was in the beginning with God. All things were made by Him, and without Him was not anything made that was made. In *Him* was life, and the life was the light of men."

Tell me not of a dark, blank, cold, and cheerless

past eternity, with one only, eternal, self-inclusive, self-contemplating Person dwelling in it, however you may accumulate into your description of His being all possible perfections. The more you tell me that He is self-subsisting, self-sufficient, self-complete, and absolutely independent, so much the more do you remove Him far away from every idea of blessedness that reason, as it seems to me, can frame or can accept. It is a dark abyss of solitude and silence, from which I shrink back in terror, and from which I cannot possibly believe that any bright and blessed creation could ever spring—any bright beginning, or blessed work, could ever emanate. I demand some inward, living, bright, and blessed relation in the eternal God himself ere I can imagine Him beginning to give birth to blessed and bright created beings. And if the problem of an absolute *unity*, such as reason tells that Godhead must necessarily be, combined with *relation*, such as reason and heart alike demand, be a problem insoluble, in which I can but doubtfully and darkly grope my way, my reason is more than satisfied, and my heart is more than joyful, when from what were otherwise the dark and blank abyss of uni-personal solitude and silence I hear an eternal Person—an eternal Word—saying: "The Lord possessed *me* in the beginning of His way, *before* His work of old. I was set up from everlasting, from the beginning, ere ever the earth was. When there were no depths, I was brought forth; when there were no fountains abounding with water. When He prepared the heavens, I was there; when He set a compass on the face of the depth, when He appointed the foundations of the earth, then I was with Him as one brought up with Him, I was daily His delight"—

blessed art Thou herein, O God!—"I was daily His delight, rejoicing always before Him" (Prov. viii. 22–32).

O Thou everlasting Son of God!—Thou art the deepest depth of all philosophy truly so called; the solution of all profoundest problems; the satisfaction of our reason; the joy of our heart; the Saviour of Thy people. Thou art alike the light of men and the explanation of the Godhead's blessedness; Thou fillest with boundless uncreated bliss Thy Father's boundless bosom. Blessed art Thou, O Thou Father of an Infinite Majesty: and Thou, O Word of God, His true and honourable Son: also the Holy Ghost. For the communion of two Personalities is saved from being a mere mutual enjoyment of reflected self-hood, by being communion concerning a third Personality. The fellowship of two, each of whom can say, "I AM," and each of whom can say, "THOU ART," seems incomplete, and still only a kind of reciprocal and mutually reflected self-hood, till, going beyond themselves, they can add that other great word, "HE IS." But in Trinity there is provision for this also. And the Father and the Son having fellowship in the Spirit and concerning Him; the Father and the Spirit, concerning the Son; and the Son and the Spirit, concerning the Father: blessedness in Godhead is in all relations and every light complete; complete in every kind and in every degree—complete in every kind beyond degree. "Blessed art Thou, O Lord."

Part Second.

God's Law, Statute Law.

I fasten on the leading thought, the thought suggested by the word *statutes*—"Thy statutes." So that the law of God is statute law—statute and ordained. It is strictly moral law; it is commandment; it is judicial, authoritative, peremptory. It is statute and ordained: "Thou shalt." Thou shalt love the Lord thy God: thou shalt not covet.

Two modern errors contradictory of this simple truth present themselves.

I. There are those who hold that the moral law is of the same kind and nature as natural and physical laws: and they would explain the consequence of breach of it, not as punishment, penalty, retribution, wrath inflicted by a personal offended lawgiver; but as the reaction caused by striking against the law itself; as when one leaning incautiously over from the summit of a lofty tower, falls by the law of gravitation, and by the law of the impenetrability of matter is dashed to pieces, or taken up bruised and bleeding. So, they hold, does God rule intelligent men, much as He rules the planets,—as when, "from His rounded palm, He bowled them flaming on the plains of night," leaving them to circle round the sun in virtue of the laws of attraction and inertia; or, as when He gave properties to fire which substantially say to man, Thou shalt not touch me, for when thou touchest me thou shalt be burned.

Now, I ask, Is this a fair account of moral law? Does God as little consult my will, does He lay as little responsibility upon me, as when He rolls the moons and planets in their orbits, or sends a comet forth into the distant realms of space? and does He, by moral law, address Himself, to me no more directly or personally, than when He leaves me to find that by violating the

law of fire I am burned, or violating the law of inertia
and of prudence alike I dash my foot against a stone?
Away with the futile absurdity! It is most miserable
science—still more wretched philosophy. It is the
destruction of morals; it makes Christianity an impertinence, an impossibility. Nay, it overthrows all evidence of the personality of God, and refuses all
recognition of the personality of man. For if God
deals with me in such a fashion, I may recognise Him
as a Power, but I am not shut up to see Him as a
Person. And I do not see that He deals with me as
with a PERSON; He seems to count me only a THING.
I ask also, Is this the sort of law by which earthly
monarchs rule, and earthly kingdoms are conducted
and conserved? Are the laws—the statutes—the laws
statute and ordained in this favoured land of ours, like
physical and material laws that lay no responsibility
upon us, and address themselves in no respect to our
free-will and sense of obligation? Does our earthly
monarch rule her subjects after such a fashion? When
our gracious Queen desired to send a General to give
deliverance to the captives and to quell the savage,
did she bowl him into the distant land bound to a
camel or a car, and leave him there to work as laws of
gravitation, of metals, of fire, of projectiles, might
allow,—observing these laws, but without any law or
commandment authoritative from his sovereign? Nay.
She called him to her counsels. Personally she gave
commandment; she dealt with him as her responsible
subject—a free-agent, able to accept or to refuse responsibility. And in mutual action of her sovereign
free-will and his subject free-will, she laid responsibility
upon him, and duty:—Thy duty shall be to give

deliverance to the captive and to quell the heathen's pride. And he accepted the responsibility; and under the weighty burden of it, his soldier-soul sprang up elastic in its chivalry; and he went, bound in duty, free in will; and in full free-will he did his duty, and he did it all; and he gave deliverance to the captive, and he quelled the savage, and he sheltered and comforted the heathen widow's death-bed, and he took her son to be the ward and pupil of a man of God and missionary of the Cross;* and he praised the Lord Most High for his success, and he praised his soldiers under Him; and he shall return to hear his monarch's "Well done, good and faithful servant," and to hear his country's proud acclaim of gratitude and praise. Wot ye not how his monarch honoured him by saying to him, "Thou shalt?"

It is even so that God puts honour—perilous, yet grandest honour—on intelligent responsible man; not dealing with him as with dead material substance, but consulting his free-will, calling it into play, laying it under obligation. He shows me that I am under law; I, personally under law to Him, a living Person, Sovereign, and giving me commandment. He shows me that I have broken that commandment, and He is justified in thence condemning me. He shows me also a glorious One to whom He gave commandment also—a very different commandment—a commandment to lay down His life for the sheep; and He accepted the commandment and the responsibility; and not at the loss of the sinner's life, but the surrender of His own, He brings deliverance to the captive, and quells the sinner's pride, and maketh him the ward and the pupil, not of

* This discourse was written and preached at the close of the Abyssinian war.

U

any man of God merely, but of the everlasting Father, and the Prince of Peace. He shows me a warfare in which not a single life was lost, but one was freely given; and from the altar, where that life was given, He takes a live coal and lays it on my lips, and He says, "Lo! this hath touched thy lips, and thine iniquity is taken away, and thy sin is purged." Then I hear Him saying, "Who will go for us, and whom shall we send?" And He enables me in personal responsibility, and personal free-will to say, "Here am I, send me." And He answers, "Thou shalt go unto all to whom I send thee, and thou shalt preach the preaching that I bid thee—deliverance to the captive, and the opening of the prison to them that are bound; and all that I shall say unto thee thou shalt speak." He gives me peremptory authoritative commandment. I am under law to Him, He is always saying to me; "Thou shalt." He is my Lord, my Sovereign, my Lawgiver, my King; and when my commission is at last finished, if it has been at all faithfully fulfilled, He will say: "Thou hast been faithful over a few things:" "Go thy way; thou shalt stand in thy lot in the end of days."

And *that*, I submit, is more honourable to my nature and my person far, than if, making me swift as Mercury, and bright as Sirius, He moved me about upon the broad plains of His government as if I were susceptible of but planetary and stellar movements, rather than of free and willing obedience to His sovereign word and will. It concerns me greatly to prefer being under express, authoritative, statute law to the "blessed and only Potentate, the King of kings, and Lord of lords." Yes; "blessed art Thou, O Lord," my Lawgiver and King; "teach me Thy statutes."

II. There is a second perversion of this truth. Some would have it that although the moral law is categorically imperative in itself, it is not so to the believer. Regenerated by the Spirit of God, the law is *in* his heart as the law *of* his heart; and now he needs no outward commandment to rule, and bind, and obligate him. Inward principle moves him spontaneously; and external imperative law is removed.

Is it so? Was it so with the first Adam? or with the second Adam? either of them?—and they are the two representative men of the race.

(1.) How was it with our first parent? If ever outward law, categorical and imperative, might have been dispensed with, it might in his case. God's law was in his heart. In all the compass of his holy blessed nature, there was nothing adverse to the law of God? He was a law unto himself. He was the moral law unto himself; loving God with all his heart, and his neighbour as himself, in all things content, in nothing coveting. Was imperative, authoritative, sovereign commandment therefore utterly unnecessary? Did God see it to be needless to say to him, Thou shalt, or Thou shalt not? It was the very thing that infinite wisdom saw he still needed; ere being proved thereby he might obtain the crown of life, otherwise incompetent to him and unattainable. And therefore did He give commandment, sheer and sovereign, commandment that was not written on his heart and could not be by nature, but must be enjoined upon him from without by sovereignty: "Thou shalt not eat of it: for in the day thou eatest thereof thou shalt surely die."

(2.) How was it with the second Adam? All God's law was in His heart. Operating there, an inward principle of grace, acted in Him by the Spirit of holiness His immeasurably, He surely, if any, might have dispensed with strict, imperative, authoritative law and commandment. "I delight to do Thy will, O God; Thy law also is within my heart." Was no commandment, therefore, laid upon—no obedience statute and ordained unto Him? Or, did He complain if there was? Nay; I hear Him specially rejoicing in it. Every word He uttered, every work He did, was by commandment; and I hear Him rejoicing that it was so. "My Father which sent Me, He gave me commandment what I should say and what I should do; as He gave Me commandment therefore, so I speak." And grand beyond compare as was His willing priestly act of laying down His life; and only second to it in grandeur as was His kingly act of taking it again; both these acts of Zion's royal High Priest were done in obedience to strict imperative commandment, statute and ordained. "I lay down My life of Myself, and I take it again: this commandment received I of My Father." Ay, and at this moment, while He pleads at the right hand of the throne, an Advocate for sinners, He is acting by commandment, by the imperative law and obligation of official duty; and the vilest sinner seeking His aid can appeal to Him by the obligation of His office and by the force of His Father's commandment, that "him that cometh to Him He may in no wise cast out." *He* at least counts it not dishonour to be under imperative commandment—to hear the Father saying to Him, "Thou shalt." And, oh, how blessed for me it is that it should be so! For I hear the Father's "Thou shalt" unto the Son take gracious, glorious forms like these: "The bruised reed Thou shalt not break, and the smoking flax Thou shalt not quench, till Thou bring forth judgment unto truth."

(3.) And shall His members, though the regenerating Spirit dwells in them, claim an exemption from what the Son was not exempt, from what the Son counts it honourable not to be exempt even in His heavenly glory? for even there He shall for ever be "subject to the Father, that God may be all in all." Shall believers, because the Spirit puts the law into their hearts, claim a right to act merely at the dictate of inward gracious principle, untrammelled, uncontrolled by outward peremptory statute? I appeal to Paul in the seventh chapter of the Romans, where he says, "The law is holy," and adds, as if to show that it was no inward actuating law of the heart, but God's outward commanding law to the will: "The law is holy, and the *commandment* is holy, and just, and good." And I appeal to the sweet singer of Israel, a man whose heart was after God's own heart, yet trusted not his obedience in the keeping of inward principle, but bowed to outward categorical commandment. For I find in this psalm, which is all throughout the breathing of a heart in which the law of God is written—I find him, over and above that, owning himself with joy as under peremptory external law: "Thou hast COMMANDED us to keep Thy precepts diligently. O that my ways were directed to keep Thy statutes. Then shall I not be ashamed, when I have respect to all Thy *commandments*."

Part Third.

Relations between God's Blessedness and His Statutes.

What the relations, the practical relations, between these two topics? They are not expressly indicated in the text. The two topics are simply placed in juxtaposition, without any formal link of connection. The bond that binds them is like a deep sea electric line; yet the soul that understandeth will read without difficulty the silent telegraphic message that hidden line conveys. It is a twofold message or lesson—its parts reciprocal and mutually supplementary—and may be stated thus: (1.) If I would effectually learn His "statutes," let me constantly contemplate His "blessedness;" (2.) If I would safely contemplate His "blessedness," let me habitually cherish subjection to His "statutes."

I. If I would effectually and loyally learn His statutes, let me contemplate Him as the blessed God. If I would in good faith and love accept Him as my only King and Potentate, let me dwell much upon the thought He is the "blessed" and only Potentate. For if I am to be His obedient servant hearkening to the voice of His commandment, under stringent, strict, imperative law to fulfil His will, it concerns me much to know what sort of God He is, and, in particular, whether He be "blessed for evermore." My perceptions of His blessedness will enter deeply into the style of spirit with which I set myself to learn His statutes.

Take the case as it appears in the infinitely lower sphere of relation to a human teacher or master. I am to be indentured to a master as his servant or his pupil. I ask not only, Is he just-minded? Is he kindly? But is he a happy-minded man? Is he equable in temperament and temper? Is he genial and joyful?— in a word, a blessed man? Or, righteous and good, it may be, in the main,—is he dark, moody, gloomy, fitful? Is he such that, like the schoolboys in the "Deserted Village," I might " learn to trace the day's disaster in the morning face?" That, certainly, would make my obedience to him greatly more difficult, my relation to him greatly more uncomfortable.

I have seen—thank God, oftener than once—I have seen a truly blessed man, a father, a brother in the ministry; his face gleaming with gladness and with love; and as he turned it upon me, I could have gladly served him to the uttermost that health of body and power of soul could have permitted me. And as the sweet memory has come across me of that shining countenance,—ripe alike in the rich joy of pious silvered age, and in the golden youthfulness that "shall be fat and full of sap, and aye be flourishing,"—I have felt as if I could understand somewhat of the depth of that prayer: "God be merciful unto us and bless us, and *cause Thy face to shine* upon us." And if a brother's or a father's blessedness could make me serve him gladly, if God would but show me the blessedness of the blessed and the only Potentate, I think I would cry out imperiously: "O blessed God, I will not let Thee go until Thou bless me; till Thou bless me by teaching me Thy statutes. The commandments of a God so blessed cannot possibly be grievous. Thy statutes cannot but be blessed too."

II. If I would safely contemplate His blessedness, let me cherish subjection to His statutes. I say "safely." For there is risk, there is danger—the danger of envy, dark, malignant envy—grudging God His blessedness.

Is this said to be a devilish and fanciful idea? Devilish? Yes. 'Tis precisely that which made angels devils. Fanciful? No. 'Tis too terribly real, as must be confessed by the children of two bright blessed beings who fell from their integrity by their desire to be "as gods" themselves; and it is too truly but the veritable reading of the carnal mind, which is enmity against God, and is not subject to the statute-law of God, neither indeed can be. Rightly probed, and rightly interpreted, that carnal mind is envious of God, envious of His inviolable, independent blessedness, and would excuse its own unholiness, if it dare, by saying, It is very easy for such a God to be holy—blasphemously fretting and grudging that it is not independently blessed too,—or at least comfortable.

It is a most insidious form of our malignant unbelief and vanity—this envious desire to be ourselves independent. And both by law and by gospel, both by wrath and by grace, God will have it avenged or annihilated. The very reconciliation proclaimed in "the gospel of the blessed God" is expressly framed and instinct all throughout with faculty and force for overthrowing it. For that reconciliation takes place as a justification;—legal, judicial, in terms of law;— contemplating the saved sinner as a subject under strict, imperative, inviolable law—standing at his Sovereign's throne condemned and self-condemned. Never more is the soul of man made to feel subject to the law of God, than in being justified freely by His grace. The believer, in the very act of receiving forgiveness and acceptance in the Beloved, is presented to God, to himself, to all the universe, in the most express conceivable aspect and attitude of a subject of his Sovereign, under peremptory obligation to authority and law, even by his very faith " submitting himself to the righteousness of God" (Rom. x. 3). Never am I more profoundly in subjection than when tremblingly I take hold on that righteousness of Christ. Never do I more profoundly own the stringency and strict severity of law, than when I essay to make use of that death of Christ which in such severity and stringency the law demanded in the case of Him who took my place, and came to magnify the law and make it honourable. Most blessed is our reconciliation to God. It is a *real* reconciliation. It is the sweet composing of a quarrel the most painful. It is the sweet and happy restoration of friendship with the Most High. All elements of handsomeness, generousness, good taste, good feeling —of finest feeling and delight—are in it; and "*blessed* is the man whose iniquity is forgiven, whose sin is covered, to whom the Lord imputeth no iniquity." Nevertheless, formally, and fundamentally, and primarily, it is a *justification*—a legal act, a sovereign deed; in terms of law, in court of law, where all is statute and ordained.

Is not that, indeed, its charm and its strength—its exhaustless charm, its strength eternal? And again, I say, it is good that it should be so, for this as for other reasons—good, I mean, that I should be made to feel under imperative commandment, under authoritative law to God—because, save for that conviction, I might come to envy Him His blessedness by very reason of its supreme and infinite independence; its high, supernal, inviolable repose; its absolute and indestructible equipoise; resting, as it does, on eternal, unchangeable perfection, and on sovereign supremacy above all creatures, all influences whatsoever; enshrined in fellowship of infinitely equal and adequate reciprocal delights unfathomable. What is my relief against the snare and risk of envying the blessedness of God? Is it, on the one hand, the conviction that He rules me only as He rules material substances, binding me like a planet or a satellite, as by hard and iron fate, to circle round His throne? That, certainly, will never teach me to rejoice in contemplating His blessedness, as He is "God over all, blessed for evermore." Is it, on the other hand, an indolent resigning of myself up to some inward principle, be it even the grace of this blessed God himself, within my heart? Nay; as little will that even qualify me to rejoice in the blessedness of "the blessed and only Potentate." What I need is a cordial recognition, a personal, practical acknowledgment of His supremacy, His absolute sovereignty—a personal, cordial recognition that the Lord God omnipotent reigneth; that He reigneth over me; that I am under statute-law in His kingdom, "hearkening," like the angels, "to the voice of His commandment." That, and that alone, will keep me safe, as I gaze into the bright and fathomless abyss of the blessedness of God. That, and that alone, shall be my own reflected blessedness; while beholding the blessedness of God, I am changed into the same image from glory to glory, from blessedness to blessedness, as by the Spirit of the Lord. I may be in some measure like unto God in righteousness, by cultivating similar righteousness; or like unto God in wisdom, by cultivating similiar wisdom, in my measure, by the Spirit of wisdom. I may be like unto God in holiness by sharing His holiness, being made partaker of His holiness, "partaker of a divine nature through His exceeding great

and precious promises." In all these I may be like unto
God by cultivating similarity. But I can be like unto
God, I can bear the image of God, in His sovereignty,
as the blessed and only Potentate, only by cultivating
dissimilarity. That is the paradox, and it has its real
ground in reason. I sympathise with God in righteousness, in holiness, in wisdom, by sharing these attributes
in their *direct* reflection. I sympathise with Him in His
sovereignty only by a reverse reflection or obverse
image here. I sympathise with His sovereignty only
by being in subjection—subjection absolute, unconditional, unqualified, even as His sovereignty is absolute,
unqualified, unconditional. By affecting to share with
Him here, I would be repudiating His sovereignty,
envying Him His independence, invading, if I could,
the inviolable blessedness which is His as the only
Potentate. I have no relief against this risk and snare
but learning His statutes; and the more I learn, and
the more I am subject, the more do I see, and the more
deeply do I rejoice in seeing, that He is the blessed
and the only Potentate. I can safely see His blessedness then. Blessed art Thou, O Lord; teach me Thy
statutes.

I close with two brief appeals.

First; I appeal to you to cherish a deep sense of
God's statutes as authoritative, imperative, of absolute
and unchangeable obligation. "Thou hast *commanded*
us to keep Thy precepts." They are His "commandments," for ever binding all men, regenerate and unre-
generate alike; and they are enforced by authority
most absolute, from which there is and can be no
appeal. Unless we feel that we are in this sense under

law to God, piety or spiritual life is utterly impossible to us. We are under an error not merely of great magnitude, but an error that is fundamental, all-pervasive, and fatal. Unless we realise God's law as continually and absolutely binding, we will be incapable of understanding what sin is, for sin is the transgression of the law; incapable of conviction of sin; incapable of self-condemnation; incapable of contrition of repentance unto life; incapable of faith in Jesus Christ, who magnified the law; incapable of receiving the sprinkling of His blood, which is just God's infinitely wise device for placing a once dishonoured law again in perfect honour in the conscience, unto its perfect peace and salvation and adoring gratitude for ever. We will be incapable, therefore, of sanctification; for a man is sanctified in so far as, and no further than, he is obedient to the law of God. I know of no spirituality that is not unqualified, unconditional obedience to God's unconditional, sovereign authority. "If any man think himself to be spiritual, let him acknowledge that the things that I write unto you are the *commandments* of God."

Secondly ; I appeal to you to ascribe blessedness to our God. My text is not a cold, didactic assertion of the proposition that God is a blessed Being. It is the warm, adoring, direct ascription of blessedness to Him by a soul in communion with Him, rejoicing in His blessedness: "Blessed art Thou, O Lord." Therefore, brethren, join with me in thus ascribing blessedness unto our God. Bless ye God in the congregations, even the Lord from the fountain of Israel. Bless the Lord, O my soul; and all that is within me, bless His holy name. Yea, blessed be the Lord God of Israel, for He hath visited and redeemed His people, and hath raised up an horn of salvation for us in the house of His servant David. And blessed be the God and Father of our Lord Jesus Christ, who, according to His abundant mercy, hath begotten us again to a lively hope by the resurrection of Christ from the dead. And blessed be the God and Father of our Lord Jesus Christ, who keepeth not His blessedness unto Himself, but hath blessed us with all spiritual blessings in heavenly places in Christ Jesus. His name shall endure for ever; His name shall be continued as long as the sun; and man shall be blessed in Him—all nations shall call Him blessed. Blessed be the Lord God, the God of Israel, who only doeth wondrous things; and blessed be His glorious name for ever. Blessed be the Lord God of Israel from everlasting to everlasting, and let all the people say, Amen. Let the **re**deemed of the Lord say so, whom He hath redeemed from the hand of the enemy. From every voice upon the crowded battlements of Zion let the joyful shout ascend, and let it be echoed back from all that are around the throne. BLESS the Lord, ye His angels that excel in strength, and do His COMMANDMENTS, hearkening unto the voice of His word. Bless ye the Lord, all ye His hosts; ye ministers of His that do His pleasure. Bless the Lord, all His works, in all places of His dominions. Bless the Lord, O my soul. Amen **and amen.**